MISSION, RACE AND COLONIALISM IN MALAWI

Scottish Religious Cultures *Historical Perspectives*

Series Editors: Scott R. Spurlock and Crawford Gribben

Religion has played a key formational role in the development of Scottish society shaping cultural norms, defining individual and corporate identities, and underpinning legal and political institutions. This series presents the very best scholarship on the role of religion as a formative and yet divisive force in Scottish society and highlights its positive and negative functions in the development of the nation's culture. The impact of the Scots diaspora on the wider world means that the subject has major significance far outwith Scotland.

Available titles

George Mackay Brown and the Scottish Catholic Imagination
Linden Bicket

Poor Relief and the Church in Scotland, 1560–1650
John McCallum

Jewish Orthodoxy in Scotland: Rabbi Dr Salis Daiches and Religious Leadership
Hannah Holtschneider

John Kennedy of Dingwall, 1819–1884: Evangelicalism in the Scottish Highlands
Alasdair J. Macleod

Miracles of Healing: Psychotherapy and Religion in Twentieth-century Scotland
Gavin Miller

George Strachan of the Mearns: Seventeenth-century Orientalist
Tom McInally

Scottish Liturgical Traditions and Religious Politics: From Reformers to Jacobites, 1560–1764
Edited by Allan I. Macinnes, Patricia Barton and Kieran German

Dissent after Disruption: Church and State in Scotland, 1843–63
Ryan Mallon

Scottish Presbyterianism: The Case of Dunblane and Stirling, 1690–1710
Andrew Muirhead

The Scots Afrikaners: Identity Politics and Intertwined Religious Cultures in Southern and Central Africa
Retief Müller

The Revival of Evangelicalism: Mission and Piety in the Victorian Church of Scotland
Andrew Michael Jones

The Bantu Presbyterian Church of South Africa: A History of the Free Church of Scotland Mission
Graham A. Duncan

Mission, Race and Colonialism in Malawi: Alexander Hetherwick of Blantyre
Kenneth R. Ross

Forthcoming titles

The Dynamics of Dissent: Politics, Religion and the Law in Restoration Scotland
Neil McIntyre

William Guild and Moderate Divinity in Early Modern Scotland
Russell Newton

Protestantism, Revolution and Scottish Political Thought: The European Context, 1637–1651
Karie Schultz

edinburghuniversitypress.com/series/src

MISSION, RACE AND COLONIALISM IN MALAWI

Alexander Hetherwick of Blantyre

KENNETH R. ROSS

EDINBURGH
University Press

Edinburgh University Press is one of the leading university presses in the UK. We publish academic books and journals in our selected subject areas across the humanities and social sciences, combining cutting-edge scholarship with high editorial and production values to produce academic works of lasting importance. For more information visit our website: edinburghuniversitypress.com

© Kenneth R. Ross, 2023, 2024

Edinburgh University Press Ltd
13 Infirmary Street, Edinburgh, EH1 1LT

First published in hardback by Edinburgh University Press 2023

Typeset in 10/12 ITC New Baskerville by
Cheshire Typesetting Ltd, Cuddington, Cheshire

A CIP record for this book is available from the British Library

ISBN 978 1 3995 1741 6 (hardback)
ISBN 978 1 3995 1742 3 (paperback)
ISBN 978 1 3995 1743 0 (webready PDF)
ISBN 978 1 3995 1744 7 (epub)

The right of Kenneth R. Ross to be identified as author of this work has been asserted in accordance with the Copyright, Designs and Patents Act 1988 and the Copyright and Related Rights Regulations 2003 (SI No. 2498).

Contents

Preface		vi
1	Introduction	1
2	The Pioneer Missionary: Domasi Days	9
3	The Right-hand Man: Scott and Hetherwick	25
4	The Mission Leader: Father Figure	42
5	The Public Figure: Critic and Campaigner	62
6	Malawi Visionary: Standing Up for Cinderella	82
7	The Linguist and Bible Translator: Words Must Be Christianised	101
8	The Mission Thinker: Priorities and Policy	121
9	The Church Leader: Imagination and Reality	139
10	Missionary *and* Empire Builder? Tensions and Contradictions	159
Bibliography		189
Index		197

Preface

The sense I have with this book is that it somehow pursued me, demanding to be written. My interest in the early history of Blantyre Mission goes back to the late 1980s and 1990s when I was becoming acquainted with Malawi in general and serving as a minister of the CCAP Blantyre Synod in particular. At a time when Malawi was struggling with questions of identity, I found that interactions with Malawian colleagues prompted me to think again about the role of Blantyre Mission in the making of the nation 100 years earlier. On return visits to Scotland, I enjoyed long conversations with Andrew Ross who, thirty years earlier, had done his PhD research, at that time unpublished, on Blantyre Mission history. It was a pleasure to collaborate with Andrew on the publication of his doctoral thesis as one of the first books in the Kachere Series, which was launched in the mid-1990s.[1]

This stimulated my own research and I published a series of articles on different aspects of Blantyre Mission history: 'Vernacular Translation in Christian Mission: the Case of David Clement Scott and the Blantyre Mission 1888–98';[2] 'The African Church and Eastern Orthodoxy: Reflections on the Centenary of St Michael and All Angels';[3] 'Where were the Prophets and Martyrs in Banda's Malawi: Four Presbyterian Ministers';[4] 'Crisis and Identity: Presbyterian Ecclesiology in Southern Malawi 1891–1993'.[5]

On my return to Scotland, Malawi history continued to be often on my mind, leading, amongst other things, to the publication of my attempt at a comprehensive account of the 150-year-old relationship between Scotland and Malawi: *Malawi and Scotland: Together in the Talking Place since 1859*.[6] Through all this research and writing the figure of Alexander Hetherwick was always present, clearly a major influence but somehow not fully accounted for. Periodic conversations with Malawi historians like the late John McCracken and the late Jack Thompson sometimes came round to the question of whether it was time for a new biography of Alexander Hetherwick.

It was, however, my return to Malawi in 2019 that provided the impetus needed to make it happen. From June to December 2019 I was living on the Blantyre Mission. My everyday surroundings, particularly the ever-astonishing church of St Michael and All Angels, inevitably called David Clement Scott and Alexander Hetherwick to mind. I was a worshipper and occasional preacher at St Michael's during those months and was stimulated by the congregation's strong sense of its special history, which included emerging plans to develop a museum. From the beginning of 2020 I was based in Zomba, which gave me ready opportunity to consult Hetherwick's extensive correspondence held by the Malawi National Archives. The onset of the coronavirus pandemic in March 2020 frustrated many plans but it also created an opportunity for research and writing. Other projects at first demanded precedence but my work on Hetherwick was slowly maturing in the background. When Malawi's third wave of coronavirus arrived in July 2021 it presented for me the opportunity to knuckle down and see if I could turn my research notebooks into a worthwhile biography.

Since the seminal work of Andrew Ross in the early 1960s, the two outstanding figures in the early history of Blantyre Mission, David Clement Scott and Alexander Hetherwick, have received rather little scholarly attention. By some unaccountable alignment of the stars, two of us were drawn to address this deficiency almost at the same time. While I was turning my attention to Alexander Hetherwick, Harri Englund, Professor of Anthropology at the University of Cambridge, set about offering a fresh consideration of the life and work of David Clement Scott. Professor Englund was ahead of me and was kind enough in September 2021 to allow me to read an advanced, but not yet finalised, manuscript of his forthcoming book on Scott: *Visions for Racial Equality: David Clement Scott and the Struggle for Justice in Nineteenth Century Malawi* (Cambridge University Press).

This made fascinating reading for me and there are many points of connection with the present book. Since *Visions for Racial Equality* was still in a pre-final state when I had the opportunity to read it, I have not made any reference to it in this book. However, I do refer to a published chapter by Professor Englund, which is to some extent an embryonic version of the forthcoming book: '"Africa Is an Education": Vernacular Language and the Missionary Encounter in Nineteenth-century Malawi'.[7] To a great extent our two books are complementary since the one concentrates on Scott and his period as Head of Blantyre Mission from 1881 to 1898 while the other concentrates on Hetherwick and his period as Head from 1898 to 1928. There is, however, a considerable overlap in that the two men were in Malawi together from 1883 to 1898 and it is very difficult to consider one of them without considerable reference to the other. My hope is that the two books, with their sometimes contrasting conclusions, can stimulate further scholarly study of this decisive period in Malawi's history. At all events, I am deeply grateful to Professor Englund for his generous scholarly collaboration and for giving us the first book-length study of the remarkable life and thought of David Clement Scott.

The book would not exist without the help I received from the staff of libraries and archives who enabled me to have access to the primary sources. The Malawi National Archives in Zomba became my second home at times during 2020–21 and I record my sincere thanks to the Director Dr Paul Lihoma, Robert Matiki and Zibson Barthrow Kalion for their unfailing welcome, courtesy and resourcefulness. The spectacular outlook over the Old Town of Edinburgh from the reading room of the National Library of

Scotland Special Collections was well matched by the efficiency and care of the staff in locating and supplying relevant documents. Particular thanks are due to Celia Phillips. It was amidst tight corona-related restrictions that I was a regular visitor to the Centre for Research Collections at the University of Edinburgh Library where the staff carefully observed all protocols while setting me up with the microfilm that contains the only complete run of *Life and Work in British Central Africa*. Hetherwick's two substantial submissions to the Edinburgh 1910 World Missionary Conference can only be found at the Library of the Ecumenical Institute, Bossey, Switzerland, and I am grateful to Pedro Nari, the Librarian, for making it possible for me to consult them.

I am also much in the debt of colleagues who have deepened my understanding of Malawi's history. Among many others these include Professors Kings Phiri, Wapulumuka Mulwafu and Silas Ncozana. I was able to give an airing to some of the main issues raised by the life of Hetherwick at the Zomba Theological College Research Seminar held on 11 August 2021 and am grateful for the critical insights offered by colleagues on that occasion. I am also greatly indebted to my longstanding collaborator, Professor Klaus Fiedler of Mzuni Press. In 2022 the two of us mark the 30th anniversary of the start of our scholarly collaboration and I continue to benefit immeasurably from Professor Fiedler's encouragement and guidance. He was involved in the development of this book from its inception and provided detailed analysis and critique. We did not always agree on everything, but the book is much the better for his comments and suggestions. I am greatly indebted to colleagues who read the manuscript and gave me their critical feedback: Rev Dr Billy Gama, Fr Francis Bonongwe, Rev Master Jumbe, Prof Harri Englund and Prof Dana Robert.

I am grateful also to Prof Scott Spurlock of Glasgow University, Series Editor of EUP's Scottish Religious Cultures Series, who saw the potential for the book to become part of the Series. Ersev Ersoy, Isobel Birks and all their colleagues at EUP turned the idea into reality with great efficiency and unfailing good humour. I also appreciate very much the co-publication agreement between EUP and Mzuni Press, which will allow the book to be readily available in Malawi as well as to an international readership. As is customary, I insist that any remaining deficiencies of the book are entirely my own responsibility. My hope is simply that the book might be one contribution to increasing our understanding of a history that continues to carry importance for Malawi and beyond.

Zomba
May 2022

Notes

1. Andrew C. Ross, *Blantyre Mission and the Making of Modern Malawi*, Blantyre: CLAIM-Kachere, 1996, repr. Mzuzu: Luviri Press, 2018.

2. Kenneth R. Ross, 'Vernacular Translation in Christian Mission: the Case of David Clement Scott and the Blantyre Mission 1888–98', *Missionalia* 21/1 (April 1993), 5–18, also in Kenneth R. Ross, *Gospel Ferment in Malawi: Theological Essays*, Gweru: Mambo-Kachere, 1995, repr. Mzuzu: Luviri Press, 2018, 107–26.
3. Kenneth R. Ross, 'The African Church and Eastern Orthodoxy: Reflections on the Centenary of St Michael and All Angels', *Africa Theological Journal* 22/1 (1993), 10–20, also in Kenneth R. Ross, *Gospel Ferment in Malawi: Theological Essays*, 127–38.
4. Kenneth R. Ross, 'Where were the Prophets and Martyrs in Banda's Malawi: Four Presbyterian Ministers', *Missionalia* 24/2 (August 1996), 113–28, also in Kenneth R. Ross, *Here Comes Your King! Christ, Church and Nation in Malawi*, Blantyre: CLAIM-Kachere, 1998, repr. Mzuzu: Luviri Press, 2020, 154–74.
5. Kenneth R. Ross, 'Crisis and Identity: Presbyterian Ecclesiology in Southern Malawi 1891–1993', *Missionalia* 25/3 (1997), 375–91, also in Kenneth R. Ross, *Here Comes Your King!* 85–106.
6. Kenneth R. Ross, *Malawi and Scotland: Together in the Talking Place since 1859*, Mzuzu: Mzuni Press, 2013.
7. Harri Englund, '"Africa Is an Education": Vernacular Language and the Missionary Encounter in Nineteenth-century Malawi', in Kenneth R. Ross and Wapulumuka O. Mulwafu (eds), *Politics, Christianity and Society in Malawi: Essays in Honour of John McCracken*, Mzuzu: Mzuni Press, 2020, 138–62.

CHAPTER ONE

Introduction

At a time of renewed awareness of issues of race and racism in many societies worldwide, a reassessment of the Western missionary movement is called for. It has long been acknowledged that the movement carried an equivocal character when it comes to the question of racism. On the one hand, it was built on a conviction that 'black lives matter'. Otherwise, why would anyone risk their life to embark on a mission among black communities of the Global South? On the other hand, the missionary movement was an expression of the sense of superiority, not to say supremacy, of the white communities of the Global North and intimately connected with European colonial rule. Scholars and commentators have tended to latch on to one hand or the other. Some have understood the missionary movement as nothing but the religious wing of colonialism and imperialism, viewing everything through this lens. Others have focused on the sacrifice and solidarity that brought missionaries to devote their lives to service among black communities, often to transformational effect. There is therefore something of an unresolved polarity. This might be unlikely to be resolved by arguing in general terms since it is often the premise that determines the outcome. This book aims to interrogate the matter through a reassessment of one particular missionary: Alexander Hetherwick of Blantyre.

In the Malawi context, Hetherwick is an inviting choice since, on any reckoning, he is a major figure in Malawi history and certainly one of the most influential missionaries. Serving with Blantyre Mission for forty-five years (1883–1928) and the Head of the Mission for thirty years (1898–1928), he was a witness and a participant in the emergence of Malawi as a nation state. Based for most of the time in Blantyre, he played a part in the creation of Malawi's first urban community and was never far from the centre of political, economic and cultural affairs. 'No name,' opined Stephen Green, 'is more closely identified with Blantyre than that of Alexander Hetherwick.'[1] When President Kamuzu Banda greeted visiting Church of Scotland Moderators with the words, 'Had there been no Church of Scotland there would have been no Malawi', it was the memory of Alexander Hetherwick as well as that of Robert Laws that he invoked.[2]

It is well known that much of Africa came under European colonial rule towards the end of the nineteenth century, in Malawi's case with the declaration of the British Protectorate in 1891. Not always recognised is the fact that this development coincided with a marked change in prevailing racial attitudes. Colonialism and racism were so intertwined that it is not always easy to tease out the specifically racial dimension. However, social Darwinism steadily took hold following the publication of Charles Darwin's *Origin of Species* in 1859. While Darwin's work was biological, the principle of evolution was given wider application and came to be seen as the key to understanding many aspects of human life. In particular, it was applied to racial distinctions on the basis that different races were at different stages of evolution in terms of their intellectual and technological development. Europeans came to understand themselves as a higher race, which was far advanced, and to regard non-Caucasians as lower races, which were viewed as being still at a backward stage. A similar frame of analysis was applied to religion so that there were higher religions, where philosophical and ethical systems were highly developed, and lower religions, which had no developed philosophy or literature. Both in terms of race and religion, Africans were generally regarded as being at the lower end of the scale.

Andrew Ross has explored this in terms of missionary attitudes.[3] Belief in the essential equality of all human beings irrespective of race was a hallmark of early European missionaries in southern Africa such as John Philip. David Livingstone stood in this tradition, as did the Missions founded in his memory that began their work in Malawi in the mid-1870s. Notwithstanding obvious cultural differences, Blantyre Mission worked on the basis of the oneness of humanity, expecting that the Africans with whom they made connections had the potential to advance in education and flourish in professional life no less than Europeans might. Meanwhile, however, a very different view of race had been gaining ground in Europe, first in intellectual circles and then in the wider culture. This maintained that humanity was not one but that each race was a distinct species. As Andrew Ross explains, 'These species were usually ranked on an ascending scale by both moral and intellectual ability, the European always at the top and the African always at or near the bottom . . .'[4] His point is well illustrated by the title of Edwin Smith's 1923 book, *The Religion of the Lower Races*.[5]

This understanding of race became so pervasive that it was very difficult to avoid being influenced by it. In its more extreme forms, it justified the extermination of indigenous people on the grounds that they were subhuman and could be hunted and killed as if they were animals. In its more moderate and 'benevolent' forms, it imposed on the supposedly superior races a duty to elevate those believed to be inferior. This supplied a supposedly benign and humanitarian interpretation of colonial rule, which could provide camouflage for the oppression, violence and exploitation that the European imperial powers inflicted on peoples whom they colonised. It allowed many of those involved in imposing colonial rule to imagine that they were taking up the so-called 'white man's burden' whereby Europeans were expected to rule over less developed races in order that they might advance and prosper. It was with this latter approach, sometimes described as stadialism, that the missionary movement could most easily align.[6]

When the Western missionary movement held its most definitive and most representative gathering in Edinburgh in 1910, what was striking was that the racially inflected hierarchy of civilisations that provided the organisational principle for one of the major reports went unchallenged and unquestioned.[7] For the European and American missionaries from every part of the world who assembled at Edinburgh, the racially defined hierarchical understanding of the world's 'civilisations' was axiomatic.[8] Far from being in any way controversial or debatable, it was universally accepted as a starting point. Hetherwick would have cut an extraordinary figure had he stood apart from this consensus. Even someone as committed to promoting mutually respectful and constructive racial attitudes as missionary leader J. H. Oldham nonetheless regarded race as definitive for human identity and human relations, and adopted a stadialist outlook.[9] 'It is recognised,' wrote Oldham, 'that the care and advancement of weaker peoples are an obligation and responsibility resting on those who are more advanced.'[10]

Perceptive Africans, including those identified with Blantyre Mission, could perceive a difference between the early missionaries who related to them fundamentally as equals and those arriving from the late 1890s onwards who were more conscious of the supposed gulf between Europeans and Africans. The latter adopted a paternalistic approach, regarding Africans as children for whose development they accepted responsibility. What this meant in Blantyre is evoked by Andrew Ross when he writes,

> In the 1890s European visitors were taken aback to enter Scott's manse in Blantyre to find a Kololo chief and his retinue or Scott's 'deacons' and their wives sipping tea in Mrs Scott's best china. By 1930 such European visitors were much more at home when they saw venerable African ministers, like any other 'boy', standing at the foot of the veranda steps wondering if the 'Bwana was in'.[11]

Alexander Hetherwick's long period of service straddled these two periods. His life therefore offers an opportunity to explore how the inter-relation of mission, race and colonialism played out during a formative time in Malawi's history.

Despite his prominence, history has not been particularly kind to Hetherwick. In the popular imagination he has rather been overshadowed by his near-contemporary Robert Laws of Livingstonia, an iconic figure especially for the northern part of Malawi. In the standard history of Blantyre Mission by Andrew Ross, Hetherwick is contrasted very unfavourably with his long-time colleague and predecessor as Head of Blantyre Mission, David Clement Scott.[12] This unfavourable contrast has been echoed by subsequent scholars.[13] The gist of the critique is that, whereas Scott was anti-racist and pro-African, Hetherwick adapted himself to the racism and paternalism of the colonial age.[14] One aim of this book is to suggest that it was not quite as simple as that. In making this suggestion it will also challenge the polarity that entails viewing the missionaries either as agents of Western colonialism or as self-sacrificial heroes devoted to the cause of their adopted communities.

Another, simpler, aim is to offer an account and assessment of the life of someone who played a leading role in the making of Malawi and a foundational role in the life of one of its major church communities, the Blantyre Synod of the Church of Central Africa Presbyterian (CCAP). His life and career form a prism through which many of the issues that faced church and nation in the late nineteenth and early twentieth century can be considered. The book is therefore written with the hope that it might fill a gap in Malawi's historiography. Missionary biographies, including Hetherwick's,[15] were plentiful during the heyday of the missionary movement, often written in glowing terms to encourage supporters. From the 1960s and 1970s attention turned to the African participants in the missionary enterprise, a welcome and necessary turn that has been very fruitful and is far from exhausted. At the same time, there is much to be learned by examining afresh the expatriate missionaries who left their mark on Malawi. Hamish McIntosh's biography of Robert Laws, Peter Forster's of Cullen Young and Harry Langworthy's of Joseph Booth have demonstrated the value of such endeavour.[16] The scale of Hetherwick's contribution to the making of Malawi demands that he too should be given such treatment.

In particular, the book can be a contribution to the growing literature on the history of the CCAP Synod of Blantyre. Given its role and influence in the country across almost 150 years, it deserves substantial study. Hetherwick himself was an early contributor with his semi-autobiographical account of the first fifty years of Blantyre Mission history, written soon after his retirement in 1928.[17] He was also an informant for his own biography, written by the journalist and editor W. P. Livingstone and published around the same time.[18] In 1951, Harry Kambwiri Matecheta, the first African ordained minister within the Blantyre Mission, published an account of its early history.[19] Factually, it has much in common with Hetherwick's account but is written from the perspective of an African participant and described by the editors of the recent new edition as a 're-righting' of the history.[20]

A decade later, Andrew Ross, in the research for his doctoral thesis, also took a revisionist approach, seeking to retrieve the African experience and with special attention to the mission philosophy of David Clement Scott who led the Mission from 1881 until 1898.[21] Particularly since its belated publication in 1996, this has become the standard history of the early period of Blantyre Mission, unlikely ever to be replaced since Ross had access to oral sources that will not be available in future. Meanwhile, in 1976, another Scottish missionary, Tom Colvin, published a more popular account of the early history.[22] More recently, Gilbert Phiri has turned his attention to the social impact of Blantyre Mission. His University of Malawi 2007 Master's thesis focuses on the impact of Domasi Mission in countering poverty in its sphere of influence while his Mzuzu University 2020 PhD thesis offers a comprehensive history of the educational work of Blantyre

Mission/Synod.²³ The present book seeks to add to this literature through a close examination of the issues that were at stake during the period of Hetherwick's leadership of the Mission from 1898 to 1928 as well as by attempting to get the measure of the man who, along with Clement Scott, played a definitive role in making Blantyre Mission what it was.

The book might also be a small contribution to the ongoing assessment of the modern Western Christian missionary movement. This has often suffered from an excess of generalisation and perhaps what can take the discussion forward is a close examination of the contribution of particular missionaries. Alexander Hetherwick is one who invites such examination in view of the range and vigour of his engagement with the Malawi context across five decades. Though he spent his whole time in one particular geographical territory, it gave him an extraordinary range of interest so that his work spanned such areas as public theology, language studies, development economics, anthropology, human rights, nation-building, missiology, inculturation and ecclesiology, which continue to be sites of active debate today. To retrieve Hetherwick's story and examine how he handled the issues of his day might be one way of shedding light on those of ours.

I acknowledge, as author, that the nature and range of Hetherwick's interests and involvements hold particular interest for me. Though separated by almost exactly 100 years, I have much in common with my subject: like him, I am a Presbyterian minister from Scotland and have spent a significant part of my life in Malawi serving with the Church of Central Africa Presbyterian. Like him I have been greatly interested in the life of the church in Malawi, the role of the church in relation to public life and the nature of the missionary enterprise. As I have wrestled with such issues in my own time, I find myself drawn to Hetherwick to discover how he handled them in his. For me, he is also a lens through which to examine what was happening in Malawi during the highly formative years when he was involved. Personal interest is a key motivator for research and writing but it can also draw the researcher so close to the subject that critical perspective is lost. This book will very likely be viewed as a sympathetic account of Hetherwick's life and contribution. It therefore stands ready to be corrected by those who might bring greater critical distance. In particular, I am conscious of the limitations of one *mzungu* (white person) writing about another in what Hetherwick himself always called 'a black man's country'.²⁴ It is Malawian scholars who are best placed to assess Hetherwick's contribution, for good or ill, to the history of their country. This book's job will be done if it provides some food for thought in that process.

To that end, what is attempted in this book is an intellectual biography. It does not attempt to give a blow-by-blow account of Hetherwick's life story with everything arranged chronologically. This has already been done in the existing biography by W. P. Livingstone and does not need to be repeated.²⁵ Instead, it identifies eight aspects or facets of Hetherwick's role in Malawi: pioneer missionary, 'right-hand man', mission leader, public figure, Malawi visionary, linguist and Bible translator, mission thinker and church leader. Inevitably there is overlap between these different categories but the framework aims to enable a focus on how Hetherwick's thinking was brought to bear on the challenges of his time. The thread holding them all together is the question of the inter-relation of mission, race and colonialism, which kept meeting Hetherwick at every turn. This question will therefore be engaged from different angles before a concluding assessment is attempted in the final chapter.

Alexander Hetherwick was born on 12 April 1860 at Knoxhill in rural Aberdeenshire in the northeast of Scotland. As a young schoolboy his imagination was captured by the stories he heard of David Livingstone's travels in Africa. The spell that was cast during those early years was to shape his life. He completed his secondary education at Old Aberdeen Grammar School before going on to study at the University of Aberdeen. He remained proud of his Aberdeen formation and was prone (with tongue in cheek) to highlight the superiority of Aberdeen graduates whenever he had a chance. A notable event for him was the occasion in 1920 when James Ogilvie, a former classmate of Hetherwick's and now Convener of the Foreign Mission Committee, was visiting Blantyre at the same time as Robert Laws of Livingstonia, another Aberdeen graduate. When the European service was held that Sunday he noted with pride: 'four graduates in Divinity of Aberdeen officiated – two of them Ex-Moderators of the two General Assemblies of the two Scottish Churches. Well done, Aberdeen!'[26]

As a young man, his spiritual life was nurtured at the West Church of St Nicholas where he was profoundly influenced by the ministry of Mitford Mitchell, who later became a prominent figure at national level in the Church of Scotland. Many years later when Mitchell died, Hetherwick wrote 'How much I owe to him and to the West Kirk under him only God and myself know – but for that I should never have been here or anywhere else that I could have looked back with thankfulness as I can do today.'[27] He became President of the University Missionary Society and it became clear that he was contemplating a missionary vocation himself. At the same time, he attained much academic distinction, graduating with First Class Honours and winning the Simpson Mathematical Prize. An opportunity to proceed to postgraduate studies in mathematics at the University of Cambridge beckoned but by this time Hetherwick knew that an academic career in Britain was not for him. When colleagues remonstrated with him for giving up the prospect of a distinguished life and career in favour of obscurity in Africa, he replied robustly: 'Sacrifice? It will be a sacrifice not to go!'[28]

The Church of Scotland Foreign Mission Committee, after getting over some misapprehension that he was training as a medical doctor, accepted him to serve as a minister at Blantyre Mission.[29] On 8 May 1883 he was ordained to the ministry by the Presbytery of Aberdeen and dedicated to the work that lay ahead of him. The following week he sailed from London on the S.S. *India*. Joining him on the journey was Henry Henderson, who had selected the site for Blantyre Mission and was now returning after a furlough (leave period) in Scotland. The long days at sea gave him the opportunity to learn much about the Mission to which his life was now dedicated. Landing at Quelimane he proceeded by steamer up the Zambezi and Shire Rivers, arriving at Blantyre on 13 August 1883. Many years later he recalled that, 'The day closed with a visit to the Dormitories and a chat with the boys sitting round the fire; most of them were Makololo lads from the 'River, sons of Livingstone's Makololo.'[30] Thus began the interaction with the African community in which he was to find his vocation.[31]

Notes

1. Stephen Green, 'Blantyre Mission', *The Nyasaland Journal* 10/2 (1957), 6–17, at 9.
2. Cit. Hamish McIntosh, *Robert Laws: Servant of Africa*, Edinburgh: Handsel Press and Blantyre: Central Africana, 1993, 244; the Moderators were John R. Gray in 1977 and William J. G. McDonald in 1989.
3. Andrew C. Ross, 'Christian Missions and Mid-Nineteenth-Century Change in Attitudes to Race: the African Experience', in Andrew Porter (ed.), *The Imperial Horizons of British Protestant Missions, 1880–1914*, Grand Rapids: Eerdmans, 2003, 85–105.
4. Ibid., 89.
5. Edwin W. Smith, *The Religion of the Lower Races*, New York: Macmillan, 1923. It should be noted that Smith himself, who championed a sympathetic understanding of African religion, was greatly troubled by the title of his book, which was imposed by the publisher. See further W. John Young, *The Quiet Wise Spirit: Edwin W. Smith [1876–1957] and Africa*, Peterborough: Epworth Press, 2002.
6. See further Hilary M. Carey, *God's Empire: Religion and Colonialism in the British World c. 1801–1908*, Cambridge: Cambridge University Press, 2011.
7. Brian Stanley, 'Church, State, and the Hierarchy of "Civilization": The Making of the "Missions and Governments" Report at the World Missionary Conference, Edinburgh 1910', in Andrew Porter (ed.), *The Imperial Horizons of British Protestant Missions, 1880–1914*, Grand Rapids and Cambridge: Eerdmans, 2003, 58–84.
8. See Kirsteen Kim, 'Racism Awareness in Mission: Touchstone or Cultural Blind Spot?', *International Bulletin of Mission Research* 45/4 (2021), 377–86.
9. See J. H. Oldham, *Christianity and the Race Problem*, London: SCM, 1924.
10. Ibid., 101. Oldham looked forward to the ultimate creation of 'a human fellowship in which the estranging differences of race are completely transcended' (ibid., 249), but regarded these differences as an inescapable reality in the meantime.
11. Andrew C. Ross, 'Christian Missions and Mid-Nineteenth-Century Change in Attitudes to Race', 101; based on oral testimony gathered by the author when conducting research on Blantyre Mission in the late 1950s and early 1960s.
12. See Andrew C. Ross, *Blantyre Mission and the Making of Modern Malawi*, especially 224–41.
13. See e.g. Harri Englund, '"Africa is an Education": Vernacular Translation and

Missionary Encounter in Nineteenth Century Malawi', in Kenneth R. Ross and Wapulumuka O. Mulwafu (eds), *Politics, Christianity and Society in Malawi: Essays in Honour of John McCracken*, Mzuzu: Mzuni Press, 2020, 138–62.

14. It should be noted, however, that in his 1998 article on Hetherwick, Andrew Ross took a more sympathetic approach to his subject than he did in his doctoral work during the 1960s. He makes no unfavourable comparison with Scott. Instead, he emphasises their collaboration and highlights Hetherwick's speeches to the 1915 Commission of Inquiry on the Native Rising, which he describes as, 'a startling insistence on the oneness of humanity transcending racial difference'. Andrew C. Ross, 'Alexander Hetherwick', in Gerald H. Anderson (ed.), *Biographical Dictionary of Christian Missions*, New York: Simon & Schuster, 1998, 291.
15. W. P. Livingstone, *A Prince of Missionaries: Alexander Hetherwick of Blantyre*, London: James Clarke, n.d.
16. Hamish McIntosh, *Robert Laws: Servant of Africa*, Edinburgh: Handsel Press and Blantyre: Central Africana, 1993; Peter G. Forster, *T. Cullen Young: Missionary and Anthropologist*, Hull: Hull University Press, 1989 and Blantyre: CLAIM-Kachere, 2003; Harry Langworthy, *Africa for the African: The Life of Joseph Booth*, Blantyre: CLAIM-Kachere, 2002.
17. Alexander Hetherwick, *The Romance of Blantyre: How Livingstone's Dream Came True*, London: James Clarke, n.d.
18. W. P. Livingstone, *A Prince of Missionaries*.
19. Harry Kambwiri Matecheta, *Blantyre Mission: Stories of its Beginning*, ed. by Thokozani Chilembwe and Todd Statham, Mzuzu: Luviri Press, 2020 (trsl. from Harry Kambwiri Matecheta, *Blantyre Mission. Nkhani za Ciyambi Cace*, Blantyre: Hetherwick Press, 1951.)
20. Ibid., 22.
21. Andrew C. Ross, *Blantyre Mission and the Making of Modern Malawi*.
22. Tom Colvin, *A Record of Fathers and Founders of Blantyre Synod*, Blantyre: CCAP Synod of Blantyre, 1976.
23. Gilbert Davison Foster Phiri, 'The Involvement of the Church in the Empowerment of the Poor through Self-Reliance Education, Health Services and Agriculture: The Case of Blantyre Synod in Domasi Presbytery', MA, University of Malawi, 2007; Gilbert Davison Foster Phiri, 'A History of Education in Blantyre Synod (1876–2018)', PhD, Mzuzu University, 2020.
24. See for example *Life and Work in British Central Africa*, August 1902.
25. W. P. Livingstone, *A Prince of Missionaries*.
26. Alexander Hetherwick to W. M. McLachlan, 26 August 1920, MNA BMC/50/2/1/180; both Ogilvie and Laws had been Moderators of their respective General Assemblies.
27. Alexander Hetherwick to James Ogilvie, 11 November 1914, MNA BMC/50/2/1/135.
28. W. P. Livingstone, *A Prince of Missionaries*, 13.
29. Thomas McLagan to Alexander Hetherwick, 30 January 1883, NLS 7546/291.
30. Alexander Hetherwick, 'My First Day in Blantyre', *Central Africa News and Views* 2/1 (July 1936), 5.
31. See further Alexander Hetherwick, 'Livingstone's Makololo: Pioneers of Empire before Cecil Rhodes', *Other Lands*, April 1935, 115–16.

CHAPTER TWO

The Pioneer Missionary: Domasi Days

Hetherwick is so often remembered as the venerable elder statesman that it is easily forgotten that he began his life and work in Malawi as a slight young man of twenty-three, fresh out of college. His university education, which he had completed with distinction, played a vital part in his formation. Yet he had much still to learn if he were to fulfil his ambition to become a successful missionary. Both Scott and Hetherwick were fond of quoting an aphorism that originated with James Stewart of Lovedale, who played a leading role in the movement that led to the establishment of both Livingstonia and Blantyre Mission, and who pointed out that 'Africa is an education'.[1] Towards the end of his long career, Hetherwick was still recalling Scott's insistence that, 'When anyone comes out here to start work among the natives he has to go to school again.'[2]

In Hetherwick's own case, the 'school' was Domasi where he was sent to begin a new mission station in 1884, the year following his arrival at Blantyre. His appointment was a strategic decision on the part of the Mission, taken with a view to establishing a bridgehead among the Yao people with whom it had been in contact since it first began its work in the Shire Highlands. Some Yao chiefs had connections with the Arab world and participated in the slave trade. Inspired by the vision of David Livingstone, Blantyre Mission was determined to counter the slave trade by introducing Christianity and 'civilisation' to its sphere of influence. The vision behind the mission station at Domasi was nothing less than a transformation of the political, cultural, social, economic and religious landscape of the Shire Highlands. It was also seen as a strategic point from which to stop the spread of Islam, a major preoccupation of the Christian missionary movement at that time.[3] David Bone notes that, 'The most enthusiastic proponent of the use of schools to try to cordon off the spread of Islam was Dr Hetherwick of the Blantyre Mission. He saw a chain of mission schools in the area north of Zomba as an effective barrier to its southward advance.'[4] The fulfilment of the vision of transformation that had been cultivated at Blantyre Mission was entrusted to the now twenty-four-year-old newcomer who would cut his teeth as a missionary in the development of the Domasi station.

Together with the intrepid Henry Henderson, who had earlier chosen the site for Blantyre Mission, Hetherwick set out to prospect for the site of a new mission station that would allow the Mission to extend its reach northwards into the heart of the Yao territory. They trekked for 220 miles around the Phalombe plain, Lake Chilwa and Mount Chikala before finally settling on a spot on the high pass between Zomba and Malosa mountains, named Domasi after the river that supplied its water. It was a strategic spot from which to counter the slave trade. It was close to the large population of the Lake Chilwa area and the missionaries were well received by the Yao chief Malemia, who had been well disposed towards the Blantyre missionaries since their first arrival.[5] Chief Malemia allocated Hetherwick a site of some 610 acres on the banks of the Domasi River and it was here that he set about building the mission station.[6]

Many years later Hetherwick recalled his introduction to the geography of the Shire Highlands when, soon after his arrival at Blantyre in 1883, he embarked on an extensive exploration of the surrounding area in the company of the evangelist and biologist Professor Henry Drummond, who was visiting from Scotland at the time.[7] What he particularly remembered was Drummond's remark about one of their porters: 'I would give all I possess to get inside that fellow for just half an hour'.[8] For Hetherwick, this set the agenda for the missionary work that lay ahead of him:

> For five-and-forty years thereafter I was trying to 'get inside' and understand such African 'fellows' as he and at the end of all my endeavours I had oftentimes to confess myself almost as much outside them as Drummond and I were outside that 'fellow' those many years ago. To think as an African thinks, 'thinking black', as it has facetiously been called – is an achievement impossible to me as a white man. The black man's whole upbringing, environment, and outlook, have raised a high wall between his mind and mine, that I have never got over – a wall built by generations of heredity in an atmosphere vastly different from mine.[9]

This reflection indicates the tension and ambivalence that marked Hetherwick's missionary experience. He thought in racial terms of 'white' and 'black' as separate categories that precluded any complete mutual understanding between two contrasting communities. Yet he committed his life to 'trying' to understand as much as he could, a sustained attempt at empathy that began with his years at Domasi.

Perhaps it is a mark of his humility and respect for the people of Africa that he admitted in the end how incomplete was his understanding. The more you know, the more you become aware of how much you do not know. Hetherwick's modest self-assessment belies the fact that for decades he was the British administration's go-to person whenever they needed an authoritative explanation of indigenous culture or tradition. He was also, for thirty years, the President of the Examinations Board for Chinyanja and Chiyao examinations taken by government civil servants. Both during his Domasi days and later, he spent long periods of time entirely in African company, applying his keen intellect not only to learning the languages but to understanding the cultures that informed them. He had gone further than any other European in appreciating the way of thinking that prevailed in the communities of the Shire Highlands. Nevertheless, rather than posing as an expert whose long experience had enabled him to master African life and culture, he preferred to stress how much he still had to learn. In particular, he was convinced that it would be Africans themselves who would provide answers to the questions that remained for him, in the meantime, unanswered. 'We have endeavoured,' he wrote, 'to penetrate some little distance into that inner mind of his which is still an enigma to the white man, and which will ever be an unknown region to the white man until the Native himself turns his mind inward on himself and tells us what he finds there.'[10]

Getting Started

It was at Domasi that this attitude was first formed and cultivated. In July 1884 the local community was intrigued to see a European with a small group of Africans clearing the ground to pitch their tents. Soon they embarked on the building of a wattle-and-daub house that would be Hetherwick's home and base of operations in the coming years. From his bedroom-cum-office he had a spectacular view across to Lake Chilwa while two other rooms anticipated the need to accommodate boarders at the school that was planned. There was also provision of elementary hospital services.[11] Within the year he also built a temporary church, made of wooden poles, mud walls and a grass roof.[12] At first, there was little indication that the mission station was particularly welcome or likely to exercise any significant influence.

When Blantyre Mission marked the semi-jubilee (twenty-fifth anniversary) of Hetherwick's arrival in 1908, John McIlwain, who had served almost as long, spoke of the 'early and trying days' through which Dr Hetherwick had passed, especially during 'his lonely years in the founding of Domasi station and his struggles against the powerful slave-raiding chiefs of that district . . .'[13] Hetherwick himself, when he wrote the obituary of Henry Scott who succeeded him at Domasi, recalled that, 'These early years were the days of small things for the missionary – slavery, superstition, and heathenism were active and unashamed, and missionary aims and motives imperfectly understood . . . It meant a stiff stubborn uphill fight, a fight demanding grit, patience, and perseverance.'[14] While paying tribute to Henry Scott, there can be little doubt that his assessment was informed by his own experience.

Europeans were few and far between in Malawi at this time and this seems to be what is in view when reference is made to the loneliness of Hetherwick's posting. He was not really alone, however, since he was accompanied by Joseph Bismarck, an African who played a prominent role in the early years of Blantyre Mission. Bismarck had grown up in Quelimane, where he was given his unusual name on account of his apparent likeness to the German chancellor of the time. He joined the initial group of Scottish missionaries when they travelled inland to join Henry Henderson at Blantyre and became the Mission's first convert. During the turbulent early period, when none of the original group of missionaries lasted more than a few years in the service of the Mission, Bismarck was one of a small group of Africans who provided stability and continuity. He was familiar with the Domasi area, having taught in the school that John Buchanan, a member of the first missionary party who later became a planter and Acting British Consul, established at nearby Mulunguzi in Zomba in the late 1870s. The Mission sent Bismarck for further training at Lovedale in South Africa and on his return in 1884 he was appointed to teach at the new station being established at Domasi.[15]

Hetherwick therefore had at his side a near contemporary who was already seasoned in mission work. Bismarck's calibre became apparent when he was in sole charge of the new station for most of the time from 1885 to 1887 when Hetherwick was back in Blantyre covering for the absence of Clement Scott on sick leave in Scotland. The establishment and consolidation of Domasi Mission during the mid-1880s owed as much to Bismarck as it did to Hetherwick, though this is scarcely reflected in the Eurocentric historiography of the missionary period. Another of the Blantyre Mission stalwarts who worked alongside Bismarck in these early years at Domasi was Rondau Kaferanjira.[16]

Despite being in good company, it was clearly a daunting prospect for the young Scot to adapt himself to a totally new environment, an alien culture, political forces that he barely understood and a language that he had just started to learn. An autobiographical passage in the lectures he gave in 1930–31 after his retirement to Scotland reveals just how daunted he felt during his early days at Domasi:

> The young missionary has not long been settled before he realises that the African has no desire for his teaching, nor any sense of the need of that Gospel which the missionary has come to impart. His limited knowledge of the native tongue keeps him from understanding much of the talk going on daily around him. He sees enough, however, during those few months to make him conscious of the difficulty of the task he has set his face to, and to ask himself, 'How am I to begin?'[17]

Hetherwick's pragmatic turn of mind is apparent in his answer to the question he posed to himself:

> The best answer is to seek for no answer – but just to begin – to begin with the task lying immediate to his hand. This, in the experience of every pioneer missionary, is to build his station – to employ and possibly to teach his Native workers their tasks – to work alongside them, to live among them day after day, week after week – all the while watching them and studying them – learning more and more of their tribal habits and customs – getting daily nearer and nearer to them – though

feeling as if they were receding more and more from him, in thought, in feeling, and in mutual understanding one of the other.[18]

His adoption of such an approach in his young days is suggestive of the qualities that were to make Hetherwick an outstanding missionary leader. He was able to combine the pragmatic spirit of 'getting on with it' with a critical, reflective assessment of the deeper significance of the work that was being done.

Living Dangerously

The conditions under which Hetherwick and Bismarck set about establishing the Domasi mission station were far from peaceful or secure. In fact, the project was in jeopardy almost as soon as it had begun. The immediate threat came not from the Yao but from another immigrant group – the Ngoni who had established themselves in the hills on the other side of the Shire River. They were a military people, renowned for their raiding. In 1884 they launched a major raid. Their forces swept across the Shire Highlands, terrorising the people, burning their villages and pillaging their livestock and crops. Among the eyewitnesses was Harry Kambwiri Matecheta who included his observations in the history of Blantyre Mission that he published many years later.[19] The raid was on a large scale and many of the Yao people fled in terror to the mountains of Soche, Ndirande and Malabvi.

Hetherwick and his staff were directly affected because they were making their way from Blantyre to Domasi just at the time when the raid took place. He decided to leave the staff in the relative security of a bamboo thicket near Nkanda River while he himself continued to Domasi where he discovered that all the people had fled up the mountain. His staff were captured by the Ngoni forces but were quickly set free when they made it clear that they were workers of the Blantyre Mission.[20] Fortunately for them, just before the raid was launched, Clement Scott had made a long-awaited visit to Chief Chikuse, the Ngoni paramount chief, and the two had struck up an immediate friendship. As a result, when the Ngoni *impis* ('armies') swept into the Shire Highlands they were under instructions not to cause any harm to the Mission, with which their chief now enjoyed friendly relations.[21]

In the event, the Domasi mission station was unscathed, but Hetherwick surely felt that it was a close shave and he was living dangerously. History, however, was turning in a new direction and this proved to be the last major raid that the Ngoni made on the Shire Highlands. Matecheta captured the historical turning point when he reflected on his own appointment in 1893 – as a Yao – to be an evangelist among the Ngoni: 'In 1884 the Ngoni had brought their warring to our village. In 1893 we brought the Gospel to their villages.'[22] As for Hetherwick, when he stood one day in 1898 admiring the orderly scene that Zomba presented as the British developed the town as their administrative centre, he could not help recalling what he had witnessed there in 1884: 'On the spot where the Recreation ground has been laid out, old Kalimbuka and a few of his villagers made a stand against them and rescued part of their crop which the raiders were carrying off. In those days who would have dreamt of the scene of today!'[23] It was in the midst of such tumult and danger that Hetherwick applied himself to establishing the mission station that he was convinced could have transformative and beneficial effect.

Living on Terms Set by Others

After the initial excitement of dealing with the Ngoni invasion, life settled down at Domasi and Hetherwick could begin to come to terms with his assignment. The mission historian Andrew Walls has observed that: 'The fundamental missionary experience, by which the endeavour stands or falls, is to live on the terms set by someone else.'[24] This was what Hetherwick was attempting to do as he learned the Yao language and did his best to understand the life and culture of the people among whom he had made his home. He was realistic about the very low level of understanding with which he began and from which he sometimes wondered, even many years later, if he had really advanced very far. His account of the experience of a newly arrived missionary is surely informed by his own experience at Domasi: 'Around him was a native community – maybe a whole tribe, of whose tongue he had learned only a smattering – if anything at all. Of their manners, habits, and customs he knew nothing – nothing of their psychological outlook on life which was to be, even after many years, still a sealed book to him.'[25]

Having come from Europe to Africa, Hetherwick soon became aware that he had entered a context where the prevailing understanding of the world was very different from that to which he had been accustomed. He observed that,

> The African is moved and swayed by unseen and mystic influences that have no place in the white man's process of reasoning, and the path through his field of thought is one impossible for the white man to follow. The African lives in a world full of mystic potencies, and surrounded ever by unseen agencies in a world of spirit powers between whom and himself is close and constant intercommunion, and which profoundly affect his motives and actions.[26]

Africans, he quickly realised, were living in an 'enchanted' world whereas Europeans had long since abandoned such a worldview. His analysis anticipated the theory of the 'excluded middle', which has been highly influential in anthropology and mission studies since Paul Hiebert's 1982 article.[27] Hetherwick explained it in these terms:

> There appear gaps in his course of reasoning which I cannot get over, but which are filled in by him with unseen and mystic forces and fears that are to him as real as the outer material world with its laws of cause and effect is to me. I believe that from this source he fills in the middle premise which throws awry my examination of his syllogism. It is just this mystic middle premise of which the white man is ignorant, and so believes it wanting, that makes the black man's reasoning so incomprehensible to the white, and which explains the latter's failure to grasp or understand the ground or cause for the former's attitude.[28]

In contrasting the religious view of the world that was all-pervasive in Africa with the secular direction of European culture, he also anticipated Charles Taylor's monumental study of how Westerners became secular in outlook, moving 'from a society in which it was virtually impossible not to believe in God, to one in which faith, even for the staunchest believer, is one human possibility among others.'[29]

At Domasi during the 1880s and 1890s Hetherwick was wrestling with the strong religious sensibility that he found in the Yao community and asking himself how it related to the Christian understanding. He summarised his findings in a paper on 'The Native Idea of God and the Soul' which he contributed to the Anthropological Institute in 1902 and reproduced in the *Life and Work in British Central Africa*:

> ... the term Mulungu is ... used to denote the spirit world in general, or more properly speaking 'the aggregate of all spirits of all the dead'. The plural form of the word is rarely heard unless the attention is being specially directed to the denizens of the spirit world in their separate individualities. By its form the word does not denote personality for it does not belong to the personal class of nouns. Its form denotes rather a state or property inhering in something as the life or health of a person inheres in his body, or as the heart in the body is regarded as the seat of conscience ... Once after endeavouring to impress on an old Yao headman the idea of the personality of the Godhead in the Christian sense of the word, my listener thereupon began to talk of 'Che Mulungu', 'Mr God', as showing that the original form in his mind had no association whatever with personality ... And yet the Yao approaches close to the conception of personality when he speaks of what Mulungu has done and is doing. It is Mulungu he says who has made the world, and man and animals.[30]

Hetherwick thus used his linguistic ability to interrogate the understanding of the divine that prevailed in the Yao community. It led him to conclude that there were three stages in the belief structure of the Yao people: (1) the human *lisoka* or soul, the agent of dreams, delirium and so on; (2) this *lisoka* regarded as the *Mulungu* or object of worship and reverence – the controller of the affairs of this world, the active agent in the affairs of the next; (3) lastly *Mulungu* as the great spirit agency – the creator of life, the source of all things animate and inanimate.[31]

He was also able to observe that, in the course of everyday life, offerings were made to the spirit world in general under the name *Mulungu*. He noticed that often 'the first fruits of the new crop – green maize, pumpkins, beans, peas etc. – were placed in a small grass hut as a thanksgiving for the new harvest'.[32] Here he discerned a point of continuity between the traditions of the people and Christian worship:

> The Harvest Thanksgiving always appeals to the hearts of the people. The idea of thanking God for the food they have just been gathering in is simple and easily understood by all of them. Nor is it a new idea. Amongst themselves they have a custom very much akin to our harvest thanksgiving. Before reaping the millet grain, the chief commonly calls on his people to bring the first fruits of the crop to his courtyard, whence a portion of it is carried to the grave of the late chief, and there offered to the spirits of the dead . . . We find there is no religious service which calls forth so hearty a response as the Thanksgiving for the Harvest.[33]

Such observation opened up for Hetherwick the whole question of the relation between the religious traditions of the people and the faith that he proclaimed as a Christian missionary.

He asked himself the question, 'What are the grounds on which the missionary appeal from the heathen world may be based?' It was common at the time to paint 'heathen' life in very dark colours in order to highlight the need for missionary work. Hetherwick took the point but was concerned that this approach tended to give a very one-sided account: '. . . it leads the mind to dwell only on that darker side of the picture, forgetting that on many parts of heathen life the shadows grow much lighter.'[34] His experience of life at Domasi had allowed him to appreciate that there was another side to the story:

> None who have lived for any length of time in the midst of native life and who possess the least spark of human sympathy, can fail to mark the great good humour, the kindness and mutual helpfulness, the politeness, the patience that are everywhere patent on the surface. The bright faces of the children, the hearty sometimes mischievous laugh of boy or girl, the loyalty of men or women to the chief and head, the grim stoicism that turns the native face to the uncertain future without a doubt or fear, are all seeds of rich hope.[35]

His appreciation of the rich human quality of the community around him did not, however, lead him to doubt its need for the gospel he had come to proclaim: 'The watering and the tending must come from Christ'.[36]

The missionary vision that formed in his mind as he grew familiar with the people with whom he was working was akin to what has been called fulfilment theology. It was not a matter of replacing the existing traditions with an entirely new system of thought. It was more a matter of the new being the fulfilment of the old. He imagined a process through which all that made for human flourishing in the African tradition could be affirmed while the renewing power of the gospel could expose and eliminate all that was life-denying and destructive. Hetherwick put it in these terms: 'Just as in the world of science and arts the aim of the discoverer is towards a reduction of the great waste of energy that goes on in the world, so does the aim of missions tend to draw these wandering energies and impulses of heathenism into the service of Christ and humanity. The faith of the Gospel would draw all these into a new channel – from which on either side life and growth would spring.'[37] This gave Hetherwick an essentially positive assessment of African life and community as fruitful ground in which Christian faith could grow.

He counselled against a negative or condemnatory approach. When he addressed his fellow missionaries at their conference in Blantyre on 22 October 1904, he advised them that, 'We need wide sympathy to see the good in our people. We must not forget that we are dealing with men and women of another race and another outlook on life. We must abstain from dwelling on the darker side of our peoples' lives, from continually carping at their weaknesses and their failures. We must see a possible Christ in every man.'[38] Such a vision called for sophistication in missionary work. There was a need to recognise and embrace the strengths of the inherited tradition in Africa while introducing the renewing and transforming effects of the Christian gospel.

It also involved a canny recognition that there are two sides to the missionary encounter. Hetherwick learned during his years at Domasi that the Africans among whom he was working were not just passive recipients. Rather they were active agents and well capable of making their own assessment of the newcomer in their midst. The missionary, he advised, ought to be aware that,

> . . . while he is studying them – they are studying him – with that wonderful instinct of theirs for character, they are reading him through and through. With keen microscopic eyes they mark his little traits of character – any weaknesses he may display are rapidly noted – characteristics he may hardly be aware of himself at all. Every hour of the day he is under observation. And then in the evening round the village fire, or on the flat rock where the women place the mortars in which they pound their household grain, he is discussed, his character for patience or kindliness or courtesy, or that 'good heart' which stands so high in Native estimation. These are all weighed and measured with an accuracy that would astonish the subject of it all and make him think more humbly of himself.[39]

Such awareness that he was engaged with people of high character and sharp judgement was to shape Hetherwick's missionary leadership in the many years that lay ahead of him. It would have been much the poorer had he lacked the 'education' that he received through his immersion in local community life at Domasi.

The Steady Routine

Malawi was passing through eventful times during the years that Hetherwick was based at Domasi. He had his part to play in the major historical events that proved transformative for Malawi but it is important to recognise that there were also many very ordinary days on the little mission station at Domasi where life followed a steady routine. Here Hetherwick found his forte and he was inclined to champion the virtues of dogged commitment to the steady round of everyday work:

> Too many missionary biographies and histories deal only with the exciting, the heroic, and the romantic – all to rouse the interest. Hence the 'commonplaceness' of everyday missionary duty finds no place in the Church's battle with heathenism . . . with the great battles of Christianity with heathenism – the dull routine of everyday work is that which wins the battle, not the brilliant charge nor the self-sacrifice that wins the Victoria cross.[40]

As with many a mission station in those days, the first endeavour was to start a school. Hetherwick recalled that, 'At Domasi it began in the missionary's bedroom – of all places! – but he was young and new to the country then, and did not know that almost every native in his raw unwashed state does not move about alone . . .'[41] There were livestock to consider so the lessons were soon removed to the back verandah. An alphabet card was stuck on the wall with a piece of bamboo, and another longer piece did duty as a pointer. Hetherwick recalled that, 'In the hot weather both teacher and pupils would fall asleep from very weariness . . .'[42] 'Elementary work it seemed for a distinguished University graduate,' commented his biographer, 'but he always saw far beyond the drudgery of the moment.'[43]

It was not long before the apparently feeble beginning gave rise to a major educational movement. By 1891 the Domasi school was well established and additional schools had been started at Kaungulu and at Mulunguzi.[44] When Melville Anderson took over the leadership of Domasi Mission in the early years of the twentieth century he made this assessment:

> What is the normal evolution of a Christian village in these parts? It would seem to be of this nature. Some boys learn to read a little. They start up in others the desire to learn. They hear about the schools in other villages and say, 'Why should we not have a school?' They build a school of trees, bamboos and grass. The Mission provides teachers. The teacher not only does school work, but conducts services and starts a class for enquirers. Thus in time we find in the village a day school,

in which also regular services are held on Sundays and in which the Hearer's Class meets and also, when these exist, the Catechumen Class and Sunday School meet.[45]

This was the movement that Hetherwick had set in motion with his classes on the verandah that had seemed to send everyone to sleep.

It took time before the small beginnings of church life could be discerned but at Easter 1891 five young men and one young woman presented themselves for baptism. Among them were Alexander Chitete, John Mkwatula, David Mothela, George Chikwana and James Mpinganjira who would later take up leading roles in the life of the church.[46] John McMurtrie, Convener of the Church of Scotland's Africa Committee, wrote to Hetherwick with some excitement: 'I write chiefly to congratulate you on the 6 baptisms on Easter Sunday recorded in the April Supplement. The beginning of a Domasi Church!'[47] So it proved to be as a steady stream of candidates progressed through the Hearer's Class and Catechumen's Class to be baptised and become full members of the church. Soon Christian weddings were being celebrated at Domasi, with two of the newly baptised Christians leading the way in September 1891 when Alexander Chitete married Chesoyaga and John Mkwatula married Chiseweka.[48]

To see the Mission Station develop from its humble beginnings to become a thriving centre with church, school and industrial activity must have been a rewarding experience. A leprosy clinic was opened in 1887 to care for the significant number of people who were suffering from leprosy at that time.[49] A major agricultural enterprise was developed to introduce new crops and new methods as well as to provide for the needs of the mission community. Maize, beans and rice were grown, there was a cattle farm and horticultural produce included cabbage, turnips, tomatoes, carrots, lettuce, mustard and rape, oranges, lemons, paw-paws, guavas, loquats, nectarines, custard apples, granadillas, apricots, bananas and mangoes.[50] Soon the Mission was opening out-stations in the surrounding area at such places as Bamba, Nsondole, Kasonga, Sakata, Mpyupyu and Chisi, with churches being built at each and many being attracted by revival (*chitsitsimutso*) meetings.[51] Hetherwick, however, was not at all inclined to rest on his laurels. He was thinking already of ways in which the Mission could further extend its influence: 'I am sent not as a stationary,' he liked to say, 'but as a missionary.'[52] He developed a keen instinct that mission thrives on extension, on finding new frontiers to cross and new challenges to meet. This would inform his thinking in later years when it fell to him to shape the policy and strategy of Blantyre Mission.

It's People that Count

At the same time, mission takes effect not only through cultural analysis or strategic thinking but particularly through the network of relationships and friendships that are formed.[53] A Scottish missionary in Malawi of a later generation, Andrew Doig, coined the phrase 'it's people that count' and used it as the title of his autobiography.[54] It could well be applied to much missionary experience, including Hetherwick's years at Domasi. When he had just newly arrived and was still living in his tent, a curious young man visited one day and the two struck up a conversation. Hetherwick was impressed with his visitor and invited him to come and live at the Mission. The young man was interested but indicated that he would have to seek permission from his chief. Time passed and Hetherwick had almost forgotten the incident when one day, at sunset, he heard 'a cheerful shout, "I have come to stay!"'[55] When the first six baptisms took place at Domasi on Easter Sunday 1891, among the candidates was this young man. The human contact made in the first encounter proved to have far-reaching effect.

Another young man whom Hetherwick remembered well was Auka, who had first arrived at Domasi Mission in dramatic circumstances at the age of eleven or twelve. From a young age he had been subject to epileptic fits and one of these had caused him to fall into a fire, resulting in severe burning to the backs of his legs. This led to the formation of large, raw ulcers on his legs and he lost the ability to walk. His fellow villagers concluded that his case was hopeless and that he must have been bewitched. They took him into the bush, tied him to a tree and left him to die. After some days he managed to set himself free, assisted, he believed, by the spirits. He could not walk but decided to crawl to the Mission where he arrived in a desperate condition just as the little congregation was gathering for the evening service. He was welcomed into the Mission community, which was able to provide medical treatment. This brought complete healing to one leg, while the other had to be amputated at the knee. After this he enjoyed freedom of movement once again and was able to train in the boot repair shop that was part of the industrial activity of the Mission. 'When one sees a boy's life recovered and himself beginning to fill a useful sphere,' remarked Hetherwick, 'one cannot but reflect on the number of lives awaiting to be redeemed from heathenism in order to fulfil higher purposes.'[56]

It was also at Domasi in the 1880s that Hetherwick met Stephen Kundecha, who would later, along with Harry Kambwiri Matecheta, be one of the first two students to train for ordination to the ministry at Blantyre Mission. When Hetherwick first met Kundecha, the latter was a small boy, with curiosity bringing him to the new Mission each day to see what was going on. Almost fifty years later Hetherwick remembered the moment during the building of the mission station when Kundecha was watching him sharpening a plane iron and he used some oil from the sharpening stone to trace the sign of the cross on Kundecha's forehead, telling him that he now had a new tribal mark and should start coming to school. The next morning Kundecha presented himself at the school and was enrolled as a pupil.[57] It was the first step on a journey that led him to become teacher, headmaster, minister and scholar. At every step of the way Hetherwick was there for him as friend and mentor. It was through such relationships that the Mission gradually made its impact on the community in which it was set.

Meanwhile there was one person who 'counted' in a special way for Alexander Hetherwick during his Domasi years. This was Elizabeth Fenwick (née Pithie) to whom he was married in 1893. The two had first met in very sad circumstances when Hetherwick, just recently arrived in Blantyre, was invited to conduct the funeral of Elizabeth's infant son George who had been born during her disastrous first marriage to George Fenwick, who had been among the first members of the Blantyre Mission staff and had later established himself as an independent hunter. Early the following year Fenwick, who was notorious for his temper and drunkenness, murdered the Makololo chief Chipatula after a drunken argument and was killed soon afterwards as Chipatula's men took revenge. This left Elizabeth in a precarious position since the senior Makololo chief Ramakukan demanded that she be handed over to him along with all of Fenwick's property.

At this moment of crisis Clement and Bella Scott invited Elizabeth to live with them, which she did for the next four years. As Scott and Hetherwick forged their remarkable missionary partnership during the mid-1880s, Hetherwick had the opportunity to get to know the young woman who was part of the Scott household. During this period, she developed into a respected member of the missionary community. When she went on leave to Scotland in 1888, Clement Scott remarked: 'Mrs Fenwick leaves for home . . . she has been working now almost nine years and the people are greatly attached to her. Her knowledge of the language, her sympathy with the people and her gentleness of disposition have made them regard her as belonging to them, and her going seems almost the losing of one of themselves.'[58]

In fact, it appears that the years Elizabeth spent as a member of the Scott household proved to be something of a turning point for her after a troubled early life.[59] Her father had drowned when he fell into Aberdeen Harbour when she was only two weeks old. This left her mother to bring her up as a single parent in conditions of considerable poverty. Things took a turn for the worse when Elizabeth was eleven and her mother died. Thereafter her education was dependent on charity and it was a charitable group in Aberdeen that offered to pay her salary as a teacher at the recently founded Blantyre Mission. Here she arrived as an eighteen-year-old in 1879, the first unmarried woman to join the staff. Life was far from easy for a lonely young woman in such a context but became much worse during her short-lived marriage to Fenwick, which saw the births and deaths of their two children. Her turbulent life presented quite a contrast to Hetherwick's stable family background but the two of them were drawn to one another and a slow-burning romance appears to have begun.

When they were both due for home leave in 1888, they sailed to Scotland and back on the same ship and the many days at sea on the long voyages provided an opportunity for them to deepen their friendship. After their return it was noticed that Elizabeth, still based in Blantyre, was making rather frequent visits to the Domasi Mission. Finally, their engagement was announced and their marriage on 22 June 1893 was a momentous event in the history of the Mission. Two Malawian couples were married on the same day and the three couples held a shared reception, a powerful demonstration of the non-racial Christian community that Scott and Hetherwick were seeking to foster and to which Elizabeth gave her wholehearted support. Some schoolgirls walked fifty miles from Domasi to attend the wedding celebration. The Hetherwicks' joy was complete when their son Clement was born in 1895, named after their colleague and leader to whom they both owed so much.

Hetherwick was reserved, as was customary at the time, in making reference to his wife. Indeed, she is not mentioned at all in his book about the early history of Blantyre Mission, despite her not insignificant role.[60] In a patriarchal culture it was not unusual for the role of women to be overlooked. However, Elizabeth did enjoy a rare moment of recognition when she completed twenty years in the service of the Mission in 1899. She was presented with a silver rose bowl and *Life and Work* commented that 'She only of the present staff has seen the Blantyre of the past, shared its excitements, troubles and successes'.[61] The following year, when the Livingstonia missionary Angus Elmslie was making preparations for the Missionary Conference to be held at Livingstonia, he was keen that Elizabeth should be one of the speakers, telling Hetherwick 'we look to her as the most experienced lady worker in the country'.[62]

At that point she was the longest-serving member of staff and, by the time she left Blantyre for the last time in 1910, she had completed thirty-one years of missionary service. For the next eighteen years she remained in Scotland overseeing the education of the children (the family was completed with the birth of their daughter May in 1901) while Hetherwick continued alone at Blantyre, with periodic furloughs in Scotland. Between them the couple accumulated vast missionary experience and unrivalled knowledge of the early history of Blantyre. They were reunited in Scotland for the last decade of Hetherwick's life, with no shortage of shared memories on which they could reflect during their years of retirement. From the evidence of Hetherwick's post-retirement lectures it appears that Domasi remained often on their minds.[63]

Notes

1. See for example Alexander Hetherwick, *The Romance of Blantyre: How Livingstone's Dream Came True*, London: James Clarke, n.d., 155.
2. Alexander Hetherwick (ed.), *Robert Hellier Napier in Nyasaland: Being his Letters to his Home Circle*, Edinburgh and London: William Blackwood Sons, 1925, 15.
3. See further Alexander Hetherwick, 'Islam and Christianity in Nyasaland', *Muslim World* 17/2 (April 1927), 184–86.

4. David S. Bone, 'The Development of Islam in Malawi and the Response of the Christian Churches c. 1860–1986', in David S. Bone (ed.), *Malawi's Muslims: Historical Perspectives*, Blantyre: CLAIM-Kachere, 2000, 113–51, at 131.
5. W. P. Livingstone, *A Prince of Missionaries: Alexander Hetherwick of Blantyre*, London: James Clarke, n.d., 35.
6. Daniel Gunya, 'Christian Missions and Land Ownership: The Case of Blantyre Mission's Land in Blantyre and Zomba Districts, 1876–1940', History Seminar Paper, presented at Chancellor College, CC/H/730/94, 18.
7. Alexander Hetherwick, *The Gospel and the African: the Croall Lectures for 1930–31*, Edinburgh: T. & T. Clark, 1932, 1–2.
8. Ibid., 2.
9. Ibid.
10. Ibid., 126.
11. Gilbert Davison Foster Phiri, 'The Involvement of the Church in the Empowerment of the Poor through Self-Reliance Education, Health Services and Agriculture: The Case of Blantyre Synod in Domasi Presbytery', MA, University of Malawi, 2007, 35.
12. Ibid.
13. *Life and Work in Nyasaland*, July–August 1908.
14. *Life and Work in Nyasaland*, April–May 1911.
15. See Joseph Bismarck, *A Brief History of Joseph Bismarck* (4 March 1932), Zomba: Occasional Papers of the Department of Antiquities, 1968.
16. Gilbert Phiri, 'The Involvement of the Church in the Empowerment of the Poor', 35.
17. Alexander Hetherwick, *The Gospel and the African*, 128–29.
18. Ibid., 129.
19. Harry Kambwiri Matecheta, *Blantyre Mission: Stories of its Beginning*, ed. by Thokozani Chilembwe and Todd Statham, Mzuzu: Luviri Press, 2020 (trsl. from Harry Kambwiri Matecheta, *Blantyre Mission. Nkhani za Ciyambi Cace*, Blantyre: Hetherwick Press, 1951), 37–39.
20. Alexander Hetherwick, *The Romance of Blantyre*, 50–52.
21. Andrew C. Ross, *Blantyre Mission and the Making of Modern Malawi*, Blantyre: CLAIM-Kachere, 1996, repr. Mzuzu: Luviri Press, 2018, 101–3.
22. Harry Kambwiri Matecheta, *Blantyre Mission: Stories of its Beginning*, 68.
23. *Life and Work in British Central Africa*, October 1898.
24. Andrew F. Walls, *The Missionary Movement in Christian History: Studies in the Transmission of Faith*, Maryknoll, NY: Orbis and Edinburgh: T. & T. Clark, 1996, xix.
25. Alexander Hetherwick, *The Gospel and the African*, 127.
26. Ibid., 3.
27. Paul Hiebert, 'The Flaw of the Excluded Middle', *Missiology: An International Review* 10/1 (1982), 35–47. Hiebert explains ways in which Western scholars are largely ignorant of how African and other people explain events with reference to the activities of spirits and witches. He terms this arena of activity the 'excluded middle'.
28. Hetherwick, *The Gospel and the African*, 4.
29. Charles Taylor, *A Secular Age*, Cambridge, MA and London: The Belknap Press of Harvard University Press, 2007, 3.
30. *Life and Work in British Central Africa*, September 1902. See also Alexander

Hetherwick, 'Some Animistic Beliefs among the Yaos of British Central Africa', *The Journal of the Anthropological Institute of Great Britain and Ireland* 32 (January–June 1902), 89–95.
31. Ibid.
32. Ibid.
33. *Life and Work in British Central Africa*, July 1903.
34. *Life and Work in British Central Africa*, November 1898.
35. Ibid.
36. Ibid.
37. Ibid.
38. *Life and Work in British Central Africa*, October-November 1904.
39. Alexander Hetherwick, *The Gospel and the African*, 129–30.
40. *Life and Work in British Central Africa*, April 1899.
41. *Life and Work in British Central Africa*, August 1892.
42. Ibid.
43. W. P. Livingstone, *A Prince of Missionaries*, 37
44. Gilbert Phiri, 'The Involvement of the Church in the Empowerment of the Poor', 36.
45. *Life and Work in British Central Africa*, December 1905.
46. Gilbert Phiri, 'The Involvement of the Church in the Empowerment of the Poor', 36
47. John McMurtie to Alexander Hetherwick 19 June 1891, NLS 7534/606.
48. Gilbert Phiri, 'The Involvement of the Church in the Empowerment of the Poor', 36.
49. Ibid., 53.
50. Ibid., 55.
51. Ibid., 37.
52. Cit. W. P. Livingstone, *A Prince of Missionaries*, 37.
53. See further Kenneth R. Ross, *Mission as God's Spiral of Renewal*, Mzuzu: Mzuni Press, 2019, 31–45.
54. Andrew B. Doig, *It's People That Count*, Edinburgh: The Pentland Press, 1997.
55. W. P. Livingstone, *A Prince of Missionaries*, 64.
56. *Life and Work in British Central Africa*, September 1902.
57. Hetherwick, *The Romance of Blantyre: How Livingstone's Dream Came True*, London: James Clarke, n.d., 171.
58. *Life and Work in British Central Africa*, February 1888.
59. See further John McCracken, 'Class, Violence and Gender in Early Colonial Malawi: The Curious Case of Elizabeth Pithie', *Society of Malawi Journal* 64/2 (2011), 1–16.
60. See Alexander Hetherwick, *The Romance of Blantyre*, passim.
61. *Life and Work in British Central Africa*, October 1899.
62. W. A. Elmslie to Alexander Hetherwick, 16 April 1900, MNA 50/BMC/2/1/33.
63. Alexander Hetherwick, *The Gospel and the African*, passim.

CHAPTER THREE

The Right-hand Man: Scott and Hetherwick

During the 1880s and 1890s, in addition to his pioneering work at Domasi, Hetherwick also had significant responsibilities in the leadership of Blantyre Mission as a whole. He quickly established himself as the right-hand man of David Clement Scott, the inspirational leader of the Mission, and acted as deputy for Scott during the latter's sometimes lengthy furloughs. Indeed, in the perception of both friend and foe, the two men came to be regarded, for practical purposes, as a single unit. This applied equally to the missionaries, such as John McIlwain or Janet Beck, who were devoted and loyal to their leadership and to those, such as R. S. Hynde or George Robertson, who became fiercely opposed to it. Likewise, in the wider community it was recognised that Scott and Hetherwick were a 'double-act'. When they adopted a critical attitude to some of the policies of the British administration during its early years in the 1890s, the two were regarded equally as a thorn in the side, one as bad as the other. Therefore, during the 1880s and 1890s, in addition to his particular responsibility for the Domasi station, Hetherwick was a major player in the overall leadership of the Mission, albeit at this point he was the 'right-hand man' rather than the principal. When Scott left Blantyre in early 1898, it was obvious to everyone that Hetherwick would be his successor and, in many ways, he simply carried on with what he had already been doing as the close associate and deputy of Scott.

Those close to Blantyre Mission were in no doubt in 1898 that it had lost a brilliant and inspiring leader, even if the bright light had dimmed somewhat since 1895 when both his wife and brother died in the same month while at the same time the campaign against him and Hetherwick for alleged 'ritualism' was reaching a crescendo in Scotland. On Scott's departure the Mission's staff and supporters were reassured that Hetherwick was perfectly placed to step into his shoes so that the Mission would continue on the lines that by then were well established. Subsequent scholarship, however, has suggested that there was a wide difference between the two. In his authoritative history of the early history of Blantyre Mission, Andrew Ross argued that Scott's departure in 1898 marked a profound change in the life and policy of the Mission. It was 'not simply the interchange of two men'.[1]

Ross acknowledged that the change that was occurring around 1898 was attributable in part to wider historical forces, particularly the advent of the colonial age and the consolidation of the British colonial regime in Malawi. It was clear that the hopes that Scott and Hetherwick had entertained a decade earlier for a 'Palmerstonian' form of Protectorate, where the internal life of the territory continued on its traditional lines while being protected from external interference, were no longer realistic. Instead, the direction of travel was clearly towards a Crown Colony where power would be concentrated in the hands of the British colonial administration.[2] However, Ross suggests that the change that occurred in the Mission at this time is attributable in large measure to differences between Scott and Hetherwick. He remarks that, 'Hetherwick was D. C. Scott's right-hand man, but after Scott's departure the real differences between the two men became more clear. Hetherwick never achieved the close personal relations with Africans that Scott did, and was never so passionately and understandingly negrophile as was Scott.'[3]

Ross concedes that Hetherwick did continue to speak out as an advocate for the African community but suggests that this was 'very much a matter of knowing what was good for the African even if the African did not'.[4] 'Hetherwick,' he states, 'was a man of integrity with a passion for justice, but he lacked the imaginative sympathy which was so dominantly a characteristic of D.C. Scott.'[5] This flaw in Hetherwick's make-up, Ross argues, led him to abandon the distinctively pro-African approach that had marked the life of Blantyre Mission under Scott's leadership and to fall in line with the racist and colonialist attitudes that were becoming the order of the day. He remarks that, 'This difference was not simply one that followed automatically from the new, stable political situation. The change was much more profound and meant that the mission was now part of the imperial establishment.'[6]

More recently, in his work on Scott's linguistic philosophy, Harri Englund has similarly drawn a sharp contrast between the philosophy that guided Blantyre Mission under Scott's leadership with that which prevailed under Hetherwick: 'Where Scott was a visionary, Hetherwick was paternalistic in his approach to Africans.'[7] Englund pays particular attention to the differences he detects in the linguistic work of the two men:

> In Scott's inspired celebration of African linguistic resources and Hetherwick's dour committee work lies a contrast that was to become all the more pronounced as the twentieth century dawned. It is a contrast between the ethos of attributing a basic unity to humankind and a paternalistic (and, in some cases, racist) division of humanity into civilized and uncivilized tongues and peoples.[8]

While both men devoted great attention to vernacular languages and attained a high level of competence, Englund argues that there was a crucial difference in their fundamental attitude. Where Scott viewed the vernacular language as a vehicle for faith and thought that had universal scope, Hetherwick was inclined to dwell on the limitations of the vernacular as demonstrating the lack of sophistication and 'civilisation' in the African community.

Englund argues that under Hetherwick the Mission departed from the vision of common humanity that inspired Scott's leadership and fell in line with the racist and hierarchical thinking of the colonial era, emphasising a supposed sharp division between the races and the superiority of white over black. A construction of the early history of Blantyre Mission is thus offered in which, in terms of its ideals and philosophy, the Mission moved from a golden era in the late nineteenth century to a dark age in the early twentieth. This dramatic change and decline is represented and personified in a contrast between the successive leaders of the Mission, Scott and Hetherwick. The question has to be asked, however, as to whether it is valid to interpret this history as a matter of the former as hero and the latter as villain? Was it really as simple as that?

The Double Act

This is a question to which this book will be returning and which it will consider from different angles. First of all, closer consideration needs to be given to the relationship between the two men. While Scott was the Head of the Mission and Hetherwick his junior, having arrived two years later than his boss, the two operated very much as a double act during the fifteen years from 1883 to 1898. In terms of the policy, direction and management of the Mission there seems to be no evidence that there was ever any serious difference between the two of them. Whether it was Scott or Hetherwick at the helm, the leadership of Blantyre Mission during this period appears to have been a seamless operation. This is remarkable given that both were exceptionally strong personalities who, not infrequently, completely fell out with people, including their fellow missionaries. However, there is no evidence that they ever fell out with each other. The harmony and common mind that they enjoyed stands out because these were stormy years at Blantyre Mission, particularly in the 1890s when the Mission had tense relationships both with the new British administration at the political level and with the Church of Scotland authorities at the ecclesiastical level. Yet it appears that Scott and Hetherwick stood shoulder to shoulder throughout the entire period. In 1893 when Scott was hard-pressed by the Church of Scotland Foreign Mission Committee concerning the need to reduce the costs of the Mission because of budgetary constraints, he wrote to the Convener: 'We can do without the Europeans, except those who work for nothing; and with them I will work the Mission (together with Mr Hetherwick) if it must be so.'[9] He could imagine dispensing, if need be, with all the other salaried Scottish missionaries, but not with Hetherwick.

In fact, the two were often the co-accused so far as critics of the Mission were concerned. As will be discussed further in Chapter Five, despite having been instrumental in the establishment of the British Protectorate, during its early years in the 1890s Scott and Hetherwick were outspoken in their criticism of administration policy. So much so that the British Commissioner Harry Johnston advised that, 'there would be no permanent and satisfactory state of things with regard to this mission until two missionaries, the Rev. D. C. Scott and the Rev. Alexander Hetherwick were removed from the country'.[10] The British Administration was clearly aware that it was a 'double act' with which it had to contend at Blantyre Mission. The strength of feeling at this time can be gauged from the description which Wordsworth Poole, one of the more expressive members of the British administration, gave of Hetherwick when he described him as 'a loathsome little brute'.[11]

Relations between Mission and Administration were tense, to say the least. Even John McMurtrie, the Foreign Mission Committee Convener in Scotland, who sympathised with the missionaries' viewpoint, had to advise Hetherwick to 'let irritation be avoided as far as possible without sacrifice of important principles'.[12] For Scott and Hetherwick, the principle at stake was that they had assured the African communities with whom they were connected that the British Protectorate would be to their advantage and they felt obliged to speak out on behalf of those communities when they found that in practice they were disadvantaged by policies of the new administration. This they did to the extent that Alfred Sharpe alleged that, 'the missionaries are taking a course that makes them appear in the eyes of the natives of this Protectorate as an Opposition Party to H.M. Administration'.[13] To some extent, this was a role that they relished as Scott deployed his rhetorical ability to castigate the administration in the columns of *Life and Work* while Hetherwick felt justified in indulging his more combative instincts. It would have been a stormy enough spell even if their own Mission staff had been united and harmonious. In fact, this was far from the case.

At the very same time that Scott and Hetherwick were confronting the British administration, a controversy within the ranks of their own Mission was coming to a head. It was one that would pitch the two of them against a significant section of their own staff. Discontent with the direction of the Mission under Scott's leadership was concentrated at the Mulanje Mission where George Robertson and Henry Herd were vocal in their criticism. The difference centred much around racial attitudes and relations with the local community, where Scott and Hetherwick felt that the colonialist attitudes of their colleagues were undermining the confidence that they had built up with the African community. Indeed, Hetherwick went so far as to describe George Robertson's attitude as 'anti-mission, anti-native, anti-Christian', a remark that drew a rebuke from Archibald Scott, the Africa Committee Convener in Scotland who was trying to resolve the conflict.[14] As the missionaries opposed to Scott and Hetherwick joined forces with the growing number of settlers who disliked the pro-African stance of the Blantyre Mission, they found that a sensitive point to attack was the emerging pattern of worship. Rather than replicating Scottish Presbyterian worship in all its details, both Scott and Hetherwick had taken a more open and expansive approach. They consciously sought to draw on the entire ecumenical heritage of the Christian church and to make space for a creative African reception of the faith. To their critics this resulted in 'ritualism' in worship, which was code for a drift towards Anglicanism or Catholicism and at that time guaranteed to set off alarm bells among devout Presbyterians.

As news of the controversy spread in Scotland it became clear that it had touched a raw nerve among supporters of the Blantyre Mission. By 1893 the Foreign Mission Committee Convener John McMurtrie was warning Hetherwick that in regard to ritual, 'unfriendly eyes are upon the Mission'.[15] He explained that, 'The bulk of our contributions comes from persons who are "low Church" in doctrine and practice. Things in themselves unimportant, such as turning to the East, or giving the Communion Table the appearance of an "altar" in a high episcopal church, would give great offence.'[16] It was a source of exasperation to the officials in Scotland that their unceasing efforts to raise financial support for the Mission were being undermined by the alleged ritualism of the mission leadership. Soon Hetherwick himself felt the heat when he arrived in Scotland on leave with Elizabeth and their new baby Clement in 1896, and was gravely handed a set of questions to answer:

Is it true that there is in Blantyre Church the following:

1. An Altar?
2. on the Altar – Candles?
3. Waiting upon the same Surpliced Choristers, Blacks – who kneel before the Altar as they worship?
4. Is there a portion of the Church for the White worshippers, and a portion for the Black worshippers?
5. Do all the worshippers kneel to the Altar on entering the Church?[17]

The controversy continued to fester until George Robertson and Henry Herd, together with Revd Dr D. J. Rankin, a prominent supporter of the Mission, made a formal complaint to the General Assembly. This resulted in Scott and Hetherwick being investigated by a Church of Scotland Commission of Inquiry in 1897.

Andrew Ross has summarised the complaints that were made: 'the Mission was an autocracy because there was no Session; it was Anglicising and therefore distasteful to the Scottish Community; *Life and Work in British Central Africa* was a badly conducted periodical; and the mission was not effective as a missionary enterprise.'[18] Hetherwick was still in Scotland and appeared before the Commission to calmly rebut all the charges that had been levelled against Scott and himself.[19] The outcome was that they were formally exonerated by the Commission of Inquiry, which found that none of the complaints could be substantiated. However, its report was negative in tone and found many grounds for censure. *The Scotsman* newspaper fairly summarised the outcome as one of 'Not Guilty; but don't do it again'.[20] Its assessment of Scott and Hetherwick, and accusations that they were harsh and authoritarian towards their fellow missionaries, is revealing:

> The impression we have formed about Dr D. C. Scott and Mr Hetherwick is that they are both men of strong determination, and perhaps like such, impatient of contradiction; they further appear to be men who will not hesitate to point out and check anything that they think wrong; and of course they sometimes fail in temper or commit an error of judgement; but they are men of the highest character, and, without going to the length of saying that we can defend all their actions, we feel that it would require more cogent evidence than was laid before us to convince us that they would habitually act towards their subordinates . . . in the way suggested.[21]

Though they were cleared of the charges laid against them, it was hardly a ringing endorsement of their leadership of the Mission.

No wonder that when the Mission Council met at Blantyre on 7 April 1897 and received the findings of the Commission of Inquiry, it heard that Hetherwick had seriously considered resigning his position. The members of the Council, no longer including the critics who by then had left the service of the Mission, rallied to his defence. They hastened to assure him of

> their devotion to him in fellow work and full appreciation of his power in Mission work and management, of his wide experience, his tried courage, his wise policy, his soundness and orthodoxy and his high character, seen both in his own original work at Domasi, and in his carrying on of the Blantyre work at various intervals in the absence of the Blantyre head; and they are ready to side with him in any serious issues in Church Courts or in public Church appeal.[22]

Scott was highly defensive in his response to the Commission's findings but it was clear that both men were bruised and chastened by the experience. They realised that the freedom and imagination that had earlier marked their leadership would become a thing of the past as Edinburgh took a firm grip. Soon Scott found to his dismay that even his sermons and magazine columns were now subject to supervision and censorship by the authorities in Edinburgh.[23] For him it was a shattering experience, leading to the breakdown of his health and his final departure from Blantyre in January 1898.

The friendship and collaboration of the two men was forged in these fires of controversy and it is difficult to imagine that an extraordinary personal closeness did not develop as they met so many crises together. Indeed, Scott was unstinting in his appreciation of Hetherwick's contribution: 'Mr Hetherwick has come in from Domasi . . . His presence is most helpful to the Mission, body, soul and spirit, so that we are in no hurry to let him away.'[24] It is also significant that Hetherwick was Scott's deputy, which meant that he was at the helm when Scott was on furlough in Scotland. On account of his rather fragile health, Scott spent some extended spells in Scotland, leaving the affairs of the Mission in Hetherwick's hands at a time when communication between Scotland and Blantyre was slow and infrequent. This included a two-year period from 1885 to 1887 when the Mission was still very much at a formative stage. Had there been significant differences of approach or policy between the two, Hetherwick had ample opportunity to take a different line during Scott's lengthy absence. There is no evidence that this ever happened.[25]

On the contrary, the philosophy, policy and practice of the Mission appear to have developed seamlessly, regardless of whether Scott or Hetherwick was in charge. This is seen, for example, in the editorial columns of *Life and Work in British Central Africa*, written by Scott when he was present and by Hetherwick when Scott was away. A difference in style is evident. Hetherwick could never match Scott for philosophical panache, poetic genius or rhetorical flourish.[26] In terms of substance of policy, however, there is formidable unity between the two. Indeed, the terms in which Hetherwick later wrote of Scott in *The Romance of Blantyre* suggest that the latter was not only his friend and colleague but also his hero.[27] When Scott died in Kenya in 1907, Hetherwick wrote to his missionary colleagues there: 'You in Kikuyu did not know him as I knew him in the best and fullest days of his life in Blantyre – those days when he drew the loyalty and homage of all he met as few men ever were able to do.'[28] When this was his sentiment, it seems implausible that Hetherwick would adopt an entirely different approach to the leadership of the Mission after Scott's departure in 1898.

A striking instance of the common mind shared by the two missionaries is seen in one of the most remarkable projects in Blantyre Mission's early period: the construction of the church later known as St Michael and All Angels. It was Scott's genius that envisaged and designed the church. Hetherwick never got over his admiration for the imagination that made it possible. But he entered into the project so wholeheartedly that he made it his own. 'He loved it with a surpassing love,' wrote fellow missionary Dr Elizabeth McCurrach, 'and liked to tell visitors of the manner of its construction and show them its beauties from every possible angle.'[29] It is often forgotten, when paying tribute to Scott's unique achievement, that it was only the outer shell of the church that he was able to complete. It was left to Hetherwick to complete the interior – to panel, decorate and furnish it. Yet, as his biographer remarks, 'His spirit was so akin to Scott's that all this secondary but important work was executed in perfect harmony with the mind of the master-builder.'[30] It was he who oversaw the addition of 'some exquisite carving, a seven light stained glass window in the apse and a five light window in the west gable.'[31] When he was building the bell and clock tower adjacent to the church in 1921–22 he was conscious that this had been 'in the mind of Dr Clement Scott as an adjunct to his beautiful church.'[32] He remembered a rough sketch that Scott had made of such a tower and did his best to use it as the basis for his design.[33] When he came to write his small book about the church building in 1926 it was clear that he himself was identified with it no less than Scott.[34] Their roles were different but complementary. The church became a physical expression of the spiritual vision that they shared.

Somewhat parallel to their shared commitment to the Blantyre church building was the literary project of the Chinyanja dictionary. Once again, it owed its origins to Scott's genius and his 1892 *Cyclopaedic Dictionary of the Mang'anja Language* has been hailed as a masterpiece not only of linguistics but also of cultural anthropology.[35] Once again, it fell to Hetherwick to continue what his friend had started. Methodically he continued to expand and elaborate the dictionary, eventually publishing the revised edition in 1930, after he had retired to Scotland, under the title *Dictionary of the Nyanja Language*.[36] In order to do this he had to inhabit the thinking of Scott to an unusual degree. He never ceased to marvel at the insightful and innovative work that his friend had done even as he developed and augmented it. The fact that through all the years Hetherwick was engaged in this extraordinary linguistic and cultural collaboration again makes it implausible that he would lead the Mission in an entirely different direction from that which had been charted by Scott.

There was also a family dimension to the relationship. When Alexander and Elizabeth Hetherwick's first child, a son, was born in 1895, they named him Clement. They could scarcely have done more to demonstrate their personal regard and admiration for Scott. We can only surmise what lay behind the choice of name. We do know, however, that in addition to the extraordinarily close working relationship that Hetherwick had enjoyed with Scott over the preceding twelve years, Elizabeth was also very close to Scott and his wife Bella. She had been in a desperate situation in 1884 when her first husband George Fenwick was murdered soon after their two young children had died and Elizabeth herself had been seriously ill. The Scotts invited her to come and live with them in their home, which she did for the next five years. Her early life had been difficult in many ways but the years she spent in the Scott household seem to have been a turning point, described by John McCracken as 'the fulcrum for her later achievements'.[37] By the late 1880s she had become a well-respected member of the Mission, fluent in Chinyanja, a capable teacher and enjoying good rapport with the African community. Having been orphaned as a child and then having lost all her family to death in Malawi as a young adult, we can only imagine that the family-type relationship that she enjoyed as a member of the Scott household in the mid-1880s meant a lot to her. The choice of Clement as the name of her baby son in 1895 can be understood in this context. These very personal ties that united Hetherwick and Scott again make it implausible that the former would set about reversing the legacy of the latter when the baton of leadership passed from the one to the other.

It is also clear that Hetherwick himself had no sense of having abandoned or departed from the distinctive approach to the work of the Mission that had been developed under Scott's leadership. In the account of Blantyre Mission that he wrote in his retirement in the 1930s, Hetherwick is fulsome in expressing his admiration for Scott: 'The word that best describes Clement Scott is "genius", for there were few things he put his hand to which he did not adorn.'[38] Scott's highly philosophical turn of mind that some found off-putting was well appreciated by Hetherwick: 'His mind and soul dwelt among and found their inspiration in the higher entities of life. He lived and moved on a plane high above his fellows – and in consequence very many failed to understand him. In his preaching, and especially when addressing a European congregation, he soared far above his audience.'[39] Nonetheless, in Hetherwick's estimation he was also strongly practical when it came to the ordinary business of life and, crucially, 'to his Africans he was their "Mfumu", their chief, and he was a hero'.[40]

By way of example, after many years Hetherwick retained a vivid memory:

> The writer remembers him once standing on the top of an ant hill, addressing a crowd of armed natives whom he was persuading to desist from attacking a native village, and to submit their case to his arbitration on the morrow. He recalled to mind one of the old Homeric heroes seeking to sway a Greek or Trojan audience with his 'winged words', only his were for peace and not for war.[41]

The warmth and admiration in his evocation of his colleague and leader makes it hard to imagine that Hetherwick had intentionally departed from the philosophy and policy that Scott represented and which the two had shared in their fifteen years of working together. In fact, Hetherwick found a way of saying that Scott had remained his inspiration: 'One who was privileged to be his colleague and to work alongside him when he was at his best, before the sorrow of his life fell as a shadow over him, may here well testify to the influence he exerted, and the high ideals of African service, which have never been forgotten.'[42]

As for Scott's perspective, we find a glimpse in a short letter he wrote to Hetherwick in 1899, after his final departure from Blantyre but while he was evidently still maintaining a hope to return. It was a letter of introduction for a Blantyre-bound visitor, which concludes with a reflection on his relationship with Hetherwick: 'I hope to be out again old man. Do advocate our alternating two years. You remember how ... we proposed the ... dance together, you concave and I convex. In spite of our mutual convexity, yea rather because of it, let us still pirouette Africa together old man.'[43] The imagery of the dance and the pirouette is typical Scott. Clearly the letter conveys affection and a high degree of mutual confidence. It also seems to show an appreciation that the two of them were very different in temperament and aptitude yet that this had served to good effect in the 'dance'. He would have loved to continue their partnership. As it turned out, he would never see Blantyre again. Hetherwick had to dance alone. Though he would enjoy some warm friendships with other members of staff, there would never again be anything remotely akin to the partnership he had known with Scott.

A Different Day

Given what we know about the relationship between Scott and Hetherwick, it seems reasonable to begin with a working assumption that there was continuity in the leadership of the Mission over the almost half-century when the two were successively at the helm. What is clear, however, is that the circumstances that prevailed in Hetherwick's time as Head of the Mission during the early decades of the twentieth century were significantly different from those of the earlier period. Probably the most crucial point is that colonial rule was the established reality with which Hetherwick had to work, whether he liked it or not. It is important to remember that the two of them started their missionary work in a pre-colonial context in the 1880s and carried their mode of operation into the early years of the British administration in the early 1890s when it was in process of establishing itself. By the end of the 1890s, however, Nyasaland was becoming a colonial society. During the early years of the twentieth century, it became ever clearer that this was the direction of travel. The historian Melvin Page remarks:

> Especially after 1907, when control of Nyasaland passed from the British Foreign Office to the Colonial Office, European intervention [was] more keenly felt. More officials arrived, and commercial activities drew other Europeans into the country. If it were not clear before, it was becoming abundantly evident: the changes in Malawian life were fundamental, and probably irreversible.[44]

Hetherwick's task was to maintain and advance the purpose and policy of the Blantyre Mission in this new context.

Interestingly, Scott too had to adapt to a very different context as he took up a new assignment at Kikuyu in Kenya. He seems to have done little to re-apply the Blantyre Mission philosophy with its orientation to African culture and African leadership. He is remembered there for his acquisition of a huge tract of land for the mission and gained the nickname 'Watenga' ('the clearer').[45] He became Vice President of the (European) Planters' and Farmers' Association. The historian Adrian Hastings observed that, 'no mission was more settler-minded and no mission had obtained ownership of more African land'.[46] Besides the 3,000-acre estate that he persuaded the government to grant to the mission, Scott acquired a further 1,000-acre estate as his own private property.[47] In the highly populated Kikuyu area this meant conditions of land and labour for the African community that were not unlike those so heavily criticised by Scott and Hetherwick during the early years of the British Administration in Malawi in the 1890s. This evidence suggests that Scott, like Hetherwick, found that he had to adjust his approach in light of the changing realities around him. It can only be a matter of speculation how he would have approached matters had he remained at Blantyre but it cannot be easily assumed that he would have taken a very different line to Hetherwick's.

Another significant change that was beyond Hetherwick's control was the decision of the General Assembly and its Foreign Mission Committee in Edinburgh that the Blantyre Mission must develop on strictly Presbyterian lines. Scott had championed a much freer approach where an African church would form its own identity as it drew on the entire ecumenical heritage of Christianity. Hetherwick, it is important to note, also promoted this approach. They both came under fire from members of the Mission who were more conservative in their Presbyterianism and from the growing numbers of Scottish settlers who were looking for a form of church life that closely resembled what they had known at home in Scotland. The result was Scott and Hetherwick being subject to the formal Commission of Inquiry, which found in their favour but with a stern warning that the Mission in future must be developed strictly on the lines of Scottish Presbyterianism.

The findings of the Commission's Report were upheld by the General Assembly, which was under pressure to take a firm grip of the conduct of the Blantyre Mission. Whoever led the Mission thereafter had to comply with the General Assembly instructions. It was not a freestanding Mission but one that was directed and funded by the Church of Scotland. Both Scott and Hetherwick were outraged by the proceedings of the Inquiry but, at the end of the day, they had to abide by its findings. Their Committee Convener, Archibald Scott, was categorical on this point: 'Our Church in Africa is to develop according to the Constitution of the Church of Scotland.'[48] Henceforth, under Hetherwick's leadership, church life developed much more on the lines of Scottish Presbyterianism. There was nothing else for it.

At the first meeting of the Mission Council chaired by Hetherwick, following Scott's departure, it was agreed to hold the meetings of Council on the second Wednesday of each quarter.[49] One of the criticisms of the Commission of Inquiry was that the Mission Council rarely met, with the result that some missionaries felt excluded and alienated. Rather than working through regular meetings of a formal governing body, in earlier years the Mission had developed through a free-flowing interaction of Scots and Africans under Scott's benevolent direction. Whatever the virtues of such an approach, it was not acceptable to the General Assembly. Hetherwick had little alternative but to activate the Mission Council as an effective governing body for the affairs of the Mission. Indeed, Scott had already taken steps in this direction prior to his resignation. It soon became clear that the work of the Mission was firmly in the hands of an all-European Council, working in a very European way. This, of course, sat well with the presuppositions of a colonial society where it was assumed that it was best for Europeans to be firmly in charge.

At the same meeting it was decided to take steps to form a Presbytery, which in due course would become the Blantyre Synod of the Church of Central Africa Presbyterian. Again, this was a decisive change from the creative and experimental approach to church life that had characterised the 1880s and 1890s to a commitment to introduce a form of church life closely modelled on that of the Church of Scotland. Again, this was a direction clearly set by the General Assembly, so Hetherwick was bound to comply. Admittedly, he seems to have embraced the new direction quite comfortably. Compared with the speculative and imaginative thinking that marked Scott's leadership, Hetherwick's approach was more pragmatic and organisational so the remit to introduce the Presbyterian system of church government may not have been entirely uncongenial. Nonetheless, even if Scott had remained in post, he could not have gone against a clear direction set by the General Assembly. The question so far as Hetherwick is concerned, is not whether he continued the free approach to ecclesiology that had prevailed in the 1880s. Rather it is whether or not he found ways to maintain the old ideals in the very different conditions that applied after the Commission of Inquiry.

A related consideration is the nature of the project cycle. Very often, projects begin with a period of great imagination and creativity but, as time goes on, there is a need to settle down into a period of steady consolidation and less exciting application of the principles that have been developed. In the case of Blantyre Mission, the personalities of Scott and Hetherwick very much played into this cycle. Scott was a mystic who was in his element when imagination and creativity were required. Under his leadership, the Blantyre Mission made a series of bold moves, for example in entrusting at an early stage major responsibilities to emerging African leaders or setting about building the St Michael and All Angels Church as a symbol of the mission philosophy. Hetherwick was fully supportive of his chief in these initiatives but his gifts were more suited to the steady work of consolidation and administration. There was undoubtedly less drama and excitement in the life of the Mission after 1900 than there was before, but it was under Hetherwick's leadership that it steadily expanded its network of schools and churches, engaging ever-growing numbers from the local communities. By 1905 Hetherwick himself was aware that a different day had arrived:

> There was a time when the appeal for Africa was to the sentiment and sympathies of the church at large – the glamour of the Dark Continent was still on the minds of those who made its appeal to the charity of Christendom, and the sacrifice made for Christ and the Gospel's sake was no small influence in touching the hearts and rousing the interests of a flagging sense of duty. Those days are gone – and the cold glare of

the common place and the daily round has replaced the warm colours of light and shade that so long were used in bringing home to the minds of the Church the sense of their obligations to the people of the Dark Continent. Romance has given place to reality and sentiment to figures– yet each is a sacrament – 'the outward sign of an inward grace'.[50]

'The common place and the daily round' were not uncongenial to Hetherwick. In fact, it can be argued that he found his forte in the deep sense of duty and consistency that marked his leadership over the thirty-year period from 1898 to 1928. This change of gear need not imply that he had abandoned or betrayed the ideals that had guided the mission in its early days. Another possibility to consider is that he maintained the ideals and adapted their application to a different period in the project cycle.

The Emerging European Community

A key feature of the different day that had now arrived was that there was a growing European community in the Shire Highlands. Though small compared with settler communities emerging elsewhere at this time, it was still highly significant in the Malawi context. The commercial prospects of the country were tied, to a great extent, to the attempt being made by European settlers to develop estate agriculture while civil government was now centred on the British administration with its growing corps of officials. Anyone operating in the country had to come to terms with this new reality. Nonetheless, Andrew Ross expresses dismay at the role that Hetherwick played in relation to the European society that was emerging in Nyasaland during the early twentieth century.[51] This included being a member of Blantyre Town Council, two spells of service on the Legislative Council and a leading role in the establishment and operation of the Chamber of Commerce, which represented the interests of European planters and traders. For Ross this was '. . . a drastic departure from D. C. Scott's vision of Africa's future, where the role of the European was to be an aid to African development and always secondary to African needs'.[52]

However, for the Mission to have cordial relationships with the European community was not a new development. It had equally been a feature of the period when Scott was Head of the Mission. At Christmas 1890 the Mission invited all the Europeans in the Blantyre area for Christmas dinner (thirty-three people at that time).[53] The Blantyre missionary Alice de Planta, who arrived in 1896, noted in her diary that 'the Mission was on the friendliest terms with all the planters and, indeed, with all the Europeans in the Country. Anyone was welcome at the Manse and the other houses and a bed and board were given to an utter stranger, who would be treated as an honoured guest though nothing whatever was known about him.'[54] She went on to observe that 'there was at the Manse a lending library, quite free of charge and most of the planters from Cholo and Mulanje and the neighbourhood availed themselves of the opportunity so obligingly given, to get books once or twice a month to read'.[55] There were only fifty-seven Europeans in the country when it became a British Protectorate in 1891.[56] Though the number had increased to 237 by 1894,[57] it was a small community in an exposed situation and therefore unsurprising that they developed a certain solidarity, notwithstanding differences of outlook that would soon become apparent between administration, settlers and missionaries.

All of the friendly interaction between the Mission and the European planters was consistent with David Livingstone's vision, which had a place for European commercial planters as well as for Christian missions. Scott himself, responding to accusations that the Mission was not on friendly terms with the Europeans, remarked that 'there are very few of the planters who come in from a distance on business who go away without calling upon us at the manse, and we are always glad to see them'.[58] Hetherwick's membership and leadership in the Chamber of Commerce was, in his own view, a continuation of the close relationship the Mission had always had with the commercial development of the country and the Europeans who were involved in it. He was at pains to emphasise that

> these industries – planting, transport and trade – have been among the chief factors in the development of the country – many of them took their origin in 'ventures of faith' to aid in the progress of civilisation and legitimate trade among the peoples of the Dark Continent. They deserve every support and encouragement that the Government here and at home can give them.[59]

There was therefore nothing novel or inconsistent about Hetherwick fostering positive relations with the emerging European settler community during the early twentieth century. The question is whether or not this led him to betray the interests of the African community, for which the Blantyre Mission had been a conspicuous champion during the early years of the British administration. More will be said later about Hetherwick's role as a champion of African interests. Suffice to say here that even his critic Andrew Ross acknowledged that Hetherwick 'continued to be critical of many of the actions of the settlers and in turn to be attacked by them as being pro-native'.[60] In fact, Ross offers an astute assessment of what was in the mind of Hetherwick when he chose to become involved in the development of the Chamber of Commerce:

> Hetherwick decided by 1900 that the early idea of Livingstone and the first missionaries of development through the growth of peasant African agriculture, served by European commerce, was simply not possible. Already the main area of economic activity was plantation-based, and he accepted this as the only possible way forward. Having decided thus, he had no alternative but to make this work as well as

possible in addition to doing all he could to ameliorate its impact upon the African people. He wanted the latter to have security of tenure on their land, good wages and good living conditions. But these things could only happen if the plantation economy itself worked profitably. It was for this reason that he became a member of the Chamber of Commerce and devoted much time and energy towards helping the planters achieve that prosperity.[61]

A key point in this analysis is that economic and political conditions were rapidly changing. To ask whether Hetherwick's approach was the same after 1900 as that which he and Clement Scott had taken in the pre-colonial situation of the 1880s is to pose an anachronistic question. It was part of the given reality that he would have to adjust to a new situation.

The more pertinent question is whether or not he was able in the new circumstances to sustain the ideals that had defined the Blantyre Mission in its formative period? Or did his attempt to come to terms with a colonial society and a settler economy lead him to compromise or betray those ideals? These are questions that will follow us through this book. At this stage, we can simply register that a presentation of Blantyre Mission history that portrays Scott as hero and Hetherwick as villain is, at the very least, complicated by the extraordinarily close relationship that the two men enjoyed as they built up the life of the Mission in the definitive years from 1883 to 1898. Alice de Planta observed that 'Dr Scott's great ambition was to see "the Church of Africa" established from North to South and behind this great dream there was no doubt there was also the faint hope that he might possibly some day be the first Bishop of that new Church.'[62] If he did harbour any such hopes they were dashed by the events of 1897. It was Hetherwick who, despite a firmly Presbyterian system coming into place, would exercise a bishop-like role in the decades that lay ahead.

Notes

1. Andrew C. Ross, *Blantyre Mission and the Making of Modern Malawi*, Blantyre: CLAIM-Kachere, 1996, repr. Mzuzu: Luviri Press, 2018, 167.
2. Ibid., 166–67
3. Ibid., 167.
4. Ibid.
5. Ibid., 168.
6. Ibid., 170.
7. Harri Englund, '"Africa Is an Education": Vernacular Language and the Missionary Encounter in Nineteenth-century Malawi', in Kenneth R. Ross and Wapulumuka O. Mulwafu (eds), *Politics, Christianity and Society in Malawi: Essays in Honour of John McCracken*, Mzuzu: Mzuni Press, 2020, 138–62, at 140.
8. Ibid., 141.
9. Rev. D. C. Scott, Blantyre to Rev Dr Archibald Scott, 17 August 1893, MNA 50/BMC/2/1/9.

10. Sharpe to Kimberley, 31 October 1894, Foreign Office 2/67, cit. Andrew C. Ross, *Blantyre Mission and the Making of Modern Malawi*, 151.
11. Wordsworth Poole to his mother, 2 September 1895, MNA, Wordsworth Poole Papers PO 1/1.
12. John McMurtrie to Alexander Hetherwick, 26 January 1893, NLS/7534/802.
13. Sharpe to Kimberley, 31 October 1894, Foreign Office 2/67, cit. Andrew C. Ross, *Blantyre Mission and the Making of Modern Malawi*, 151.
14. Archibald Scott to Alexander Hetherwick, 8 August 1895, NLS 7535/379–81.
15. John McMurtie to Alexander Hetherwick, 15 June 1893, NLS 7534/852.
16. Ibid.
17. *Life and Work in British Central Africa*, April 1894.
18. Andrew C. Ross, *Blantyre Mission and the Making of Modern Malawi*, 220.
19. See W. P. Livingstone, *A Prince of Missionaries: Alexander Hetherwick of Blantyre*, London: James Clarke, n.d., 91–92.
20. *The Scotsman*, 25 March 1897, cit. Andrew C. Ross, *Blantyre Mission and the Making of Modern Malawi*, 221.
21. Mission Council meeting at Blantyre, 19 May 1897, MNA 50/BMC/1/1/1.
22. Mission Council meeting at Blantyre, 7 April 1897, MNA 50/BMC/1/1/1.
23. See Andrew C. Ross, *Blantyre Mission and the Making of Modern Malawi*, 221–22.
24. Cit. Livingstone, *A Prince of Missionaries*, 67.
25. Even Hetherwick's critic Andrew Ross admits that '... in Scott's absence Hetherwick carried on as best he could, following as much as possible in Scott's footsteps. The routine that had been established carried on with little incident'. Andrew Ross, *Blantyre Mission and the Making of Modern Malawi*, 103.
26. For an appreciation of Scott's extraordinary qualities see Andrew C. Ross, 'The Mzungu Who Mattered', *Religion in Malawi* 8 (1998), 3–7.
27. See e.g. Hetherwick, *Romance of Blantyre: How Livingstone's Dream Came True*, London: James Clarke, n.d., 33–37.
28. Alexander Hetherwick to John Arthur (Kikuyu), 17 December 1907, MNA 50/BMC/2/1/85.
29. Livingstone, *A Prince of Missionaries*, 193.
30. Ibid., 69.
31. Richard Paterson, *Blantyre*, Sketches of the Fields No. 9, Edinburgh: Church of Scotland Foreign Mission Committee, n.d., 8.
32. Alexander Hetherwick, 'Blantyre Mission Annual Report, 1921', MNA BMC/50/2/1/194.
33. Ibid.
34. Alexander Hetherwick, *Blantyre Church, Nyasaland*, Edinburgh: Church of Scotland, 1926.
35. D. C. Scott, *A Cyclopaedic Dictionary of the Mang'anja Language*, Edinburgh: Foreign Missions Committee of the Church of Scotland, 1892.
36. D. C. Scott and Alexander Hetherwick, *Dictionary of the Nyanja Language*, London: Religious Tract Society, 1930.
37. John McCracken, 'Class, Violence and Gender in Early Colonial Malawi', 9.
38. Alexander Hetherwick, *The Romance of Blantyre*, 36.
39. Ibid., 34.
40. Ibid., 35.
41. Ibid.
42. Ibid., 36–37. The sorrow that befell Scott was the death of his wife Bella and

brother Willie within the same month in 1895. Though he remarried and returned to Blantyre for a further term of service he never regained the elan of his earlier days.

43. 'Kelementi' [David Clement Scott] to Alexander Hetherwick, 26 February 1899, MNA 50/BMC/2/1/28; letter partially damaged, two words missing. 'Kelementi' is the Chinyanja rendering of Clement.
44. Melvin E. Page, *The Chiwaya War*, 2nd ed., Mzuzu: Mzuni Press, 2021, 36.
45. See Todd Statham, 'Scott, David Clement', *Dictionary of African Christian Biography*, https://dacb.org/stories/malawi/scott-davidc/ accessed 30 April 2021.
46. Adrian Hastings, *The Church in Africa 1450–1950*, Oxford: Clarendon Press, 1994, 557.
47. Ibid., 427.
48. Archibald Scott to Alexander Hetherwick, 30 November 1898, NLS 7537/47–49.
49. Blantyre Mission Council, 6 July 1898, MNA 50/BMC/1/1/1.
50. *Life and Work in British Central Africa*, February 1905.
51. Andrew C. Ross, *Blantyre Mission and the Making of Modern Malawi*, 170–71.
52. Ibid., 171.
53. W. Henry Rankine, *A Hero of the Dark Continent: Memoir of Rev Wm Affleck Scott*, Edinburgh and London: William Blackwood, 1896, 197.
54. Nick Beaton, 'Early Reminscences of Blantyre Missionary Alice de Planta and her Husband Duncan Beaton, Manager, A.L.C.', *Society of Malawi Journal* 54/2 (2001), 1–27, at 8.
55. Ibid., 11.
56. Bridglal Pachai, *Land and Politics in Malawi, 1875–1975*, Kingston: The Limestone Press, 1978, 32.
57. Ibid.
58. Rev D. C. Scott to Rev Dr Archibald Scott, 17 August 1893, MNA 50/BMC/2/1/9.
59. *Life and Work in British Central Africa*, February 1903.
60. Andrew C. Ross, *Blantyre Mission and the Making of Modern Malawi*, 171.
61. Andrew C. Ross, 'The Blantyre Mission and the Problems of Land and Labour, 1891–1915', in Roderick J. Macdonald (ed.), *From Nyasaland to Malawi*, Nairobi: East African Publishing, 1975, 86–107, at 106–7.
62. Nick Beaton, 'Early Reminscences of Blantyre Missionary Alice de Planta', 11.

CHAPTER FOUR

The Mission Leader: Father Figure

It must have been a poignant day for Alexander Hetherwick when he received a letter from Africa Committee Convener Archibald Scott to tell him that 'Dr [Clement] Scott will not return to Africa, save for emergency service, and that, if at all, only temporarily. So I hope you will be enabled to continue after you get a rest.'[1] This did not come as a complete surprise. Like many brilliant people, Clement Scott had a certain fragility. His health had always been vulnerable. The sudden loss of both his wife and brother in 1895 had been a shattering blow. Though he remarried while on leave in Scotland, it was noticeable on his return to Blantyre in 1896 that he was not quite the force that he had been in earlier years. Matters only got worse with the ordeal of the Commission of Inquiry the following year. It was demoralising for Scott that his own church seemed to have so little understanding of what he had been trying to do at Blantyre. The tight control from Edinburgh that came into force after the Commission was so uncongenial to Scott that before long his health was breaking down and it became clear that his position in Blantyre was unsustainable.

Hetherwick witnessed what his friend, leader and confidante was passing through. He too had come through some bleak moments during the Commission of Inquiry. In character and constitution, however, he was a very different proposition. He was fortunate to enjoy robust health and very rarely fell sick. When he had a heavy cold in 1925 and had to be off work for two days, he noted that it was the first time for twenty-eight years that he had been off duty on health grounds.[2] While he lacked the extraordinary imagination and sensitivity that marked Scott's leadership, he had qualities of stamina and resilience that would stand him in good stead in the thirty years of leading the Mission that now lay in front of him.

Hetherwick's place among the staff of the Mission was very different in the years after 1898 to what it had been before, not only in the formal sense that he was the sole leader from then until his retirement in 1928. In the earlier days the leader, whether Scott when he was present or Hetherwick when Scott was absent, was a 'first among equals'. The Mission was fortunate to attract to its service a group of highly able missionaries who were near contemporaries both in terms of age and in terms of their length of service with the Mission. These included Clement Scott's brother Willie (Affleck) and brother-in-law John Bowie, John McIlwain, Robert Cleland, Henry Scott (no relation to Clement), James Reid and the redoubtable woman missionary Janet Beck. Whereas in the early years Hetherwick was among a group of peers, after 1898 he was the oldest and longest serving member of staff, with a reputation that none of the other missionaries could remotely match. Even those like John McIlwain and Janet Beck, who had entered the service of the Mission not long after Hetherwick, very much looked to him as their senior.

For those who arrived after 1900 his matchless experience of both the Mission and the country, as well as a growing difference in age as the years passed, meant that they looked to him as a father figure. He was tongue-in-cheek when he addressed his letters to his colleagues 'Dear Bairns' (the Scots word for children) but it reflected the kind of relationship they enjoyed. As Andrew Ross comments: 'From the departure of D. C. Scott in 1898 ... Alexander Hetherwick *was* in a sense the Blantyre Mission ... The length of his service, his knowledge of both Yao and Nyanja, his intimacy with so many of the chiefs whose fathers he had also known, gave him enormous prestige with the settlers and the Administration as well.'[3] Such was his stature that he came to personify the Mission during the first quarter of the twentieth century. The next chapter will consider his role in public life during this period. First, we consider his leadership within the Mission itself.

Leading the Mission

There were many sides to Hetherwick's role during his time as Head of Blantyre Mission but there is little doubt that his own consistent priority was the development of the Mission itself. To this task he brought his forceful and sometimes abrasive personality. Even his fondest admirers would have to admit that it did not take much to stir his indignation. To take but one example, when W. P. Livingstone published his biography of Robert Laws he made a passing reference to the founding of Blantyre Mission and, in Hetherwick's view, offered an incorrect account of the choice of the site for the Mission.[4]

The latter at once took up his pen and scarcely paused to commend the book before turning to 'the paragraph on page 106 where you give what I cannot but call a travesty of the choice of the present site of Blantyre'.[5] He then embarks on a long account of Henry Henderson's choice of the site of Blantyre Mission. Accuracy in references to the history of the Mission was clearly a matter that was close to his heart and anyone who fell short could expect to face both barrels. This was, after all, no more than a matter of historical detail so it is little wonder that those who crossed Hetherwick on more substantial matters discovered that they had aroused a formidable opponent.

He was certainly not someone that you would want to overcharge. The Scots have a reputation for being reluctant to part with their cash. However, among the Scots themselves this reputation is reserved especially for people from Aberdeen – which was Hetherwick's home city. When

Figure 4.1 Alexander Hetherwick in his study at Blantyre Mission

the Blantyre Mission Council met on 3 September 1890 they received a complaint from John Moir of the African Lakes Company that a group of missionaries who had recently sailed on the ALC steamer had all paid £12 rather than the £15 fare that was due. Hetherwick immediately admitted that it was he who was responsible for the £3 shortfall. His explanation was that '... as he had received no intimation that the passage was raised from £12 to £15 consequently he could not make a protest – but that as soon as he found out what they had been charged he protested by deducting the said £3.'[6] Such a combative stance was typical Hetherwick. He could not even report on an agricultural show without revealing his combative instincts: '. . . Mr Burnett's display of vegetables drove all competition from the field, and Mrs McIlwain defeated her rivals in three branches of domestic art'.[7]

His brusque and abrasive style was evident at times in his handling of the Mission staff. He did not suffer fools gladly. For example, when he wrote in 1903 to the Foreign Mission Committee Convener John McMurtrie about a temporary member of staff named Brown, he remarked that '. . . he entirely lacks the sympathetic attitude towards the natives that makes a missionary. He has absolutely no give and take – can see nothing but his own view of the native character – the very last man to draw the people around him . . . I would not have him as a member of the Blantyre staff for love or money.'[8] It is notable that it was Brown's failure to relate well to the African community that drew Hetherwick's fire. The same issue underlay the failure of Revd and Mrs Wands to fit in at Domasi Mission when they were posted there in 1925. Hetherwick was only too happy to see the back of them: 'Providence came to our aid again in helping us to get rid of unsatisfactory people without trouble.'[9]

Over the years there were quite a number of unsuccessful appointments. Elizabeth McGillivray, for example, was appointed in 1909 to work under Janet Beck in the Women's Department with particular responsibility for the sewing class. When she arrived it soon became clear that she refused to take any instructions from Miss Beck and was unwilling to have anything to do with the sewing class. No wonder Hetherwick was soon writing to Edinburgh that 'the present attitude on Miss McGillivray's part is an impossible one'.[10] She herself was very unhappy, sending a formal letter of complaint to the Mission Council and telling Hetherwick, 'I do not wish to have a personal interview with you about this matter because the last two interviews have upset me very much, I would prefer a written reply'.[11]

When her letter was discussed at the Council meeting, Hetherwick promised to call a meeting to address the issues she had raised. Two months later, nothing further had been done and she wrote to him again to express her exasperation: 'This cannot go on any longer. You have shunned and taken no notice of me, and all I have plainly stated to you about the work and if you cannot right matters, I intend at once to have the whole case thoroughly sifted and put before the people who can and will right it. Either your treatment of me must alter and I get my proper position here or extreme steps must be taken.'[12] She did not last long at Blantyre Mission. When she left in March 1913 Hetherwick wrote to the Women's Foreign Mission Committee in Edinburgh that she was 'the most insubordinate, impertinent and impossible woman I have had to deal with during the whole past thirty years of my work here in Blantyre'.[13] Missionaries as a class are notoriously prickly characters and the Blantyre Mission had its share of the 'awkward squad'. Nor can it be denied that there were occasions when Hetherwick himself displayed his prickly side.

On the other hand, there were those with whom he worked in great harmony and mutual respect over many years. He shared almost thirty years of service at Blantyre with his near-contemporary Janet Beck. When she celebrated the silver jubilee of her service in 1911, he remarked that he could 'truly say before God that Miss Beck is the greatest spiritual asset that the whole Mission has – aye that the whole of the Missions in Central Africa have'.[14] When her health broke down following a motorbike accident in 1916 and she returned to Scotland, he was unstinting in his appreciation: 'She has left a mark on the home and family life of the Christian native in these parts that will remain and grow deeper in all time to come. Her work and herself have been the envy of all the other missions in this country – none of whom have had anything like them to show. There are many native women who in after years will rise up and call her blessed. *O si sic omnes*!!! (If only all were like this.)'[15] John McIlwain was another who was 'like this'. His service was almost contemporaneous with Hetherwick's and when McIlwain died at Blantyre in 1927, the latter recorded that 'There was a crowd such as we have never had round anyone's grave – Native or European'.[16]

Hetherwick also struck up warm friendships with new missionaries who began their service during his time as Head of the Mission, such as Frederick and Nita Alexander, long-serving missionaries at Zomba, and Alex Burnett, who after many years of service at Blantyre became Hetherwick's unofficial representative in Scotland. Their correspondence reveals much affection, humour and mutual support. When Burnett left the service of the Mission in 1925, he wrote to Hetherwick: 'No words of mine can convey to you how deeply deeply grateful I am to you for all the love, loyalty and kindness you have shown me. When I think of all you have done for me my eyes fill with tears and my heart is overwhelmed with gratitude to you.'[17] The letters of other long serving Blantyre missionaries, like the Bowman brothers, Frank and Ernest, or Melville Anderson, are less affectionate but nonetheless show respect and confidence. When Frank wrote in 1926 to confide that he thought the time might be coming for him to step down, he remarked, 'I write to you quite frankly because you perhaps know me better than anyone on the field'.[18] Similarly, when his brother Ernest consulted Hetherwick in 1927 about whether he should leave the Mission in order to work for the newly established Government Department of Education he clearly did so with a deep sense of trust.[19]

Andrew Ross singles out Robert Napier from among the new missionaries as the one 'who would have been thoroughly at home with the original "Scott clan"'.[20] Yet far from this creating any kind of distance from Hetherwick, the relationship between the two was one of extraordinary affection. Napier characteristically addressed his letters to Hetherwick 'Dear Atate (father)', while Hetherwick replied 'My dear Mwana (child)'.[21]

This was somewhat light-hearted and tongue-in-cheek but nonetheless accurately suggests that the relationship of the two men was like that of father and son. When Napier was shot and killed by German forces in Portuguese East Africa towards the end of the First World War, Hetherwick remarked that 'We feel immeasurably the poorer for his loss, and we feel that the Mission has lost one who was destined to be its leader'.[22] Clearly Hetherwick had been doing succession planning and had been mentoring Napier with the idea that he would one day take over the leadership of the Mission. It was not to be. All that was left was for Hetherwick to show what Napier had meant to him by publishing a collection of his letters that reveal something of the quality of his missionary service.[23]

For those who won Hetherwick's respect he offered unyielding support and generous friendship. Dr Elizabeth McCurrach, a missionary who arrived towards the end of Hetherwick's time recalled that 'the manse was home to me for three years, and I never expect again to get so much kindness shown to me in life'.[24] Besides her own happy experience, she noted the place that Hetherwick occupied in the affections of the Mission as a whole:

> His band of loyal workers gave him a place of great honour in their hearts. No department liked a day when he was away from the station: black and white alike looked for his coming with pleasure. He was very kind to young missionaries and sympathetic with their ideas, always ready to discuss new plans. Young in mind himself he was willing that youth should have its chance.[25]

Emerging African Leaders

When David Livingstone set out the prospectus for the missions that he hoped would build on his work he was clear that the evangelisation of Africa would need to be carried out by Africans themselves. The role of any Europeans was merely auxiliary. This philosophy was taken to heart by Blantyre Mission from its beginnings and its early period was marked by the appointment of Africans to significant leadership positions. By the time Hetherwick took over as Head of the Mission, however, times had changed. A colonial society was emerging where it was commonly assumed that it was necessary for Europeans to be in charge. The time for Africans to occupy significant leadership positions was relegated to the distant future. One of the tests of Hetherwick's leadership was how far he would be able to sustain the original ideals of the mission in the new context. Andrew Ross has argued that he failed the test, contrasting his allegedly distant and stiff relationships with Africans with the freedom and confidence that characterised Scott's relationships with his African protégés. 'Hetherwick,' he concludes, 'never achieved the close personal relations with Africans that Scott did, and was never so passionately and understandingly negrophile as was Scott.'[26] There may have been personality factors at play here. Scott was a spontaneous and passionate character who won loyal friendship from those who responded to his genius, while he also tended to alienate those who did not. Hetherwick was also well capable of falling out with people but he was a more introverted and reserved character. Before concluding from this that he was unable to form close relationships with African members of the Mission, however, it is worth looking at some of the available evidence.

Mamie Martin, a perceptive participant at the Livingstonia Mission Conference of 1924, took note of an incident that sheds light on this question. During a session on how Africans came to faith, she was impressed by the speech of the Blantyre minister Harry Kambwiri Matecheta:

> Several of the native pastors told how they had come. The Blantyre one was the most interesting. He said he first came through his father who was a heathen, but who had been working at the Mission and came back to the village and taught his children the Lord's Prayer. This made the boy go to Blantyre and soon Dr Hetherwick took notice of him in the school, 'because I was a very clever boy and answered well. But I was also a very bad boy, very bad indeed. I was always fighting with other boys. I like to fight. I thought I would never be happy if I stopped fighting. However, I had a talk with Dr Hetherwick one day and after that I found a better way of being happy.'[27]

By this time Matecheta was one of the most senior African leaders in the service of the Mission, having been ordained to the ministry at Blantyre in 1911, the first African to attain this status in Malawi. In his major speech at Livingstonia, he singled out Hetherwick as a mentor who had decisively influenced him in his formative years.

Matecheta's relationship with Hetherwick is a matter to which Thokozani Chilembwe and Todd Statham turn their attention in their introduction to the account of the early years of Blantyre Mission that Matecheta published in 1951. His recent editors offer a perspective on the profile of Hetherwick that Matecheta offers:

> Hetherwick, who served the Mission for forty-five years, including many as its head . . . does appear often in *Blantyre Mission*. But he appears in a 'matter-of-fact' way, and certainly not as the face of the Mission . . . We wonder if Matecheta is reflecting the Africans' view of Hetherwick, whose more paternalistic leadership has been unfavourably contrasted to Clement Scott?[28]

This reflects the prevailing trend in historical scholarship but it seems to be at odds with some passages in Matecheta's text itself. It is true that Hetherwick is by no means a dominant figure in the account offered by Matecheta, as might be expected of the long-term Head of the Mission. However, Matecheta's project was to offer an African perspective on the history of the Mission. He therefore tends to focus on the African participants and presents the European missionaries on a human scale, mentioning for example some of their nicknames and their foibles that caused amusement among the Africans.

Hetherwick tends to be exempted from the affectionate and almost jocular tone in which some of the missionaries are described. However, Matecheta does record some incidents where Hetherwick's influence on him while he was a schoolboy at Blantyre Mission proved to be decisive, rather echoing his 1924 speech at Livingstonia. He writes:

> I was very quick to understand the sermons of Dr. A Hetherwick during the worship services that were organized daily for the workers from 1 to 2 pm ... Dr. Hetherwick always started the service by asking people what he had taught the previous day. Despite my young age, I would stand up in the midst of the crowd and say, for example: 'You preached about "The Lost Sheep"'. I described everything while he gazed me with great amazement because of my age. One day he asked my name. I said, 'I am Kambwiri'. Then he said, 'I want you to come to Maganga'.[29]

He also acknowledges that, but for Hetherwick's intervention, he might well have given up on his involvement at the Mission:

> I came to live at Maganga. Yet the fights were not yet over, perhaps because I provoked them as a son of a Yao, who did not fear even the older boys. One day, tired with this sort of life, I just tied up my things and went to bid farewell to Dr Hetherwick – he stopped me from leaving ... Another time I left without his knowledge, but after two days he sent messengers to get me; my father also insisted that I should return. I agreed and that is why I am here right up to this day! I thank him for his persistence and patience with me.[30]

Such recollections do not suggest that Hetherwick was aloof and unapproachable, lacking in sympathy for Africans who became involved with the Mission. It seems to accord more with the reminiscence of his friend and fellow-missionary Alex Burnett:

> He knows every evangelist and teacher intimately; he knows their difficulties and temptations in their isolated outposts, and no one is more welcome when he visits them. He is their champion and friend; one whom they can absolutely trust and confide in. They call him *Mzungu Wamkuru*, the Great White Man ['senior European' might be a better translation], whom they love and revere. I accompany him on many of his tours and it is a joy to see the reception the people give him and how they listen to his addresses.[31]

It is true that the revitalisation of the Mission Council that was mandated by the General Assembly after the Report of the 1897 Commission of Inquiry meant that the Mission became more European-run and this introduced a certain distance between the European missionaries and the African church leaders that chimed well with the emerging colonial society of the early twentieth century. However, this does not mean that Hetherwick had lost the confidence in African leadership that had marked the earlier years of the mission. One of his first initiatives when he took over the headship of the Mission in 1898 was to reopen the sub-station at Nthumbi in Angoniland (Ntcheu) and to put it under the charge of none other than Matecheta, who by this time was among the Mission's most trusted teacher-evangelists.

Going against the now prevailing wisdom that it was necessary to have a European in charge of such a project, he acknowledged that this decision was a 'venture'. But he went on to proudly claim that, 'The venture was fully justified by its results. The name of "Father Harry", as he is lovingly called by the people, has been a power for spiritual influence in the whole district.'[32] Far from departing from the vision that inspired Clement Scott, Hetherwick was convinced that the work of Matecheta among the Ngoni represented its fulfilment: 'Clement Scott's vision of his early days of a mission to the Angoni, who caused him and the Blantyre people many anxious days and sleepless nights, has been fulfilled beyond his utmost hopes.'[33]

At the same time, in the post-1898 context, relations with African leaders within the Mission were not always so happy. A case in point is Mungo Murray Chisuse, who had been a leading figure at Blantyre Mission all through the 1880s and 1890s. He had been trained as a printer and took charge of the Mission Press, a high-profile and influential part of its work. Chisuse was an epitome of what could be achieved in terms of Africans being trained and taking up significant leadership roles. However, by 1907 Hetherwick had become convinced that a European printer was needed and Hamilton Currie was appointed.[34] This meant, in effect, a demotion for Chisuse and unsurprisingly he began to look outside the Mission for opportunities to use his skills, with the result that he became the first successful independent photographer in Malawi.[35] Reading between the lines, he felt he had been ousted at Hetherwick's instigation and inevitably this led to a certain souring of relations. This appears to be an instance where Hetherwick was susceptible to the now-ascendant colonial attitude that it was preferable to have Europeans in charge.

Colonialist language also came to be accepted. There are times when the generalising way of referring to 'the native' appears to be demeaning and compliant with racist tropes but on other occasions it can be subversive of racial stereotypes. When a new teacher, named Walker, came out from Scotland to serve with the Mission when it was short-staffed during the war, Hetherwick made the telling remark: 'He is a gentleman which goes a long way with the natives who are quick to recognise the man they have to deal with and what kind he is.'[36] The category of 'gentleman' was one normally reserved for Europeans in the racial thinking of the time but this is subverted by Hetherwick when he suggests that the qualities of a gentleman were well appreciated by 'the natives' (echoing his famous riposte at the Chilembwe Commission of Inquiry – see below).

In terms of personality, it may well be that Hetherwick lacked the sympathy and sense of adventure with which David Clement Scott entered into relationships with his African protégés. In fact, very few could be a match for Scott in this regard. Nonetheless, Hetherwick's correspondence files are full of letters in Chinyanja from people like Harry Kambwiri Matecheta and John Gray Kufa who had been members of Scott's deacons' class. Though they are usually writing about routine matters concerning the running of their stations, it is clear that they looked to Hetherwick as their leader and mentor. As for Lewis Mataka Bandawe, who arrived at Blantyre Mission just as Hetherwick took over the leadership, his recollection was that, 'Really, the Mission was like paradise. When we used to sing the hymn, "There is a city bright", we often said that the Mission was just like that city.'[37]

Notwithstanding such happy memories, it has to be acknowledged that the Mission was not immune to the linguistic codes that inscribed racist and colonialist thinking on the community in Nyasaland. One of these was the convention of referring to African men as 'boys' regardless of their age or seniority. This was pervasive in the life of the Mission, with Hetherwick using this language as much as anyone else. To some extent it became a linguistic convention and survives to this day, for example with domestic staff being routinely described as 'houseboy' or 'gardenboy' according to role. In the life of the Mission it was often used without any intention to be demeaning but nonetheless in a colonial society it was a device that expressed the supposed superiority of the European as the adult and the supposed inferiority of the African as the child.

Likewise, at a time when Europeans were always addressed outside their immediate family circle by their title and surname, with only children being addressed by their first name, it was common practice to address Africans by their first name, thereby infantilising them. Even after Harry Kambwiri Matecheta and Stephen Kundecha were ordained to the ministry, becoming ecclesiastically fully equal to their European colleagues, the missionaries, Hetherwick included, continued to refer to them as 'Harry' and 'Stephen'. This was not intentional belittling or disrespect, but it showed how far racist and colonialist thinking had seeped into the attitude and language of a Mission that, in principle, had very different values.

On the other hand, under Hetherwick's leadership the Mission invested massively in the training of Matecheta and Kundecha so that they would be able to occupy roles that had hitherto been reserved for Europeans. The empowerment of Africans as leaders, that had marked the early years of the Mission, had not been forgotten. In fact, Hetherwick made the theological class for the two men his top priority when it started in 1907, complaining that it demanded three hours of teaching and two hours of preparatory work every day. The fact that he dedicated such time to this task amidst the many other demands that were made on the Head of the Mission, demonstrates how much he put a premium on the equipping of African leaders. When the two men wrote their first exams, Hetherwick remarked that, 'It has far surpassed my utmost expectations, and confirms me in the policy that our Mission should adopt now – the extension of our sphere not by European stations but by native workers and native outstations.'[38]

His vision for the future of the Mission was that it would be driven by African leadership and he set the priorities for his own work accordingly. While the Mission was unable to escape the influence of racist and colonialist attitudes and language, at a deeper level it was fostering the emergence of an African leadership to which the future would belong. In 1921 Hetherwick led a two-week retreat at Chiradzulu for the five ordained African ministers who were serving at that time. They lived in community for the fortnight and followed a programme of spiritual exercise and theological reading.[39] Harry Mtuwa reported that it was 'a most strenuous "Retreat" and that he has enjoyed it immensely'.[40] Hetherwick had clearly been in his element.

Policy and Strategy

During Hetherwick's early years the strategy of the Mission was to extend its influence from its initial base at Blantyre by establishing mission stations in key positions in the wider Shire Highlands area. His own pioneering work at Domasi had been the first move in this direction and it was followed by a short-lived attempt at Chiradzulu that led to a permanent mission station being established at Mulanje. A sub-station at Nthumbi in 'Angoniland' (now Ntcheu District) further extended the reach of the Mission as did attempts to develop work at Chiromo in the Shire valley. The guiding idea initially was that each of these centres might develop the range of programmes and services that were proving successful at Blantyre itself – church, school, clinic, industrial training, community outreach. By the early years of the twentieth century, however, Hetherwick was coming to the conclusion that this approach was dissipating resources and compromising quality. He came to the view that a centralisation of education and training at Blantyre would better provide the Mission as a whole with the human resources that it needed in order to advance. He set out his thinking in a letter to James Robertson, who had succeeded Archibald Scott as Convener of the Africa Committee in Edinburgh:

> I have only begun, and in the years that are spared to me here I hope to see the edifice finished. Let me once more put my policy before you. There are four lines of development on which this place is moving.
>   As a spiritual centre for the whole district that falls within the sphere of the Blantyre station. (Blantyre pop 73,380, West Shire 20,995, Southern Angoniland 68,000, Chiromo 40,000 (est). In this district we have the following native stations as centres of spiritual

work, Chiradzulo 13 miles distant, Nsoni 18 miles, Pantumbi 90 miles, Lichenza 21 miles.

We have in all 360 Church members on the Communion roll, over 400 Catechumens now, and 2199 scholars in the school while we have 55 preaching centres in the villages on Sundays.

As an Institution for the Educational and Industrial training of the natives – chiefly those who make up the membership of the Native Church. These are trained on a definite system – a three-year course of manual education in one or other of the trades which we profess. Each department follows a fixed and recognized code of instruction, and gives its pupils a thorough training such as will fit him or her to meet the flowing tide of civilization that is covering the whole of the native life of the land.

As an Institution for the training of the future teaching staff of the Church. We need trained teachers for the development of education of the Country – a matter which is vital to the welfare of the people and the good of the native Church.

As a College for the training of the future ministry of the Church. At this we are doing only a very little – how can I? I have one [Harry Kambwiri Matecheta] to whom the prospect of the Christian ministry is a near one – but I can hardly get at him at all – his sphere of labour where he is showing the grit that is in him, is over ninety miles from here . . .[41]

Hetherwick was among those who championed the philosophy of centralisation at the Missionary Conference that was hosted at Livingstonia later the same year. He was heartened that this approach was endorsed by the conference as a principle to guide the work of all the Missions in the country. At the start of 1905 he wrote a memorandum to the Foreign Mission Committee on the issues of centralisation of training. He argued that there were two major factors that were inhibiting the progress of the Mission: there was no extension into new districts and there was no trained and educated native ministry. The reason why no progress was being made on these fronts, he suggested, was fourfold:

Lack of unity of plan and policy of development for the whole Mission. Each Station is working on its own lines with an overlapping of its energies and a wastage of power.

By attempting to work each of the present Stations on the same lines as Educational, Medical and Industrial Training Centres, with a proportionate European staff, the efforts of the members of the staffs are too much concentrated on the stations, and too little devoted to the supervision of native workers at the various sub-stations in their different spheres.

This mistake of attempting to work all the stations on precisely the same lines has prevented the provision at any of the stations of a

European staff sufficient and qualified to train the necessary numbers of native workers – or to make provision for a native ministry.

The resulting lack of trained native staff has stood in the way of the Europeans being set free for extension into other spheres.[42]

By contrast, the new scheme that he was proposing,

... aims at centralising all the higher departments of training – Evangelistic, Medical, Educational and Industrial – at the mother station of Blantyre, with the intention of providing a better trained and more responsible native staff for the work of the other stations, so as to enable them to devote their time wholly to the supervision of their native workers in their various districts. By this means also, in a few years, provision will be made whereby with the present European staff, extension into new spheres will be made possible.[43]

At the heart of the policy was a vision for an expansion of the work of the Mission through the leadership of suitably trained African ministers, evangelists and teachers. At the end of October 1905 Hetherwick heard from John McMurtrie in Edinburgh that the Foreign Mission Committee had approved his proposal.[44] Much of his work during the next few years was concerned with the development of the Henry Henderson Institute where this vision would be put into effect. 'By 1910,' writes Kelvin Banda, 'Blantyre station had become one of the notable educational institutions in Southern Africa. It had become the centre of not only educational and religious affairs but also political and social life of the Southern Region.'[45]

A Passion for Extension

Though at first sight it appears paradoxical, the aim of centralising the training operations of the Mission at Blantyre was to achieve the extension of its work into new areas. The central plank of the strategy was the equipment of African leaders who could spearhead the advance. In 1908, when Hetherwick marked the silver jubilee (twenty-fifth anniversary) of his arrival in Blantyre, he recalled his very first evening. He had sat up late into the night talking with Clement Scott, Alexander Peden and Henry Henderson about 'hopes and vision of future work and extensions'. Now he could reflect that, 'More than any of us ever ventured to hope and dream have the visions of that evening been realised for the Mission and the Church in this place.'[46] The passion for extension was undimmed, however, and when it met on 15 January 1908 the Mission Council unanimously agreed:

That the future policy of the Mission with regard to extension be directed towards (1) the occupying of the whole country by planting native stations such as Panthumbi, Chiradzulo, etc, under trained native Evangelists, Teachers, Ministers, etc. (2) the better training and equipment of native workers for this work, and (3) the more effectual and regular supervision of these stations by the European Missionary from the various European centres of the districts.

That the work of the present European stations be devoted more and more to the effective superintendence of the district work in their respective spheres, leaving the work of training Evangelists, Teachers etc more and more to the Central Institution at Blantyre.[47]

The strategy was to use Blantyre as a base to prepare the human resources that would enable an ever-wider extension of the work of the Mission within its sphere of influence. The vision, however, did not stop there.

Almost from the beginning, Blantyre Mission had been aware that its primary sphere of operation in the Shire Highlands was a relatively small area in relation to the vast territory in which it was set. In particular, geographically it was almost like an island surrounded by the much more extensive territory of Portuguese East Africa. Tentative beginnings had been made during Scott's time as missionaries carried out exploratory visits and initial outposts were established by emerging African leaders such as John Gray Kufa. Under Hetherwick's leadership the dream of extending the Mission's work into surrounding areas of PEA continued to catch the imagination. When the Mission Council met on 17 November 1910 it was inspired by the great World Missionary Conference that had been hosted in Edinburgh earlier that year, giving new impetus to the missionary movement in terms of extending its reach.[48] For the Blantyre Mission staff this meant a renewed commitment to their vision for work in Portuguese East Africa and they took the unusual step of composing a formal appeal to the Church of Scotland. It was signed by all the staff, including Elizabeth Hetherwick, whose formal status was that of spouse but who, after thirty-one years, was the longest serving missionary. The appeal was in the following terms:

> We the Members of the Mission Staff of the Church of Scotland Mission, Nyasaland, being assembled this day in conference at Blantyre . . . are persuaded that the time has now come for an advance into new fields, and we therefore make this appeal to the Foreign Mission Committee and to the Church of Scotland to sanction a fresh extension of their work into the Portuguese territory which lies immediately adjacent to the present sphere . . . Our present sphere in Nyasaland is surrounded on all other sides by other missionary agencies, there is therefore no other opening for us in our own Protectorate. Moreover, this large part of Portuguese East Africa lies entirely untouched by any missionary influence . . . One European station in Lomweland east of Lake Shirwa, another in the Bororo country south of Mlanje, to be followed by a third in the west country towards the Zambezi River, will give the Church of Scotland a claim to this field as a sphere for evangelisation worthy of her missionary traditions.[49]

These ambitious ideas never completely came to fruition but the first part, the station in Lomweland, was successfully put into effect over the next few years.[50]

The enthusiasm of the Mission Council was matched by that of Africans in the service of the Mission. Robert Napier had a map in his study that showed 'the smallness of the present sphere, and the huge area of the Portuguese country'.[51] He used it to foster enthusiasm among African leaders in the Mission for the proposed extension. One day he noted that 'the teacher in one of our district schools made me write down his name as a volunteer whenever we go'.[52] Meanwhile Hetherwick wrote a memorandum in which he systematically laid out the rationale for the extension into Portuguese East Africa and the means by which it could be achieved.[53] This laid out the arguments of centralisation with a view to extension, the lack of opportunity for pioneering work in the existing sphere and – a principle of great importance to Hetherwick – '. . . there must be a constant extension if the mission is to keep up its vitality in this country'.[54] Despite hesitation in Scotland where the church officials were all too aware that they struggled to support the existing operations without adding to them, Hetherwick's argument eventually won the day. It was a momentous day at Blantyre Mission in April 1912 when he received a telegram telling him, '£300 already promised proceed Lomweland'.[55]

Resisting Roman Catholic Advance

So far as missionary work is concerned, Blantyre Mission had the Shire Highlands to itself during its early years. Hetherwick was irritated when Joseph Booth founded his Zambezi Industrial Mission close to Blantyre in 1892.[56] A constant refrain in *Life and Work* was dismay that, with the whole of Africa to choose from, so many missions based themselves in Blantyre. Much more substantial competition came, however, with the arrival of the Roman Catholic Montfortian Mission in 1901.[57] From small beginnings, this Mission developed a Catholic presence that would eventually overtake the Blantyre Mission in terms of institutional strength and membership numbers. In Hetherwick's time the competition became intense and stirred his combative instincts. Typical was the comment he made in 1925 to his colleague Revd J. A. Smith: 'The RCs are making a determined attack on Mulanje and we need all our forces there to counteract their schemes. Unless we are able to make good at this time the whole of our Mlanje work will fall to pieces by the machinations of the Romanists who are without scruples or honesty pushing for a place – even in defiance of the Government.'[58] Military language was his preferred form of expression when it came to assessing the growth of the Catholic missions (as it was with the Catholics vice versa). Looking ahead to an educational conference in 1927, he wrote to fellow missionary Barbara Low, 'The Educational Conference will be a big thing – and a big battle. The RCs are getting ready their weapons and unless we are a united front against them we shall be routed and may just shut up shop.'[59] When the Governor Sir Charles Bowring suggested that Hetherwick might meet with Bishop Auneau to see if they could reach an understanding, he received a blistering response: 'Your suggestion of a meeting between myself and Bishop Auneau I would look on favourably if I thought that any good would come of it. But I can imagine no hope of such an issue. When a man is out to burn your house about your ears, it is little use sitting down with him to discuss how much he may be allowed to burn.'[60]

When he wrote to headquarters during the last years of his service to lament the lack of new missionary recruits, he highlighted the threat posed by the growth of the Catholic missions:

> When one sees here as I do every day the determined efforts made by the Romanists to get a hold of Nyasaland one trembles for the future of Protestant Missions in this land. They are throwing out lines and putting in stakes all over the country while we have been standing still for the past good many years . . . They appeal to the Government because they have so large a staff of Europeans that they can give the European superintendence that Government loves.[61]

He was perturbed that the government was inclined to favour the Catholic schools since, in his view, the education they offered was far inferior to that of the Blantyre Mission. Particularly galling to Hetherwick was the fact that the government usually recruited its own staff from among those educated in Blantyre Mission schools, yet its policy favoured the allegedly inferior schools of the Catholics.[62] He set out his strategy to counter their initiatives in a letter to Barbara Low:

> I am sorry to hear of the RCs giving trouble. They will do so I fear for some time till the superiority of our schools tells the native that we are better than they. It is in this way alone that we shall be able to meet them and their wiles. We can put down any school with a certificate teacher in any village where they are putting up a prayer house and in this way we can empty their so called school. But, oh, they are wiley with all the wiles of the Evil One.[63]

Perhaps the exasperation indicates that Hetherwick knew he was fighting a losing battle. Still, his fighting spirit continued to the last.

Reporting to HQ

The fighting spirit also found expression in communications with the Church of Scotland headquarters in Edinburgh, which were a constant preoccupation for Hetherwick. He did not hesitate to take his bosses to task when he thought it was warranted. In 1903 he wrote to James Robertson, Convener of the Africa Committee, indicating the extent of the fast-growing work and protesting:

> And in all this what help, what consideration, what support have I had from you? None – absolutely none ... I do blame you, and your indifference to a work that God is forcing on us here ... Do you not think it an extraordinary thing that the Senior Missionary of your church in Africa should have to say that those who support him the least in the work and development of the Mission are those who have been entrusted by the Church at home with the care and interests of the Mission?[64]

All too often he felt badly let down when required support was not forthcoming, lamenting in 1926 for example that, 'The Committee's bankruptcy of resources has been a sore blow to any hopes I had cherished for the future of the Mission. I sometimes feel I am at the end of my tether.'[65] Though relations with the officials in Edinburgh were bruising at times, there was also a softer side. When John McMurtrie stepped down after many years as Convener of the Foreign Mission Committee, Hetherwick wrote to tell him that,

> I recall my almost midnight visit to your little study in Inverleith Row and your prayer for me before I started. It was to me the beginning of a new life and I can only think with humble gratitude to God for His goodness to me all these intervening years. Never did I dream that I should be spared to see what I see around me today in the Mission here and outside it. God has been very good to us all.[66]

Notes

1. Archibald Scott to Alexander Hetherwick, 30 November 1898, NLS 7537/399.
2. Alexander Hetherwick to Sir Charles Bowring, 5 August 1925, MNA BMC/50/2/1/234.
3. Andrew C. Ross, *Blantyre Mission and the Making of Modern Malawi*, Blantyre: CLAIM-Kachere, 1996, repr. Mzuzu: Luviri Press, 2018, 171, my italics.
4. W. P. Livingstone maintained that Magomero was Henderson's choice for the site of the Mission and that they only ended up at Blantyre (Kapeni's) because they were exhausted by their journey up from the Lower Shire and could go no further. See Andrew C. Ross, *Blantyre Mission and the Making of Modern Malawi*, 54.
5. Alexander Hetherwick to W. P. Livingstone, 10 January 1922, MNA 50/BMC/2/1/95.
6. Mission Council meeting at Blantyre, 3 September 1890, MNA 50/BMC/1/1/.
7. *Life and Work in Nyasaland*, July–August 1909.
8. Alexander Hetherwick to John McMurtrie, 1 June 1903, MNA 50/BMC/2/1/48.
9. Alexander Hetherwick to Barbara Low, 10 November 1925, MNA 50/BMC/2/2/15.
10. Alexander Hetherwick to Miss Macpherson, Women's Foreign Mission Committee, 3 February 1910, MNA 50/BMC/2/1/105.
11. Elizabeth McGillivray to Alexander Hetherwick, 15 June 1910, MNA 50/BMC/2/2/1.

12. Elizabeth McGillivray to Alexander Hetherwick, 30 September 1910, MNA 50/BMC/2/2/1.
13. Alexander Hetherwick to Miss Macpherson, 25 March 1913, MNA BMC/50/2/1/125.
14. Alexander Hetherwick to W. M. McLachlan, 9 September 1911, MNA BMC/50/2/1/120.
15. Alexander Hetherwick to W. M. McLachlan, 3 April 1916, MNA 50/BMC/2/2/9.
16. Alexander Hetherwick to W. M. McLachlan, 24 January 1927, MNA BMC/50/2/1/247.
17. Alexander Burnett to Alexander Hetherwick, [undated] February 1925, MNA BMC/50/2/1/228.
18. Frank Bowman to Alexander Hetherwick, 31 December 1926, MNA 50/BMC/2/2/24.
19. Ernest D. Bowman to Alexander Hetherwick, 5 September 1927, MNA 50/BMC/2/2/27
20. Andrew Ross, *Blantyre Mission and the Making of Modern Malawi*, 244.
21. Letters between Alexander Hetherwick and Robert Napier, 1914, 50/BMC/2/2/6.
22. *Life and Work in Nyasaland*, April–June 1918.
23. Alexander Hetherwick (ed.), *Robert Hellier Napier in Nyasaland: Being his Letters to his Home Circle*, Edinburgh and London: William Blackwood Sons, 1925.
24. W. P. Livingstone, *A Prince of Missionaries: Alexander Hetherwick of Blantyre*, London: James Clarke, n.d., 192.
25. Ibid., 193.
26. Andrew Ross, *Blantyre Mission and the Making of Modern Malawi*, 167.
27. Margaret Sinclair, *Salt and Light: The Letters of Jack and Mamie Martin in Malawi 1921–28*, Blantyre: CLAIM, 2002, 207.
28. Harry Kambwiri Matecheta, *Blantyre Mission: Stories of its Beginning*, ed. by Thokozani Chilembwe and Todd Statham, Mzuzu: Luviri Press, 2020 (trsl. from Harry Kambwiri Matecheta, *Blantyre Mission. Nkhani za Ciyambi Cace*, Blantyre: Hetherwick Press, 1951), 22.
29. Matecheta, *Blantyre Mission*, 44.
30. Matecheta, *Blantyre Mission*, 45.
31. Livingstone, *A Prince of Missionaries*, 171.
32. Alexander Hetherwick, *Romance of Blantyre: How Livingstone's Dream Came True*, London: James Clarke, n.d., 112.
33. Ibid.
34. Blantyre Mission Council, 30 January 1907, MNA 50/BMC/1/1/1.
35. See John McCracken, 'Mungo Murray Chisuse and the Early History of Photography in Malawi', *Society of Malawi Journal* 61/2 (2008), 1–18.
36. Alexander Hetherwick to J. N. Ogilvie, 15 June 1916, MNA 50/BMC/2/2/9.
37. Lewis Mataka Bandawe, 'The Memoirs of Lewis Mataka Bandawe', in Kenneth R. Ross (ed.), *Christianity in Malawi: A Sourcebook*, 2nd ed., Mzuzu: Mzuni Press, 2020, 53, extract from Lewis Mataka Bandawe, *Memoirs of a Malawian*, Blantyre: CLAIM, 1971.
38. Alexander Hetherwick to J. D. McCallum (Convener, Africa Sub-Committee), 29 August 1907, MNA 50/BMC/2/1/82.
39. Alexander Hetherwick, 'Chiradzulo 1887–1921', MNA BMC/50/2/1/193.

40. Frederick Alexander to Alexander Hetherwick, 23 November 1921, MNA BMC/50/2/1/193.
41. Alexander Hetherwick to James Robertson, Convener of African Sub-Committee, 28 April 1904, MNA 50/BMC/2/1/53.
42. Alexander Hetherwick, Memorandum for the Foreign Mission Committee Relative to the Centralisation of the Training Departments of the Mission. Minute of Blantyre Mission Council, 25 January 1905.
43. Ibid.
44. John McMurtrie to Alexander Hetherwick, 27 October 1905.
45. Kelvin N. Banda, *A Brief History of Education in Malawi*, Blantyre: Dzuka, 1982, 11.
46. Blantyre Mission Report for the Year 1908, MNA 50/BMC/2/1/96.
47. Mission Council meeting at Blantyre, 15 January 1908, MNA 50/BMC/1/1/1.
48. See W. H. Temple Gairdner, *'Edinburgh 1910': An Account and Interpretation of the World Missionary Conference*, Edinburgh and London: Oliphant, Anderson & Ferrier and Chicago and Toronto: Fleming H. Revell, 1910; Brian Stanley, *The World Missionary Conference, Edinburgh 1910*, Grand Rapids and Cambridge: Eerdmans, 2009.
49. 'Appeal to the Church of Scotland for Extension of Work into Portuguese East Africa', Mission Council meeting at Blantyre, 17 November 1910, MNA 50/BMC/1/1/1.
50. See M. Ali Nihoka, *Cristo em Moçambique através da missão escocesa: Surgimento e desenvolvimento da Igreja Evangelica de Cristo em Moçambique 1894–2013*, São Paulo: Scortecci, 2014, 23–28.
51. Alexander Hetherwick, *Robert Hellier Napier in Nyasaland*, 50.
52. Ibid., 60.
53. Alexander Hetherwick, 'Notes on the Scheme of Readjustment of Mission Methods to Allow of the Extension Into the New Territories of Portuguese East Africa', Blantyre, 28 January 1911, MNA 50/BMC/3/18/2.
54. Ibid.
55. Alexander Hetherwick to W. M. McLachlan, 30 April 1912, MNA 50/BMC/2/2/5.
56. See Harry Langworthy, *'Africa for the African.' The Life of Joseph Booth*, Blantyre: CLAIM-Kachere, 1996.
57. See Hubert Reijnaerts, Ann Nielsen and Matthew Schoffeleers, *Montfortians in Malawi: Their Spirituality and Pastoral Approach*, Blantyre: CLAIM-Kachere, 1997; repr. Mzuzu: Luviri Press, 2018.
58. Alexander Hetherwick to Revd J. A. Smith, 10 November 1925, MNA 50/BMC/2/2/16.
59. Alexander Hetherwick to Barbara Low, 6 May 1927, MNA 50/BMC/2/2/26.
60. Alexander Hetherwick to Sir Charles Bowring, 12 April 1926, MNA BMC/50/2/1/242.
61. Alexander Hetherwick to W. M. McLachlan, 20 April 1925, MNA 50/BMC 3/1/11.
62. See e.g. Alexander Hetherwick to W. M. McLachlan, 7 August 1925, MNA/BMC/3/1/11.
63. Alexander Hetherwick to Barbara Low, 24 August 1927, MNA/BMC/3/1/11.
64. Alexander Hetherwick to James Robertson (Convener, African Sub-Committee, Church of Scotland), 11 January 1903, MNA 50/BMC/2/1/46.

65. Alexander Hetherwick to Alexander Burnett, 27 April 1926, MNA 50/BMC/2/2/20.
66. Alexander Hetherwick to John McMurtrie, 30 June 1908, MNA 50/BMC/2/1/91.

CHAPTER FIVE

The Public Figure: Critic and Campaigner

While leadership and management of the Mission was a full-time job in itself, Hetherwick's attention was never confined to its internal affairs but extended to all aspects of the life of the Protectorate. Across five decades he was among Nyasaland's most prominent public figures. To some extent he occupied a special position, having been closely involved in the events that led to the creation of the Protectorate. As time went on there were fewer and fewer people who could match his longevity and historical knowledge. This gave him a certain moral high ground when it came to assessment of public issues. Besides his personal stature, Blantyre Mission was uniquely placed as it predated the British Administration and was embedded in local community life. Its geographical proximity meant that it was in more contact with the government, the settlers and the emerging colonial society than were missions based elsewhere in the Protectorate.

Especially in the 1890s when the Administration was just establishing itself, it was much more engaged with the south of the country, the Blantyre Mission sphere, than elsewhere. This gave Blantyre Mission something of a representative role where it could advocate not only its own interests but also those of the other missions based further north, which had less opportunity to be frequently in contact with the emerging public life of the Protectorate. As W. H. Murray, Head of the Dutch Reformed Mission, observed regarding Hetherwick in 1924: 'His ability, his determination, his fearlessness made him the trusted champion of mission interests. He belonged to us all and not merely to Blantyre Mission. If he was feared by government officials we knew the reason why – he knew too much of Nyasaland's history. In any case, they could not but respect him.'[1]

Another strategic advantage enjoyed by Blantyre Mission was that it published the first newspaper or magazine to be established in the Protectorate. It was published monthly from 1888 as *Life and Work in British Central Africa* until it changed its name to *Life and Work in Nyasaland* in 1907. It finally ceased publication in 1919 when it was felt that newspaper demand was being satisfied by the bi-weekly *Nyasaland Times*.[2] For more than thirty years *Life and Work* enabled the Mission to address its prophetic critique to the literate community as a whole. From the outset it was outspoken and produced sharp opinion pieces not only on religious matters but on the social, economic and political life of the Protectorate. As Hetherwick noted, with characteristic understatement, 'On more than one occasion it championed the cause of the natives when other authorities in the country appeared to be running on wrong lines.'³

His colleague Clement Scott was more emphatic when he responded with disdain to a recommendation from headquarters in Scotland that the newspaper be closed down. This was the last thing he was ever going to do. In his view, '*Life and Work* is unique, a Mission history, a Mission pulpit, a philosophy, a policy, and a salvation for the people.'⁴ Scott himself was a brilliant editor and his rhetorical flourish found full expression in many leader columns. Hetherwick was a frequent contributor during the ten years that Scott was at the helm and then took on the role of editor himself for the next twenty-one years. His trenchant and combative style was evident as the newspaper played a campaigning role on such issues as South African labour recruitment, land tenure and government policies and actions that he found objectionable. There were few public issues during this period on which Hetherwick's voice was not heard through the columns of *Life and Work*.

The Fight for Malawi

He was propelled into public life just a few years after he had arrived in Malawi when he discovered that the whole enterprise of Blantyre Mission, and the potential new country that was emerging around it, was jeopardised by political developments. Hetherwick had arrived in Malawi at a portentous time, just as the so-called 'Scramble for Africa' was about to unfold. The status of Blantyre and the surrounding area was somewhat ambiguous. On the basis of a Bull of Pope Alexander VI there had been an understanding that the whole of tropical Africa south of the Congo basin belonged to Portugal. The Portuguese, however, had concentrated their attention on the coasts and the Zambezi River, never showing much interest in the interior. Meanwhile David Livingstone's extensive travels in Central and Eastern Africa created a certain understanding that there was an emerging British sphere of influence. It was on this understanding that Blantyre and its sister Livingstonia Mission had established themselves in what is now Malawi. The carving up of the map of Africa among the European powers in the 1880s meant that there was no longer any room for ambiguity. There had to be a clearly defined border between the territory controlled by Portugal and that where British influence was recognised.⁵

By 1888 the Portuguese were flexing their muscles with a view to asserting their claim to the Shire Highlands, now seen to be of strategic importance so far as controlling Central Africa was concerned.⁶ When Hetherwick left Blantyre to go on furlough in Scotland, after more than two years when he had been Acting Head of the Mission during Clement Scott's absence on health grounds, he was already concerned about Portugal's imposition of tariffs on goods and restrictions on travel into the Shire Highlands area. When he reached the coast, he discovered that the Portuguese were organising an expedition, ostensibly for scientific purposes, but in reality as a means of asserting their control of what is now southern Malawi.[7] Hetherwick immediately realised what was brewing and when he arrived in Scotland lost no time in mobilising those who had Malawi at heart, including the Church of Scotland, the Free Church and the sponsors of the African Lakes Company. Before long, they had despatched a delegation to London to alert the British government to the threat and to lobby for decisive action.

The response of the British government was cool. The general outlook in the Foreign Office was that Britain was already overstretched by its imperial commitments and should avoid being stretched any further. A protectorate in Central Africa did not figure at all in the strategic thinking of the government. As the Prime Minister Lord Salisbury stated to the House of Lords: 'It is not our duty to do it. We should be risking tremendous sacrifices for a very doubtful gain.'[8] His strategy was to seek to secure southern Zambezia as a hinterland development of the Cape Colony and to this end he was content to leave northern Zambezia to the Portuguese.[9] When he received the Scottish delegation, he made it clear that he would, 'on no account ... annex Nyasaland or declare it British territory'.[10] The fight was on. As his biographer noted, 'Hetherwick threw himself into the campaign with tireless energy and resource'.[11] He was swiftly installed as the adviser to the Church of Scotland Foreign Mission Committee, his diary was soon full of appointments and conferences and he was frequently on the platform at public meetings.

Meanwhile, Harry Johnston, the newly appointed British Consul at Mozambique, was despatched to Lisbon to see if he could come to some accommodation with the Portuguese. When he returned, Salisbury summoned the Scottish representatives, Hetherwick among them, to London to hear the results. These were exactly the opposite to what they wanted to hear. On the table was a map of Africa with a blue line drawn to indicate the proposed boundary between Portuguese and British interests. Hetherwick immediately noticed that the line ran up the Shire River. This left the Shire Highlands, the entire sphere of operation of Blantyre Mission at that time, in the hands of the Portuguese.

Not for the last time, Johnston discovered that in Hetherwick he had an utterly determined opponent. Things were no better when Johnston travelled to Edinburgh. He felt sure that his powers of persuasion would be sufficient to convince the Scots that the Portuguese terms were reasonable. He soon learned otherwise as he met 'a large company of dour-looking men', who 'sat with faces like granite'.[12] Back in Blantyre, Clement Scott wrote in the new Blantyre Mission newspaper: 'Rumours from home reach us of a division of territory between Portugal and Britain in which the Shire is the boundary line. This is disastrous if it is true: it is indeed keeping the shell and giving the Portuguese the kernel.'[13]

Far from accepting the terms, the Scots intensified their campaign, with Hetherwick at the heart of it. He was utterly convinced that Portuguese annexation would be gravely injurious both to the work of Blantyre Mission and to the Malawian people with whom it was by now very much identified. A British Protectorate seemed the only viable alternative. The campaign involved a series of public meetings in Aberdeen, Glasgow, Edinburgh and Dundee, which culminated in 'a monster petition' signed by more than 11,000 ministers and elders of the Scottish churches, demanding British intervention in the Lake Malawi area.[14] The campaign even involved collaboration between members of the Free and Established Churches at a level that was unprecedented since the 'Disruption' that had divided the two churches in 1843. The Convention of Royal Burghs and several Chambers of Commerce lent their support.[15] When Archibald Scott, Convener of the Church of Scotland Africa Committee, presented the petition to the Prime Minister, Lord Salisbury, he was able to say: 'My Lord, this is the voice of Scotland'.[16]

Meanwhile in southern Africa, a game-changer had occurred in January 1889 when D. J. Rankin discovered the Chinde mouth of the Zambezi, which allowed the Zambezi-Shire route to be recognised as an international waterway. This meant that it was possible to reach Malawi without touching Portuguese soil. When Harry Johnston used the new route to sail up the Zambezi and Shire to stake the British claim to Malawi in August 1889, Hetherwick too was on board, returning to Blantyre after his leave in Scotland.[17] He therefore witnessed at first hand the denouement of the entire episode as Johnston confronted the Portuguese expeditionary force under Major Serpa Pinto just below the confluence of the Shire and the Ruo where he secured the Portuguese agreement to withdraw. Before long Johnston was touring Malawi securing the agreement of the chiefs to come under British protection. For Blantyre Mission this was the fulfilment of all its hopes and Hetherwick reported that, 'The manse dining-room at the mission became a factory with half a dozen sewing machines for the manufacture of Union Jacks – made of calico, red, white and blue – for presentation to the chiefs of the district who gladly welcomed these tokens of protection from the Portuguese menace.'[18]

On 19 August 1889 John Buchanan, as Acting Consul, sent a letter to Serpa Pinto announcing that, 'the Makololo country and the Shire Hills, commencing at the Ruo river, has been placed under the protection of Her Majesty the Queen'.[19] In October when Serpa Pinto defied this declaration, advanced up the Lower Shire and killed more than seventy Makololo in a battle, matters escalated rapidly. British pride was stung, Salisbury finally came round to the view that he had to protect Scottish missionary and commercial interests in the Shire area and British naval forces sailed for Gibraltar to put pressure on Lisbon. It was one of only two occasions during the scramble for Africa that there was a real possibility of European powers coming to blows.[20] In the event, Portugal backed down, its forces on the

Shire retreated and, on 20 August 1890, Britain and Portugal signed a convention that recognised what we now know as southern Malawi as British territory.[21] This did not come about without a struggle and Alexander Hetherwick had played a crucial role.

Resisting Company Rule

However, no sooner was one danger averted than another raised its head. The missionary campaign had resulted in Britain taking responsibility for the territory that was to become Malawi. The British Treasury, however, was adamant that no funds were available to support a British administration. Another way to exercise colonial rule was to give a charter to a commercial company to take on the responsibility of government. This was first mooted for Malawi in 1885 when the African Lakes Company offered to take on the running of a British Protectorate. Hetherwick was in charge at Blantyre Mission at the time and prepared a long memorandum arguing against granting the powers of a Chartered Company to the ALC on grounds of 'the manifest incapacity of the Lakes Company as presently constituted for undertaking any such administration . . .'[22] This was despatched by the British Consul Hawes to the Foreign Office in London and seems to have played a part in the proposal being refused.

This episode, however, was merely a precursor to a much more serious proposal that followed a few years later when Cecil Rhodes' British South Africa Company began to lobby for a charter to govern Malawi. By 1890 it was clear that British rule was on the way and Rhodes saw his opportunity to extend the sway of his company. It appears that lobbying from the Blantyre Mission proved decisive in the British government's decision to turn down the offer from Rhodes and establish an imperial Protectorate on 14 May 1891. As Sir Harry Johnston, the British Commissioner, later wrote to Rhodes, '. . . remember that it was Scott and Hetherwick who balked the scheme in 1890 of all British Central Africa coming under the Company's charter.'[23]

Johnston continued to take a favourable view of the idea of the fledgling Protectorate coming under the authority of the British South Africa Company, but he was met at every turn by the implacable opposition of the Blantyre Mission.[24] When Hetherwick returned to Scotland on leave, soon after his marriage to Elizabeth Fenwick in 1893, he found that, as Horace Waller wrote to Clement Scott, he was being 'roundly abused in the *Scotsman* newspaper as being one who has thwarted the Commissioner sorely'.[25] This was because of his tireless resistance to any suggestion that Malawi should come under company rule. Waller noted that, 'Hetherwick has had his say, and a very strong one too'.[26] He was very wary of the commercial motives that would likely prove decisive in shaping policy. Even the funds provided by Rhodes to support the British administration were treated with intense suspicion by the Mission. As stated in its newspaper in April 1894:

We hear that Mr Rhodes of the South African Chartered Company has given, or still continues to give, £17,000 for this country's government. Let us again warn the interests in this land that such a gift cannot be pure philanthropy. Mr Rhodes is not establishing a Christian or philanthropic or even imperial Mission. Let us remember also that the government by £17,000 of alien money must be exercised to that amount in the interests of that alien influence, and that alien interest lacks the essential elements, the dignity, the impartiality, the esprit de Coeur of a British government. The effects *cannot be good.*[27]

The Mission's suspicion of the commercial motives of the company was compounded by its antipathy to the racial policies that prevailed at the Cape, which the Blantyre missionaries regarded as very different from those that they had been cultivating in Malawi. To Johnston's intense chagrin, they remained implacably opposed to any moves towards the introduction of rule by Rhodes' British South Africa Company. Alfred Sharpe, as Acting Commissioner in 1894, wrote in exasperation:

Mr Commissioner Johnston in his despatches advised that there would be no permanent and satisfactory state of things with regard to this mission until two missionaries, the Rev D. C. Scott and the Rev. Alexander Hetherwick were removed from the country ... the missionaries are taking a course that makes them appear in the eyes of the natives of this Protectorate as an Opposition Party to H.M. Administration.[28]

Critic of the British Administration

Though the Blantyre missionaries had been instrumental in the creation of the British Protectorate, this did not mean that they were going to be its uncritical supporters. In fact, they had some very clear ideas about how British rule should be exercised in this particular context. When the reality did not meet their expectations, they were not slow to speak out and it was often Hetherwick who gave most trenchant expression to their concerns. Taxation was an early sore point. Andrew Ross remarked that, a '... terrible sense of "let-down", of having encouraged something which has turned out sour on maturing, runs through the mission's opposition to the early taxation policy of the administration.'[29] Six shillings per household was an outrageously high rate of tax and Hetherwick denounced it as 'extortionate in amount and arbitrary in its imposition'.[30] This was especially galling for the Mission since they had persuaded a number of chiefs to accept British rule on the basis that it would not involve taxation. What made matters worse, in Hetherwick's view, was that there had been no serious attempt to explain the tax in order to gain the consent of the people.[31] This was to be a running theme throughout the 1890s. Scott and Hetherwick had built relationships with chiefs through patient and extended discussions (*mlandu*) and they expected the British Administration to follow suit.

The point of departure in Hetherwick's 1891 article was the excessive level of the tax but his deeper point was that it was imposed without consultation. This led him to the underlying bone of contention between the Mission and the Administration:

> We ask too for a constitutional mode of dealing with native life around us. We ask that the authority and influence of the native chiefs in the country be recognized and their counsel sought in dealing with the people. The African, if he is anything, is constitutional – no change or step of any importance is taken without first open 'mlandu' in which the opinion of all is fully sought and expressed. We hope to see the same constitutional methods continued in all future changes. The native recognizes and obeys them, and when similar modes are followed, he will obey the new power as readily as the old. The nature of native life must be developed and not crushed.[32]

What soon became apparent, however, is that 'crushing' was the Administration's preferred method and it had no intention of adopting the consultative approach advocated by Hetherwick.[33] It did, however, concede that the six shilling rate of tax had been excessive and impractical. The rate was halved to three shillings.[34]

The early 1890s witnessed a series of harsh and violent actions on the part of the British Administration as it sought to enforce its authority in the Protectorate.[35] Some of those on the receiving end were chiefs whom Blantyre Mission regarded as friends and communities with which it had over many years built up relationships of mutual confidence. In 1892, for example, Hetherwick wrote to Edinburgh to report that, 'Mitochi our old friend refused to hoe the Zomba road and also to pay his gun taxes. An attack was made upon his village and several houses looted – ivory, gunpowder and other articles being looted and carried off until such time as Mitochi came and paid his gun taxes.'[36] He went on to cite another incident where the Administration had inflicted collective punishment on a community one of whose members had incurred its wrath. Hetherwick had witnessed the results:

> I saw the ruins and the half-burned maize lying scattered over the ground – a sore sight when one thought of the famine of the past season and yet the administration boast that they administer English law here. If a man does wrong and deserves to be punished, let him be punished, but don't punish a lot of innocent men, women and children by burning their houses and their food.[37]

Naturally, such events caused consternation in the affected communities and Hetherwick did not hold back when he expressed their concerns:

These affairs have caused great excitement in native circles and the cruelty of the English is freely commented on, and in no terms of praise. This mode of procedure will be the ruin of us all, and cannot fail to alienate the native from the European, the old confidence being broken down. The English used to be spoken of by all as the people who came with peace – now the 'war' of the English is a common phrase. There has been war at Mlanje, war on Ndirande, war at Zomba, war at Chiradzulu, war on the lake. Wherever the administration has gone it has been burning, plundering and destroying villages. And this is your English Protectorate! God help us![38]

A particularly galling incident for Hetherwick concerned Kawinga, the Yao chief based at Mount Chikhala. For years, from his base at Domasi, Hetherwick had tried to cultivate friendly relations with Kawinga but the chief was determined to have nothing to do with the European newcomers. Finally, by around 1890 the chief's attitude began to soften and there seemed to be good prospects of friendly interaction between the Mission and Kawinga's people. In 1891 he signed a treaty to stop slave-raiding and entered into friendly relations with Europeans. No sooner had relations taken this hopeful turn than the Administration carried out a military expedition against Kawinga with a view to imposing taxes.

Hetherwick immediately had his pen in hand to protest about, '... the utterly unjust and unfair treatment to which Kawinga has been subjected. I could not have considered so arbitrary proceedings as possible even in a Portuguese territory.'[39] A problem for Hetherwick and his colleagues was that the distinction between the Mission and the incoming colonial administration, which was clear enough in their own minds, was far from obvious to the African communities to whom the Europeans could appear to be a single unit. So appalled was Hetherwick by what he regarded as violent and unjust actions on the part of the British Administration that he set about distancing the Blantyre missionaries from their compatriots in the government:

> We have been compelled to separate ourselves from the Administration, and to frankly tell the natives that we cannot and do not approve of what goes on. For a long time I kept silent, and hoped that things might mend. There seems little ground for hope of that now. The European camp here is divided up. The old unity is gone. There are those whose attitude is 'only a nigger' and there are those – alas, very few – who view the natives as rational beings who have some claim for freedom to exist and who have rights of their own. I am sorry to say that the Administration officers belong to the former class – at least their actions would lead one to such belief and their actions bear out their openly expressed opinions.[40]

It is significant that, even at this early stage, Hetherwick was calling out racial attitudes on the part of the government officials that he regarded as completely at variance from what the Mission stood for. From the government point of view, as Robert Boeder writes, 'Hetherwick was acting more like a rival sovereign power than a loyal subject.'[41]

No wonder that relations between Mission and Administration became very strained. So much so that Foreign Mission Convener John McMurtrie in Edinburgh worried that Hetherwick was being unnecessarily provocative. He sought to understand Hetherwick's concerns while counselling him to calm down: '... let us always hope that the early mistakes of the Administration are to end, and that it will be possible one day for the Mission and the Administration to live in mutual helpfulness; and accordingly let irritation be avoided as far as possible without sacrifice of important principles.'[42] Hetherwick, however, was convinced of his case: 'I never wrote from "irritation". Had I done so I should never have laid my pen down; for what passed in those early days of the Administration would have drawn strong words from Job himself.'[43] He continued to relentlessly expose actions of the Administration that he considered indefensible.

For example, in 1894 when Chief Malunga of Ndirande Mountain was arrested on the dubious ground that some of his people had allegedly been involved in an attack on a group of carriers on the Matope road, Hetherwick was outraged by the conduct of the police:

> The system of administering justice is most unjust. The head of the police is both prosecutor and judge. Fairness or justice is not possible under such a system. It must be changed and that can only be done by legislation at home. You must back us up in our protest against such oppression as cannot fail to occur under such an anomalous form of Government. It is not a matter of little import: it affects the whole liberties and legal rights of the natives, and the welfare of the Christian Church in this part of Africa.[44]

From a longer historical perspective it may well appear that Hetherwick was naïve in expecting fairness and justice from a colonial government. When the whole system was oppressive and exploitative, how could it be expected to act justly in any particular instance? Hetherwick, however, held on to his expectation that the British Administration would meet high standards of justice in the conduct of its affairs and he consistently spoke out when he considered that it was falling short.

Land and labour were also sensitive points. An influx of European planters had taken possession of much of the best land in the Shire Highlands. Harry Johnston as Commissioner had attempted to secure the rights of the African population that was already occupying the land. However, in practical effect, in the view of Blantyre Mission, they were reduced to conditions close to slavery.[45] This injustice was compounded by the dependence of the European-owned estates on African labour. By 1892 Scott and Hetherwick were receiving complaints from their African friends that estate-owners were destroying their crops if they did not agree to work for the estates as and when required. The problem, as they explained in their newspaper, was that the planting season, when the estates were most in need of labour, was the same time that Africans had to take care of their own fields.[46] The Blantyre Mission accepted the new economic reality of estate-based agriculture but brought to it a concern that fair conditions of service would be applied. After all, the Mission's guiding premise was that its presence and activity would be beneficial to the African population. It brought the same expectation to the conduct of the British Administration.

A particular concern of Hetherwick's was conditions of service for the *tengatenga*. Before the advent of the railway and motorised transport, goods and even people had to be moved around by carriers. This involved the mobilisation of vast numbers of Africans and their conditions of service were very poor. Hetherwick was not unwilling to call the Administration to account:

> Surely if we use the native as a beast of burden, it is our duty to feed and house him. Instead to avoid trouble and lessen the cost, which means bigger dividends to the British shareholder, we trade upon his humanity by making him do the work of an ox and then forage for his food in a foodless country. Is this the British justice and equality which we pretend to uphold and fight for?[47]

From the viewpoint of the administration, the Blantyre Mission appeared to be criticising it at every turn. In 1894 when Clement Scott sprang to the defence of some Africans accused of robbery, Alfred Sharpe responded wearily, 'I cannot understand, and never have been able to understand, the way in which in all matters where the Administration is concerned, you take up the peculiar position of supposing that what is done by Her Majesty's Administration must be wrong.'[48]

It does seem that in the early 1890s the Blantyre Mission was so dismayed by the policy and conduct of the British Administration that, at least to some extent, it became instinctively oppositional and inclined to assume the worst whenever any complaint was made against the government. Robert Boeder, Sharpe's biographer, notes that in 1894, 'Johnston blamed "this objectionable creature" Hetherwick for all his difficulties . . .'[49] Things settled down as colonial rule became the accepted order of the day, but Hetherwick remained on the alert for anything he regarded as injustice towards the local community. In November 1902 he became engaged in what he described as 'the biggest fight for the natives that we ever had yet'.[50] The Administration had been sending a detachment of troops to Somaliland and required carriers to take their equipment to Chiromo. The carriers were recruited by force, police going into the villages and capturing able-bodied men. Excessive violence was used with men being beaten and, in a number of reported cases, women being raped.[51] 'On the Monday evening following,' reported Hetherwick, 'there was a scare that reminded me of nothing less than the old Angoni days when the people fled to the hills for refuge or came to the Mission. A crowd of people from over the stream came and slept in the Mission school for the night. Others came and slept in the kitchens of the boys houses at the back of the Mission where they thought they would be safe.'[52] He was scandalised that under the supposedly orderly British rule he should be facing a situation that reminded him of the Ngoni raids of precolonial times.

Hetherwick quickly mobilised the Chamber of Commerce on the basis that, 'It was a matter that affected the whole community as well as the natives and the voice of the European community should be heard on the occasion as well as the voice of the mission.'[53] It says something about Hetherwick's stature that he quickly won the full support of the Chamber: 'Never in the whole course of my work in Africa have I seen a stronger feeling among the European residents about Blantyre to get justice done the native at all costs.'[54]

However, when a judge-led inquiry was appointed to investigate he found that the judge, '. . . set himself to whitewash the Administration and the Armed Forces, and to blackball the European community here for taking up the case of the natives who had good ground for complaint.'[55] Hetherwick took great offence at the attitude of the judge: 'The worst feature to my mind was his open judgement that the crime of rape was lessened here by the morality of the native women. That a Judge administering the law of England should on the bench attempt to minimise the crime of rape – the worst crime of all in the native mind – is to my mind an appalling revelation of what a judicial mind may be driven to.'[56]

In the view of Blantyre Mission, the outcome of the Inquiry tended to minimise the gravity of the offences committed:

> the military were exonerated save for two cases of criminal assault on women by members of the force on Katunga's road, and the robbing of several huts and gardens at the back of Ndirande by the rear guard and baggage carriers of one of the columns. To the Blantyre police three serious charges of criminal assault on women in the villages were brought home, and exemplary punishment was inflicted. For raiding in the villages on the side and back of Soche six of the police have been put on trial. In all cases where damage has been shewn compensation has been paid by the Government.[57]

These measures indicated at least some acknowledgement that wrongs had been perpetrated by the government forces but they did little to allay Hetherwick's concerns.

The issues at stake from his perspective were those of precedent and principle. If such outrages could be perpetrated under the nose of the Blantyre community, what might be happening in the more remote parts of the country? 'If these things were done here,' asked Hetherwick, 'what would be the condition of things away in the lonely districts of the country where there was no voice of public criticism to put a check on the doings of the native police.'⁵⁸ Hence he regarded the matter as 'vital to the welfare of the native people here and all over British Central Africa . . .'⁵⁹ From his perspective it was a straightforward matter of justice: 'It is a shameful outrage on the rights and liberties of the natives. When once they have paid their taxes to the Government, they have a right to be as free as we are . . .'⁶⁰ British colonial rule, as he understood it, was supposed to function to the benefit of the local population, bringing justice, peace and prosperity. Being a 'Protectorate', so far as Hetherwick was concerned, should be about protecting the interests of the inhabitants. 'Remember,' he wrote to John McMurtrie, 'this is a question affecting the liberties and rights of the natives. The same things which we complained of have been done not once nor twice over the country, but have always been kept quiet.'⁶¹

Reflecting on the implications in *Life and Work*, Hetherwick set out the basis on which he so often took the Government to task:

> We have taken these people under our care, and we have replaced the old native jurisdiction by a system of our own. It is our solemn duty not to rest content till we have made that system a pledge of the peace of the country and its good government. It was for this end that the flag was hoisted over these highlands, and it is only a part of the 'white man's burden' which we have undertaken to carry.⁶²

Such a passage reveals the extent to which Hetherwick had identified himself with the colonial system and the paternalistic attitude that this entailed towards the indigenous people. At the same time, it demonstrates how passionately he stood up for the African community in the new social and political context and how far he identified with its interests. As Andrew Ross observes:

> Despite his membership of the Blantyre Chamber of Commerce, Hetherwick continued to serve as a scathing critic of much that the Administration did, and was so effective at harrying some of his fellows in the Chamber that again and again, in the columns of the settler newspaper, R. S. Hynde's *Central African Times*, he was attacked as being dangerously pro-native. What annoyed Hynde and the other planters above all was what had annoyed Johnston in the early days, the fact that so much of the criticism of the conduct of the settlers and the Administration was made publicly in the columns of *Life and Work*. This criticism was in consequence widely read by the constantly growing group of educated Africans.⁶³

The Legislative Council

When Nyasaland became a Crown Colony in 1907 one outcome was the establishment the following year of a Legislative Council, essentially with the function of a Parliament.⁶⁴ It was on a small scale with three government officials and three 'Un-officials' chosen by the Governor from the wider community. Nonetheless, it was hailed by Hetherwick as an historic beginning: 'Thus our Colonial Parliaments began – growing through the various stages of a Crown Colony till they reach the full status of a representative Parliament elected by the votes of a free and independent franchise.'[65] He was gratified when he was invited to be one of the first three 'Un-official' members, writing to his fellow missionary Dr Caverhill, 'I am pleased for the reason that Missions have got a place on the Legislative Council – in fact, my designation is "Senior Unofficial Member". I think it shows that the government recognise the hold that Missions have taken on the country and the part they have played in the past of its history.'[66]

The appointment cemented Hetherwick's status in the public life of the Protectorate – now 'the Honourable' as well as the Reverend Doctor. The government critic, who had earlier been roundly denounced by Alfred Sharpe, was now invited by Sharpe as Governor to become part of the government system. The fact that he had no qualms about taking on such a role, becoming formally part of the colonial system, demonstrates the extent to which he had accepted colonial rule as the order of the day. This does not mean he had forgotten the interests of the African community; in fact, his role on the Legislative Council was to represent them. It did mean, however, that he was very unlikely to share the radical critique of colonialism that was developing in the minds of African Christians such as Charles Domingo or John Chilembwe.[67]

Unsurprisingly, it was soon apparent that he would not be a quiet or passive member of 'Legco'. As he wrote to his colleague James Reid: 'We had a fairly good meeting of the Legislative Council – but the other two Un-Official Members of the Council [Kidney and Metcalfe] are not to add much to the Legislation of the Country. They sat mum during the Estimates and left me to do the questioning.'[68] He was also ready to use his new position to challenge the government when he thought it necessary. When the government indicated that it planned to open up the country to recruitment of labour for the mines of the Transvaal and South Africa, he announced with some relish that 'we are to have a battle royal over this question in the next Legislative Council'.[69] In the event he was successful in securing the prohibition of all such labour recruitment.[70] His position on the Legislative Council also gave him the opportunity to pursue one of his long-running concerns: the difficulty of Africans in accessing the land they needed for farming and their lack of security of tenure. His aim was to increase opportunities for Africans to secure individual land tenure.[71] 'This,' he noted, 'is the first time any Un-official Member has tried to initiate legislation on any point so it will be interesting to watch the attitude of the Government on the occasion.'[72]

The same session in November 1909 featured the first full-scale debate to occur at the Legislative Council and it was provoked by Hetherwick's fierce opposition to a government proposal. It proposed to introduce a Collective

Punishment Ordinance under which when a crime was committed, such as robbery or assault, the entire African community in the vicinity should be subject to punishment. The government believed that when such offences occurred it was likely that the entire local community was to some degree complicit and it could therefore be justified in imposing fines not only on the individual offenders but also on the entire community. Hetherwick was appalled. As the official record indicates:

> The Hon and Rev Dr Hetherwick in rising to oppose the Bill said it was with a feeling of astonishment that he learned a Bill of this nature should have been introduced into the Council ... He never read a proposal which filled him with such a feeling of shame as when he first read this proposed Bill in the *Nyasaland Gazette*, and he could not but feel that the whole principle involved was contrary and wrong. It was a Bill frankly by which the innocent were to be punished along with the guilty, or sometimes the innocent were to be punished for the guilty, and that, he held, was both morally and legally wrong.[73]

He pointed out that, 'a number of natives who had no knowledge and no concern with the crime would be punished by fines inflicted on them under the Ordinance'.[74] In his experience, such crimes were usually perpetrated not by those living in the vicinity but by people who had come from a distance. The effect of the proposed Ordinance would be the punishment of completely innocent people. The result would be 'simply a feeling of injustice, and resentment would be aroused in the native mind – a feeling that would last'.[75] He also made the point that the injustice was racial in nature: 'He called the attention of the Council to the fact that there was nothing in the Ordinance by which it could be applied to the European community'.[76] Despite the vehemence of Hetherwick's opposition, the Ordinance was passed but the government was put on notice that it could expect to be called to account were it to be applied in an unjust way.

Thus he quickly established his reputation as someone who could keep the government on their mettle. When Robert Laws, who succeeded Hetherwick as the missionary member of the Council in 1913, had to defend the Scottish missions following the Chilembwe Rising of 1915, '... elements in the Church of Scotland had wished that Hetherwick had been there, for they felt that he could have fought a case better than Laws'.[77] Hetherwick's critics, such as Andrew Ross, allude to his membership of the Legislative Council as if it were incontrovertible evidence that he had sold out to the colonial system.[78] In fact, Hetherwick used his membership of the Council to champion African interests on such matters as land, labour and the administration of justice. These were much the same issues as those that had driven Blantyre Mission to take a critical stance towards the British Administration when it came into place in the early 1890s.

Of course, it was a colonial arrangement that provided for a European missionary to represent African interests. But it was the only arrangement that was available to Hetherwick and he used it to fight tooth and nail for justice towards the African community that was always uppermost in his mind. From his perspective, he was simply continuing, under the new constitutional arrangements, the advocacy of the rights of the African community on which he and Clement Scott had embarked twenty years earlier. Now he had a new platform on which to pursue his campaigns. In a long and detailed article in *Life and Work* he recommended the idea that elected African representatives might sit on the Legislative Council.[79] In this, however, he was far ahead of his time. For the time being, the paternalistic model was the only one available for the political representation of the African community and he had to make the best of it.

A Laughable Mouse?

Though no longer on the Legislative Council, Hetherwick did have his opportunity to address the Commission of Inquiry that investigated the Chilembwe Rising of 1915. As will be discussed in Chapter Ten, he was able to demonstrate important differences between the philosophy of Blantyre Mission and the prevailing attitudes of the wider European community in Malawi. What he was never able to understand, however, was the motivation that inspired John Chilembwe and those who joined the Rising, many of whom had come through the Blantyre Mission educational system. Baffled by their decision, he tended to play it down and regard it as an aberration. In later years, when he reflected on the event, he was still concerned to minimise its significance and to argue that the government had got things totally out of proportion: 'it was in no sense a "Native Rising"'.[80] Pointedly he did not name either Chilembwe or the Providence Industrial Mission but simply recorded that at the beginning of 1915, 'trouble was raised by a native leader of a missionary body with its headquarters in Western America'.[81]

His framing of the events of the Rising aims to make clear that it was simply a local incident involving a disaffected individual and of no wider consequence: 'He seized advantage of the unsettled times and the absence of the local troops in German East Africa to take revenge for some private grudge by making a raid on a neighbouring planter, killing him and two other members of his staff, and carrying off two ladies to their village camp.'[82] As for the Commission of Inquiry that followed the Rising, Hetherwick remembered it simply for its unreasonable criticisms of mission education on the part of 'the ignorant and unthinking'.[83] When the Commission's Report was published early in 1916, Hetherwick delivered his verdict in Latin: *parturiunt montes nascetur ridiculous mus* (out of the labours of a mountain, a laughable mouse is born).[84] As he later explained to the International Missionary Council: 'Government lost their heads, and made more of the trouble than there was any necessity for'.[85] His conclusion was dismissive: 'Nothing came of the Commission and the whole matter was speedily forgotten in the face of the larger issues that were being fought out elsewhere.'[86]

Hetherwick's determination to downplay the significance of the Chilembwe Rising reveals his blind spot in relation to colonial rule. Even the Governor, Sir George Smith, could appreciate that the Rising 'opened a new phase in the history of Nyasaland'.[87] A generation later the monumental study of George Shepperson and Thomas Price demonstrated the extent to which the Chilembwe Rising was a definitive moment in Malawi's history.[88] For Chilembwe, those who joined him and the many others who did not join but had some degree of sympathy for his radical action, there was something wrong in principle with the colonial rule to which they found themselves subject. In fact, it was so deeply wrong in principle that it called for active resistance, even if the resistance had little chance of success. This stance, which has been recognised and affirmed by the nation as a whole in independent Malawi, was so far outside Hetherwick's comprehension that he could not make any sense of it. For all that he was robust in taking the colonial government to task for any failures to meet the standards of justice and responsibility that he expected, his goal was the effective operation of the colonial system, not any attempt to supplant it.

Nevertheless, he took to heart what had happened in the Rising and its aftermath and it gave him a certain sympathy with the Providence Industrial Mission, Chilembwe's church, when it restarted in 1926 under Daniel Malekebu. Richard Paterson was a new member of staff at Blantyre Mission at that time and recalled that, 'Dr Hetherwick himself asked me would I be friendly with them [the PIM]. Dr Hetherwick was very vexed about the Rising, you know, and the way the government handled it. The public executions, for example. He thought it was rather a shameful episode. And so I made a point of going to see Malekebu whenever I was in the area.'[89] Another little known feature of the aftermath concerns the two sons of John Chilembwe, Charles and Donald, who ended up being in the care of Blantyre Mission. Their mother had died and, when their grandmother also died, Hetherwick proposed that they should become wards of the government so that the costs of their residence and education at Blantyre Mission would be covered.[90] His plea was successful, so Charles and Donald Chilembwe grew up at Blantyre Mission with their costs being met by the government.[91] Although his public statements about the Rising were rather dismissive, these are indications that he had taken the matter very much to heart.

Notes

1. Livingstone, *A Prince of Missionaries: Alexander Hetherwick of Blantyre*, London: James Clarke, n.d., 183–84.
2. All his life Hetherwick thrived on controversy and wrote many forthright columns for *Life and Work*. However, in the atmosphere that prevailed in the aftermath of the First World War he demonstrated uncharacteristic restraint:

'I fear that "Life and Work in Nyasaland" will not appear again. There are too many delicate questions on the biards just now which we should have to speak our minds about, and as things are at present this might bring us into antagonism with the Powers that be. The atmosphere is full of the same explosiveness which is almost universal over the world, and sparks flying about might be dangerous.' Alexander Hetherwick to W. B. Stevenson, 4 July 1921, MNA BMC/50/2/1/190.

3. Alexander Hetherwick, *Romance of Blantyre: How Livingstone's Dream Came True*, London: James Clarke, n.d., 74.
4. Blantyre Mission Council meeting, 19 May 1897, MNA 50/BMC/1/1/1.
5. See John McCracken, *A History of Malawi 1859–1966*, Woodbridge: James Currey, 2012, repr. Woodbridge: James Currey and Mzuzu: Mzuni Press, 2021, 50–57.
6. See P. R. Warhurst, 'Portugal's Bid for Southern Malawi', in Bridglal Pachai, G. W. Smith and Roger K. Tangri (eds), *Malawi Past and Present*, Blantyre: Christian Literature Association in Malawi, 1971, 20–36.
7. W. P. Livingstone, *A Prince of Missionaries*, 49.
8. Lord Salisbury, cit. Ronald E. Robinson and Jack Gallagher, *Africa and the Victorians: the Official Mind of Imperialism*, London: Macmillan, 1961, 224.
9. See Andrew C. Ross, *Blantyre Mission and the Making of Modern Malawi*, Blantyre: CLAIM-Kachere, 1996, repr. Mzuzu: Luviri Press, 2018, 134.
10. Dr Lindsay, quoted in Livingstonia Sub-Committee Minutes, 26 July 1888, National Library of Scotland Ms 7912, cit. John McCracken, *A History of Malawi 1859–1966*, Rochester: James Currey, 2012, 53.
11. W. P. Livingstone, *A Prince of Missionaries*, 50.
12. Ibid., 51.
13. *Life and Work in British Central Africa*, June 1889.
14. Esther Breitenbach, *Empire and Scottish Society: The Impact of Foreign Missions at Home c.1790 to c.1914*, Edinburgh: Edinburgh University Press, 2009, 158.
15. John D. Hargreaves, *Aberdeenshire to Africa: Northeast Scots and British Overseas Expansion*, Aberdeen: Aberdeen University Press, 1981, 36.
16. Livingstone, *A Prince of Missionaries*, 52.
17. Ibid., 53–54.
18. Alexander Hetherwick, *The Romance of Blantyre*, 69.
19. Cit. A. J. Hanna, *The Beginnings of Nyasaland and Northern Rhodesia*, Oxford: Clarendon Press, 1956, 144–45.
20. John McCracken, *History of Malawi*, 56.
21. Ibid.
22. Enclosed in Hawes to Roseberry, 30 March 1886, no 13 CA, FO 84/1751, cit. Andrew Ross, *Blantyre Mission and the Making of Modern Malawi*, 122.
23. Harry Johnson to Cecil Rhodes, 7 June 1893, Salisbury Rhodesia Archives, CT/1/13/4/1, cit. Andrew Ross, *Blantyre Mission and the Making of Modern Malawi*, 150.
24. See John McCracken, *History of Malawi*, 57.
25. Horace Waller to D. C. Scott, 23 October 1893, MNA 50/BMC/2/1/9.
26. Ibid.
27. *Life and Work in British Central Africa*, July 1894.
28. Sharpe to Kimberley, 31 October 1894, FO 2/67, cit. Andrew Ross, *Blantyre Mission and the Making of Modern Malawi*, 151.

29. Andrew Ross, *Blantyre Mission and the Making of Modern Malawi*, 165.
30. *Life and Work in British Central Africa*, November 1891.
31. Ibid.
32. Ibid.
33. See further John McCracken, *History of Malawi*, 57–65.
34. Bridglal Pachai, *Malawi: The History of the Nation*, London: Longman, 1973, 113.
35. See Eric Stokes, 'Malawi Political Systems and the Introduction of Colonial Rule, 1891–1896', in Eric Stokes and Richard Brown (eds), *The Zambesian Past: Studies in Central African History*, Manchester: Manchester University Press, 1966, 352–75.
36. Alexander Hetherwick to Archibald Scott, 13 June 1892, NLS 7534/744-50.
37. Ibid.
38. Ibid.
39. Alexander Hetherwick to Archibald Scott, 28 June 1892, NLS 7534/751–57.
40. Alexander Hetherwick to Archibald Scott, 13 June 1892, NLS 7534/744–50.
41. Robert B. Boeder, *Alfred Sharpe of Nyasaland: Builder of Empire*, Blantyre: Society of Malawi, 1981, 39.
42. John McMurtrie to Alexander Hetherwick, 26 January 1893, NLS 7534/802.
43. Alexander Hetherwick cit. W. P. Livingstone, *A Prince of Missionaries*, 77.
44. Alexander Hetherwick to Archibald Scott, 19 October 1894, NLS 7535/133–35.
45. *Life and Work in British Central Africa*, December 1894.
46. *Life and Work in British Central Africa*, February 1892.
47. *Life and Work in British Central Africa*, August 1900.
48. Alfred Sharpe to D. C. Scott, 30 October 1894, MNA 50/BMC/2/1/10.
49. Robert B. Boeder, *Alfred Sharpe*, 45.
50. Alexander Hetherwick to John McMurtrie, 24 November 1902, MNA 50/BMC/2/1/45.
51. See Sean Morrow, '"War Came from the Boma": Military and Police Disturbances in Blantyre, 1902', *Society of Malawi Journal* 41/2 (1988), 16–29.
52. Ibid.
53. Ibid.
54. Ibid.
55. Alexander Hetherwick to John McMurtrie, 20 January 1903, MNA 50/BMC/2/1/46.
56. Alexander Hetherwick to John McMurtrie, 24 November 1902, MNA 50/BMC/2/1/45.
57. *Life and Work in British Central Africa*, December 1902.
58. Alexander Hetherwick to John McMurtrie, 24 November 1902, MNA 50/BMC/2/1/45.
59. Ibid.
60. Alexander Hetherwick to John McMurtrie, 14 December 1902, MNA 50/BMC/2/1/45.
61. Alexander Hetherwick to John McMurtrie, 20 January 1903, MNA 50/BMC/2/1/46.
62. *Life and Work in British Central Africa*, December 1902.
63. Andrew C. Ross, 'The Blantyre Mission and the Problems of Land and Labour, 1891–1915', in Roderick J. Macdonald (ed.), *From Nyasaland to Malawi*, Nairobi: East African Publishing, 1975, 86–107, at 104.

64. *Life and Work in Nyasaland*, March–June 1908.
65. Ibid.
66. Alexander Hetherwick to Dr Caverhill, 14 May 1908, MNA 50/BMC/2/1/89.
67. See Kenneth P. Lohrentz, 'Joseph Booth, Charles Domingo, and the Seventh Day Baptists in Northern Nyasaland, 1910–12', *Journal of African History*, XII/3 (1971), 461–80, repr. Klaus Fiedler and Kenneth R. Ross eds, *Christianity in Malawi: A Reader*, Mzuzu: Mzuni Press, 2021, 206–38; Harry W. Langworthy, 'Charles Domingo, Seventh Day Baptists and Independency', *Journal of Religion in Africa*, XV/2 (1985), 96–121, repr. Klaus Fiedler and Kenneth R. Ross eds, *Christianity in Malawi: A Reader*, 170–205; George Shepperson and Thomas Price, *Independent African: John Chilembwe and the Origins, Setting and Significance of the Nyasaland Native Rising of 1915*, Edinburgh: Edinburgh University Press, 1958; repr. Blantyre: CLAIM-Kachere, ^{6}2000 and Mzuzu: Luviri Press, ^{7}2020.
68. Alexander Hetherwick to James Reid, 11 November 1908, MNA 50/BMC/2/1/95.
69. Alexander Hetherwick to J. N. Ogilvie, 30 September 1909, MNA 50/BMC/2/1/101.
70. Alexander Hetherwick to J. D. McCallum, 9 March 1910, MNA 50/BMC/2/1/105.
71. Summary of the Proceedings of the Fourth Session of the Legislative Council, Held at Zomba on 2–4 November, 1909.
72. Alexander Hetherwick to J. D. McCallum, 26 October 1909, MNA 50/BMC/2/1/102.
73. Summary of the Proceedings of the Fourth Session of the Legislative Council, Held at Zomba on 2–4 November, 1909.
74. Ibid.
75. Ibid.
76. Ibid.
77. Letter Book No. 29, 676; cit. George Shepperson and Thomas Price, *Independent African*, 369.
78. Andrew Ross, *Blantyre Mission and the Making of Modern Malawi*, 171.
79. *Life and Work in Nyasaland*, April 1908.
80. Hetherwick, *The Romance of Blantyre*, 214.
81. Ibid., 213.
82. Ibid., 213.
83. Ibid., 215.
84. Alexander Hetherwick to W. M. McLachlan, 7 February 2016 (quotation from the Latin poet Horace), MNA 50/BMC/2/2/9.
85. Letter from Hetherwick to Miss Gibson of the International Missionary Council, 27 April 1926, cit. George Shepperson and Thomas Price, *Independent African*, 376.
86. Alexander Hetherwick, *The Romance of Blantyre*, 215.
87. Cit. George Shepperson and Thomas Price, *Independent African*, 399.
88. Ibid.
89. Personal communication in interview with Mr Richard Paterson in Edinburgh, 27 April 1967, Roderick J. Macdonald, 'Rev Dr Daniel Sharpe Malekebu and the Re-Opening of the Providence Industrial Mission 1926–39', in Roderick J. Macdonald (ed.), *From Nyasaland to Malawi*, Nairobi: East African Publishing, 1971, 215–33, at 226–27.

90. Alexander Hetherwick to Sir George Smith, 19 December 1922, MNA BMC/50/2/1/206.
91. R. H. Murray, Resident, Blantyre, to James Reid, 3 May 1923, MNA BMC/50/2/1/210.

CHAPTER SIX

The Malawi Visionary: Standing Up for Cinderella

If a nation is an 'imagined community'[1] then one of the people who first imagined Malawi was Alexander Hetherwick. He stood, of course, in the tradition of David Livingstone who had first thought of an initiative to defeat the slave trade in Central Africa by introducing Christianity, commerce and civilisation. He was always ready to acknowledge that the vision he had for the Mission derived from what the great explorer had started. Not for nothing did he give his history of the Mission the subtitle 'How Livingstone's Dream Came True'.[2] He was also greatly informed and influenced by the people of the land and their aspirations, not least the Makololo who had allied themselves with Livingstone and who were prominent at Blantyre Mission during his early years. Hetherwick's distinctive part in the process was to be in leadership at the time when the dreamt-of country actually came into being. As various forces jostled for influence, he had to imagine what kind of country it was going to be and to advocate his vision when there were other forces working to take the country in a different direction.

One thing that remained very clear in Hetherwick's mind was that the emerging country must be very different from the territories south of the Zambezi. It was partly his disaffection with the racial attitudes of the settlers in South Africa that propelled Livingstone to travel northwards seeking territory where the direction being taken by South Africa would not prevail. This left its mark on Hetherwick throughout the entire time of his leadership at Blantyre Mission. A trivial but revealing episode occurred during Hetherwick's second spell on the Legislative Council from 1922 to 1925 when it was proposed to change the time of the Protectorate from 'Zomba mean time' to 'the Standard time of South Africa' with effect from 1 July 1924. Hetherwick's handwritten note on the paper proposing the ordinance states tersely: 'Not in favour of this ordinance: why should we follow SA time. Nyasaland is no part of SA and I trust never will be any part of SA. We have had our own time all along.'[3] The strength of feeling on Hetherwick's part arose from his conviction that life in Nyasaland must run on very different lines from those that prevailed in South Africa. He made his case at the Legislative Council: 'He thought Nyasaland should keep the time that it had got ... The history of this standard went back to 1884, when Lieut. O'Neill was in Blantyre and spent many weeks ascertaining the exact longitude of Blantyre Mission.'[4] He lost the vote 4–2 but his underlying concern that Nyasaland should not be guided by the norms of South Africa was one that he was always ready to express.

Another concern of Livingstone's that was to be a constant factor in Hetherwick's mind was the challenges presented by the geography of the country. Its future prosperity, they both understood, depended on being able to sell its produce on the global market. For a landlocked country in the interior of Africa, this in turn depended on reliable and effective transportation to carry goods to the coast. Livingstone had been active at a time when neither rail nor road transport could be expected. Hence his obsession with exploring the rivers and lakes of central and eastern Africa with a view to identifying the waterways that could be future trade routes. A major factor in his attraction to the Shire Highlands and Lake Malawi was that it appeared to have a ready-made route for transportation of goods to the Indian Ocean via the Shire and Zambezi Rivers. This was always complicated by the stretch of the Shire known as the Murchison Cataracts, which is not navigable but became ever more problematic during Hetherwick's time as the water level of the Shire fell.

Disappointment about the low level of the river became a constant refrain and Hetherwick could see that this was part of a broader trend: 'It is evident there is a gradual desiccation of all the great water systems of Africa, and the fall of the level of the Lake would appear to be part of this process'.[5] Nonetheless, the point to which he always returned was that, 'the whole future of the country depends on this question of our connection with the coast'.[6] The development of railways was the great hope in Hetherwick's time and he was one of its champions. This was not unrelated to his concern to keep Nyasaland distinct from South Africa. Rather than become integrated into South Africa's transport system he advocated that Nyasaland should have its own direct route to the coast and the world beyond. His very first motion at the Legislative Council was that,

> the completion of a Railway from the Coast to Lake Nyasa is essential to the future interests, safety and prosperity of the Protectorate: and the Council accordingly urges on HM Government the advisability of taking such steps as will secure the extension of the present Shire Highlands Railway to the Coast at Beira on the one hand and to the Lake at Fort Johnston on the other at as early a date as possible.[7]

In championing the cause of Nyasaland, Hetherwick always had the sense that he was standing up for the underdog. He often evoked Harry Johnston's comparison of the Protectorate with Cinderella, the girl in the fairy tale who was overlooked in favour of her older sisters and left to clean the kitchen while they went to the ball.[8] From Hetherwick's perspective this was how Nyasaland had been treated, with the issue of the railway being a good example. The British government was promoting the development of railways in other contexts but, as he reflected at the turn of the century, 'somehow at present this Cinderella among the Protectorates is down among the pots and pans and ashes, while no fairy godmother has yet appeared, nor Prince to claim the owner of the glass slipper.'[9] Years later, as he imagined how things might develop after the end of the First World War, Hetherwick was equally gloomy: 'At present and for years Nyasaland has been "Cinderella" among the British Protectorates in Africa and has sat among the ashes.'[10] The point of the fairy tale, however, is that Cinderella does not remain forever in her lowly position. In the end she outshines her sisters and everyone else as it is she who finds favour with the prince and lives happily ever after. Though she was not initially recognised, she had the qualities to succeed and eventually she did. Hetherwick's vision was that this would, in the end, be Nyasaland's story too. But meanwhile she was neglected and despised so there were battles to be fought.

South African Labour Recruitment

Fighting for Malawi was not, of course, a new experience for Hetherwick. In his early years of service, he had fought against the prospect of Portuguese rule and he had seen off the threat of rule by a Chartered Company. He had also had many a battle as the British Protectorate was established during the early 1890s and often did not live up to his expectations. These were all struggles in which he engaged in close association with his friend and leader David Clement Scott. As the twentieth century dawned, Scott had departed and it fell to Hetherwick alone to meet a new threat to Blantyre Mission's aspirations that appeared on the horizon. As soon as the idea of recruiting labour from Malawi to meet a shortfall in the mines of South Africa was mooted in 1902, Hetherwick expressed firm opposition. 'We believe,' stated a *Life and Work* leader column, 'and we have no hesitation in saying, that such a step would be disastrous to the welfare of the people and country.'[11] The Blantyre Mission Council, meeting in early 1903, was unequivocal in its opposition to the labour recruitment proposals: 'The Council is of the opinion that such a policy would be most deleterious in its effects on the progress of the country, the moral welfare of the native population and the best interests of native Christianity.'[12] These were the first warning shots in a battle that Hetherwick was to wage relentlessly, against heavy odds, in the coming years.

In the columns of *Life and Work* and in lengthy letters to the Foreign Mission Committee in Edinburgh he set out the reasons for his strenuous opposition to the proposals. His vision for the future of Nyasaland was one where the country's rich human resources would drive its development. If these were diverted to the mines of the Rand, Nyasaland would be reduced to a 'native reserve', the purpose of which would be to supply labour to support industrial development elsewhere. Giving a free hand to labour recruiters from South Africa, in his view, would mean 'the cessation of all future development of Central Africa. The progress of the country depends on its labour.'[13] As Hetherwick wrote to John McMurtrie, 'We hold that the education of the native of Central Africa must be carried on in his own land and amid the surroundings of his own home life. It is only by the labour of his hands that the development of this country can be carried out, and once convert him into a worker in the mines of the South African Colonies, and his own true development and that of his country will at once cease.'[14]

This was not just a matter of development theory. Through the Chamber of Commerce Hetherwick was closely connected with the major employers in the country and he spoke from first-hand evidence when he told McMurtrie that, '. . . the various commercial interests and industries in the country have during the past three years suffered severely from the lack of a sufficient labour supply'.[15] To jeopardise Nyasaland's own emergent commerce and industry, in Hetherwick's view, would be to undermine all the efforts that had been put into the development of the Protectorate since it was first exposed to British influence. He argued:

> These industries – planting, transport and trade, have been among the chief factors in the development of the country – many of them took their origin in 'ventures of faith' to aid in the progress of civilisation and legitimate trade among the peoples of the Dark Continent. They deserve every support and encouragement that the Government here and at home can give them.[16]

Hetherwick's concerns extended beyond the economic impact of the migrant labour proposals. They also posed, he suggested, a 'grievous moral danger to the African race, and character'.[17] The result for the Nyasaland worker, he explained to McMurtrie would be that he would be, 'taken away from his home surroundings, conveyed into another climate with extremes of heat and cold different from his own, put to a work that he is totally unaccustomed to, made to live in an atmosphere and moral surroundings that cannot but have a degrading influence upon him and his character.'[18] He also foresaw a negative impact on the emerging Christian church: 'No native should be separated from his wife and family. In the native Christian church more harm has arisen from this than any cause of moral lapse with the church.'[19]

For all these reasons Hetherwick identified the entire cause of the Mission with the need to resist the labour recruitment initiative:

> It behoves all who have worked for the amelioration of the African race to be up and doing and bring every possible force to the aid of the native who is thus to be exploited for the profit of the mine owner and the capitalist of the South African Colonies. It was not for this that we have worked all these past twenty years to bring the light of civilisation and the gospel to the Dark Continent.[20]

His vision for the future was diametrically opposite to the plans being prepared for migrant labour in South Africa. He foresaw the flourishing of

Nyasaland through the endeavour and commitment of its people and felt he could not stand by while the Protectorate was deprived of this indispensable resource.[21]

It was time, he became convinced, to once again apply pressure to the British government. 'It is urgent,' he pressed McMurtrie, 'and you cannot take steps too soon, as the mining capitalist is putting great pressure on both the Colonial Office and the Foreign Office.'[22] Within weeks McMurtrie had joined forces with his opposite number at the United Free Church of Scotland, responsible for Livingstonia Mission, to write to the government expressing their alarm at the plans to recruit labour from British Central Africa for the mines of South Africa.[23] Meanwhile in Blantyre Hetherwick had clashed with Sir Alfred Sharpe, the Commissioner, at a meeting called by the Chamber of Commerce. Sharpe had attempted to stop Hetherwick from speaking since he did not represent any of the commercial interests in the country. Hetherwick, however, was undeterred: 'I said that I was the oldest resident in the country and had for years studied the question from all sides and was prepared to state my views on the commercial aspect of the matter.'[24] Sharpe backed down and Hetherwick 'told him plainly that this proposal meant the total ruin of the Agricultural and Commercial Industries of the Country.'[25]

The Commissioner was clearly unconvinced so Hetherwick wrote to Edinburgh in belligerent terms:

> Sharpe goes home to push the Capitalists' side of the matter. So there must be a fight. The matter is vital to the future of the country and the moral and physical welfare of the people and every step should be taken to lay the whole situation before the country and the Church. Yesterday Sharpe pooh-poohed the missionary point of view of the subject as the 'sentimental' side. He will regret his words before he is much older.[26]

Hetherwick evoked the memory of the agitation that had changed the policy of the British government in 1889 when the Portuguese threatened to take control of the Shire Highlands. The new threat from the labour recruiters was no less serious: 'This is the most critical position we have ever come to in the history of the country and we will have to fight the battle I fear alone.'[27]

Taking the fight to London, a large delegation of Scottish church leaders met with Lord Lansdowne the Foreign Secretary in March 1903. They were disappointed to learn that the Foreign Office had agreed to allow 1,000 workers to be recruited from BCA to the mines of the Rand as an 'experiment', though took some encouragement from their impression that Lansdowne himself was hoping the experiment would fail.[28] Hetherwick meanwhile took aim at Sir Alfred Sharpe: 'Commissioner Sharpe has betrayed the country and its interests into the hands of the Mine Owners. He has played a wretchedly selfish game, and has lost the confidence of the European population here ... I have done my best to support him since he became Commissioner but I am done with him now. This last betrayal of the interests of the country is to me the last straw.'[29] Matters were made worse for Hetherwick by the British government's inclination to allow another 5,000 workers to be recruited before the experiment with the first 1,000 had been completed. 'Nothing,' he declared, 'can exceed the perfidy of the Government on this point. They said they would abide the result of the "experiment" and now they are to begin to recruit before the "experiment" is complete, and the results are with-held from the Missions, who have been the lawful protectors of the natives on this question.'[30] Meanwhile he was aware of reports of many cases of death or serious illness among the 819 workers who participated in the 'experiment'. 'Is this to be allowed to go on without an appeal and protest from those at home to whom common humanity is dearer than the interests of the Mining interest that rules in Downing Street just now?'[31]

In Hetherwick's understanding he was fighting for the welfare and the future of the African people of Nyasaland, who were always foremost in his mind. The question at stake, as he put it in a letter to *The Scotsman* newspaper, was:

> Are the natives of these regions to be allowed to give their lives and their energies for the peaceful development of their own land and home, or are they to become the serfs of the gold interest of the South African Colonies? I need not point out the bearing of all this on the future of our work here. We want an independent Church and an independent people not a race which looks to the Rand for its salvation and its life.[32]

This was the vision that guided his life and work. Now he felt let down on every side. He remonstrated with Sir Alfred Sharpe, the Commissioner: 'From whatever side I look at this question, I cannot shut my eyes to the fact that it reverses the whole policy of the past that was aimed at in our occupation of British Central Africa, and I am convinced that its effect on the country and people will be disastrous.'[33] He acknowledged that Sir Alfred did not accept his view but still pressed for action, 'to secure the development of Central Africa on its own lines, and not as an appendage of the South African Colonies which have confessedly marred their own native question so ruinously.'[34] The conviction that Nyasaland must take a different direction as regards its African population from that which was obtained in South Africa was always a guiding light for Hetherwick in public affairs.

He was also bitterly disappointed in his own Church since the General Assembly of 1904 had not addressed the issue, which, he reminded McMurtrie, 'is a matter of life and death for the people of this part of Africa'.[35] He also frequently expressed his disgust at British government policy on this matter. Yet he knew that he was up against powerful economic forces and was ready to confront them too:

> It is the old story – the desire to be rich at the expense of other people's labour. If the South African Colonies are the whiteman's, then let him make them his home and let him cease to struggle to make his fortune in a few years and then rush home to build his palace in Park Lane – and with his millions from there seek to dominate the politics and welfare of the country he has fled from.[36]

Very different was the direction Hetherwick had taken in his own life. Very different was the purpose of Blantyre Mission as he saw it. Very different was the aim of British involvement in the land that would become Malawi. He urged McMurtrie:

> Remember you are fighting for the lives of the natives whom the Church takes under its care and has striven to protect all these twenty eight years. Is the Church now to allow them to become the slaves of the mine owners – the people whom it has rescued from the slaver and to whom it has given the blessing of peace and the message of the Gospel?[37]

Hetherwick was in no doubt about the answer to this question: 'It is a shameful business and we must fight it to the end.'[38] He took his own advice to heart and continued the fight when he had the opportunity, as a member of the Legislative Council, to introduce legislative proposals: 'The prohibition of all recruiting for outside the Protectorate which we got carried at the last Legislative Council should let the S.A. Colonies see that we mean to develop our own country with our own labour before permitting the Rand Mine owner to run over us in this matter.'[39] It was a battle that engaged his energies over many years, in his own mind a battle for the future prosperity of the land and its people.[40] In the longer run it was a losing battle since opportunities for employment in South Africa and Rhodesia would continue to attract Malawian workers in large numbers.[41] Pachai records that, 'By 1914, about ten thousand Malawians were working in the Transvaal mines alone and about three times that number in the Rhodesian mines'.[42] Nevertheless, Hetherwick's passionate and untiring determination to champion the interests of the land and the people, as he saw them, are amply demonstrated by his activism on the issues of migrant labour, especially during the first decade of the twentieth century.

Land Tenure

Closely related to the issue of labour was the question of land tenure.[43] While the Blantyre Mission had advocated the establishment of a British Protectorate and encouraged European settlers to come and establish estates, Scott and Hetherwick were soon concerned about the implications of these developments for the land tenure of the existing African communities. European planters, who had been arriving in increasing numbers in the late 1880s, had bought land from chiefs. These transactions, however, appear to have been based on a misunderstanding. While the Europeans understood that they were buying permanent title to the land, the chiefs, as Andrew Ross explains, 'thought they were selling the use of the land, in other words a kind of lease'.[44] When Harry Johnston set up the first British administration, he quickly established a system for assessing and certifying land claims. Under this system much of the Shire Highlands came to be owned by European planters and most of the remainder was owned by the Crown. This left the African population with very little opportunity to acquire ownership of land. The result, as Hetherwick explained in 1910, was that,

> At present the Native is landless! He cannot call an inch of the land his own – he is at the mercy of the Private Landowners or the Government who although they say the land is Crown land and the Native has the right to settle on it, yet they may evict him at a moment's notice if the land is to be sold to a European or is required for some public purpose.[45]

This state of affairs was a long-running source of concern to the Blantyre Mission. Scott and Hetherwick sought to defend the very limited rights that had been accorded to the African communities. In 1900, when Hetherwick protested about European planters clearing villages whose people were entitled to remain since they had been there at the time of the land claim, the government agreed to remind planters that they could not undertake such action without official permission.[46] A few years later, Hetherwick was alert to sense the danger entailed in a major land grant of 266,000 acres to Eugene Sharrar's railway company, with all this being carved out of Crown land. Though he was a strong advocate of the plans to build the railway, he was also mindful of the principle that the Crown would hold this land on behalf of the African people who had owned it prior to the advent of the British Administration. Now the land available to the indigenous people was growing less and less. Hetherwick warned that, 'the native will have less chance of finding room to settle if he is compelled to move from the European's land on to native reserves. This is a serious danger, and if not foreseen the native will come to occupy the position of a serf on the European's land.'[47] Though he had resigned himself to the alienation of a great deal of the ancestral land of the African communities, he was determined to do all he could to prevent matters from getting even worse.

The Native Locations Ordinance of 1904 did make provision for Africans to rent land on the basis of a lease that would run in perpetuity but very few had taken advantage of the opportunity. Hetherwick's assessment of the situation reveals both his awareness of a fundamental injustice experienced by African communities and his pragmatic acceptance of the colonial system as the inescapable order of the day. In a major *Life and Work* article in 1909 he wrote:

> On the face of it, it is an anomaly that the native should in this way have to buy back the land that was once his own. Where he once had fixity of tenure, he now has to pay for it at the rate of four shillings per annum. It is an anomaly but one of those anomalies that must be accepted and allowed for. The introduction of the white man with his new notions of private property in land was the predetermining issue, and this must be accepted as something that has come to stay.[48]

Hetherwick therefore confined his efforts to achieving some amelioration of the position of the African communities within the existing system.

He pressed for reform of the system of land tenure that would provide more opportunities for Africans to have secure title to their land. In 1905 he wrote to the Commissioner Sir Alfred Sharpe to propose a system that would allow individual Africans to hold land – 'say 10 acres, either on lease or freehold'. 'The object of this would be to give the native the advantage of some security of tenure, and lead him to adopt means of self-advancement in the way of better houses for himself and family, or improved means of cultivating his ground etc.'[49] Sharpe replied in encouraging terms – 'I am quite in sympathy with some such scheme as the one which you outline'.[50] However, nothing came of it. As Bridglal Pachai concludes in his study of the land question: 'after two decades of colonial rule the position of the majority of the Africans was still not clarified in respect of land occupation, land laws, availability of land, relief from oppressive and discriminatory provisions.'[51]

When Hetherwick was on the Legislative Council he aimed to take his chance to introduce legislation that would address the land issue.[52] 'I am to bring up at the Council the question of the Natives' place on the land,' he wrote, 'and his want of fixity of tenure. This is a problem which the Government should have tackled sooner or later and I think the time has now come when it should be taken up and dealt with by the authorities.'[53] This issue, in Hetherwick's mind was very strongly interlinked with his resistance to labour migration. He believed that if Africans had security of tenure and good prospects on their own land, they would be much less likely to be attracted to life as migrant labourers – to the benefit of both the people and the land. As he urged the Legislative Council:

> Every inducement should be given to the native population, beginning of course with a few, and extending it as far as possible, for acquiring land rights, and with a few alterations this Ordinance was the way in which these rights could be secured. This was required for the advancement of agriculture and for the sake of keeping the native in the country, which could only be done by giving him an interest in the soil of the country.[54]

When the government, after the First World War, proposed to set up a Land Commission, Hetherwick took a keen interest. He was involved in the preparation of recommendations by the Chamber of Commerce but discovered that one of the responsibilities he had proposed for the Commission was omitted when the Chamber made its submission to government. He lost no time in writing personally to the government to advocate that the omission be rectified and that the Commission be required 'to consider the position of the Natives living on European owned Estates'.[55] Urging the inclusion of this question he stated, 'I am strongly of the opinion that this is a vital part of the whole question, and one which has caused many difficulties in the past and which has never been satisfactorily settled.'[56] He followed up by writing directly to the Governor, Sir George Smith, 'I am afraid some of our friends have the idea that they have a "freehold" on the native as well as on the land.'[57]

He was eventually appointed to be a member of the Commission and had high hopes for what it might achieve: 'It is to be a big thing and I hope will have the effect of securing the native in all his rights to the land for all time to come.'[58] His hopes were vindicated when the Commission issued its report and he could feel confident that, 'If the recommendations of the Commission are given effect to by legislation they will secure to the native his rights to the land for all time to come . . . The Report will become the Magna Carta of native rights on the soil of his own country.'[59] The Natives on Private Estates Ordinance, which was passed in 1928 just a few months after Hetherwick's final departure, did provide greater security of tenure for tenants on European-owned estates."[60] It must be acknowledged, however, that conditions for these tenants were far from enviable and fell well short of the hopes Hetherwick had entertained for the Commission.[61] It was meagre reward for a lifetime of fighting for the land rights of African farmers but at least their situation was better than it might have been otherwise. 'The period after September, 1928,' concluded the historian Bridglal Pachai, 'would show how effective and useful the Ordinance was.'[62]

Cinderella and her Sisters

The questions of land and labour focused Hetherwick's mind also on the Protectorate's geopolitical situation. Returning often to the Cinderella image that had been evoked by the first Commissioner Harry Johnston, he acknowledged that,

> The epithet may still be considered applicable when we compare its size, situation, and resources with those of the two larger and wealthier sister Protectorates of Uganda and British East Africa. But as regards resourcefulness, energy, and success in self-development, Nyasaland need give place to neither of these territories.[63]

No matter the difficulties and disappointments, Hetherwick never wavered in his confidence that the Protectorate could have a flourishing future.

Nonetheless he was realistic about the challenges: 'From the very first Nyasaland has suffered by reason of its position on the map of Africa ... The Protectorate has all along been handicapped by its smallness as well as by difficulties of communication with the outer world.'[64]

Hetherwick was much occupied, as was Livingstone before him and successive generations after him, with questions of transport and communications. How could Malawi with its landlocked position be effectively connected with the world's system of trade? Livingstone's great hope had lain with the major rivers that flowed from inland Africa to the sea, in Malawi's case the Shire. This remained the strategy during the early years of Blantyre Mission but as time went on and the water level of Lake Malawi and the River Shire went up and down, it became apparent that it was not going to be dependable as a primary route. When the Shire became unnavigable for periods during the 1890s, some hoped that this was simply part of a cyclical pattern and that water levels would revive. Hetherwick was less sanguine. He foresaw drier conditions as deforestation was already taking its toll. In his view an alternative strategy had to be found.

This was the great age of the railway, with new railway lines being built all over the world and Cecil Rhodes dreaming of a Cape to Cairo line that would open up the whole of eastern Africa to his enterprises. It therefore appeared to be an obvious solution to the Protectorate's predicament. Hetherwick was one of the champions of the need to build a railway. By the turn of the century, it was being viewed as a panacea. *Life and Work* put the rhetorical question: 'When the railway comes – what is not to happen?'[65] At Hetherwick's instigation a missionary delegation met with the British government early in 1901 and, as John McMurtrie reported, 'We all set forth that the progress of the country is arrested by the want of a railway, or that the country is even going back.'[66] There was also a human rights dimension to this which Hetherwick had repeatedly pressed. Transport and communications hitherto had depended heavily on the *tengatenga* (carriers) whose conditions of service were often scarcely compatible with respect for human dignity. Therefore, the railway offered the prospect that they could be relieved of their burdens. When the missionary delegation met the British government they also 'represented strongly the evils of human porterage'.[67]

In the end, however, it was not the government that provided the solution but Eugene Sharrer of the British Central Africa Company, one of the major European commercial enterprises in the Protectorate. 'We owe our thanks to Mr Sharrer,' acknowledged Hetherwick, 'who for years, amid much discouragement that made others give up the attempt, has kept at his object, and now seems to be on the road to success.'[68] The route was to run from the lower Shire River at Chiromo to Blantyre and then past Zomba on to the south end of Lake Nyasa. In Hetherwick's imagination, 'It establishes the Lake route as the Great Highway into the Centre of Africa'.[69] To his mind, the significance of this initiative could hardly be overestimated. As he wrote to John McMurtrie at the end of 1902, 'This is the most important thing that has come to the country and the people since the establishment of the Government in 1891.'[70]

The development of the railway, however, turned into a race against the rapidly declining navigability of the Shire. Even before the line from Chiromo to Blantyre had been completed, the falling water levels on the Shire made it impossible for the steamers to reach Chiromo. The line therefore had to be extended to Port Herald. Before long the water level in the river fell further so that ships could no longer reach Port Herald. The railway line had to be extended to Chindio on the Zambezi. By now, however, the falling water levels were affecting the Zambezi also and it became questionable whether shipping would be able to reach Chindio.[71] It was becoming clear to Hetherwick that the only viable solution would be an extension of the railway line to Beira on the coast of Portuguese East Africa, thus removing entirely the use of steamers on the waterways. As he wrote in his annual report for 1908:

> To accomplish in ten hours what in the old days used to take from three to six days is a boon that no one can help valuing. But such facilities only make it more apparent that the present line will never be properly utilised till it is continued to the Lake on the one hand and to the Coast at Beira on the other – thus linking us to the South African system of Railways and opening markets to our produce that at present are closed to our planters and producers by reason of the cost and difficulties of transport to the coast. That the Government might see its way and find means to secure this is the desire of all who have the widest and best interests of the country at heart.[72]

Here there was a difficult trade-off for Hetherwick since he had always been determined that Nyasaland would keep its distance from South Africa. The railway might be a vital link to the wider world for Nyasaland but it would also connect it far more closely with the territories south of the Zambezi towards which Hetherwick had never hidden his antipathy.

In the early days of the railway development, he had been clear that:

> We don't want to be joined to the Cape – the whole conditions of Central Africa are entirely different from those of the colony south of the Zambezi. The south will become more and more a white man's land; Central Africa will remain for the most part a black man's land. The laws and regulations that will meet the needs of the mixed population on the south of the Zambezi waterway, will not fit the almost wholly native population of Central and tropical Africa. Our development here will be on lines very different from that of the colony.[73]

As he warmed to his theme, he was at pains to underline that, 'Central Africa will never become a colony in the sense that it may be colonized by a white population. Central Africa in no way can be regarded as a dwelling place for the white races – it is the home of the black man and the black man alone.'[74]

If this sounds like a robustly pro-African standpoint, his recognition that the country ultimately belongs to 'the black man' is combined with a paternalistic understanding of the role of 'the European':

> He [the black man] alone can develop its resources under the rule and the guidance of the European; he alone can till its soil and convert its wide marshes into gardens of rice for the teeming millions of the crowded cities of the colder regions of our globe. This is his place and sphere. Ours is to govern him and teach him till he sees that his lot lies in his own home and on its soil, and not in the mines of Kimberley or the Transvaal.[75]

He stood with the people of Nyasaland and was determined that they would not become subject to the conditions that prevailed for the African population of South Africa. But he was convinced that their progress, for the time being, depended on the colonial rule under which they were living. At the end of the day, the need to extend the railway line to Beira meant that there was a direct connection to South Africa through the Beira Mashonaland line. Hetherwick accepted that this was the only way forward but regarded it as a mixed blessing: 'This will mean vast changes for us – some good, some bad. It will afford easier facilities for travel and the carriage of goods to and from the Protectorate, but it will also open the gate to a flood of influence from South Africa, which will not be to the well-being of the life of the Protectorate, whether European or Native.'[76]

Through the long years of the First World War, Hetherwick was contemplating the geopolitical challenges posed by Nyasaland's situation. He kept returning to the issue of the smallness of the Protectorate in comparison to other African territories and concluded that, 'this hindrance to its future progress can only be removed by its union with one or other of the neighbouring territories administered directly or indirectly by the British Crown'.[77] He was emphatic that South Africa should be excluded from consideration in this regard:

> We may at once put aside any idea of incorporating Nyasaland within the South African Union. The conditions of the country are all against any such proposal. Nyasaland is a black man's country. There is no scope within it for the settlement of a white population such as the South African Colonies and Southern Rhodesia afford. The place of the European in the Protectorate is that of administrator of its Government or director of its commercial and agricultural enterprises. The work of development will be done by the native himself under the white man's rule and leadership. The future problems and lines of development of Nyasaland are altogether different from those of South Africa. The River Zambesi has always been a natural bound-

ary between Central and South Africa, and forms a very definite line of demarcation between two different territories.[78]

If Nyasaland could not look southwards, in what direction might attention be turned in pursuit of a wider union?

In the wartime conditions of early 1917, Hetherwick wrote in *Life and Work* that, 'We cannot help thinking of the future. After the storm is over and the strife of passion is stilled, what is to become of Nyasaland. Where is our little Protectorate to stand in the rearrangement of African territories! A movement has been set on foot here towards joining up Nyasaland and Northern Rhodesia as a British Central African Protectorate under the British Crown.'[79] He recognised that Northern Rhodesia was under the Chartered Company and not under the Crown like Nyasaland but was confident that this did not present any insurmountable issues. He proposed to 'detach Northern Rhodesia from the Chartered Company's territories, join it up to Nyasaland, and administer both as one Protectorate under the Crown.'[80] He could imagine a territory that combined what today is Malawi and Zambia as one that would have economy of scale and would command greater recognition. As he gave free rein to his imagination he contemplated a further union of 'all the British Protectorates in East and Central Africa including Uganda, British East Africa, British Central Africa, and such part or parts of the German East African possessions as might fall to be administered by Great Britain when the war is over.'[81] 'Zanzibar,' he suggested, 'would form the natural and most convenient seat for such a central administration, and thus the old base of East and Central African trade would recover somewhat of its historical prestige.'[82]

As he canvassed such thoughts, Hetherwick could not be accused of lacking imagination, albeit the imagination was constrained by his thinking only in terms of the British sphere of influence. At the same time, he was not without a canny political instinct and he also mooted the idea that Nyasaland's geographical challenges could be met by looking not to the west but to the east. As the end of the war approached, he sensed that there might be new possibilities: '. . . whilst the political position is obscure and uncertain, one hopes that if the map of Africa is to undergo any change it surely should be possible for our Colonial Office to extricate Nyasaland from its present unenviable position of being a "back lane".'[83] He had a bold and daring proposal to put on the table:

> The fact is patent to anyone that it would be of immense advantage to the country if there could be secured to it some coast line and a good harbour. Whilst it is no doubt true that a Railway connection with Beira is guaranteed and will shortly be constructed, it is nevertheless true that it must pass over alien territory and is therefore liable to trouble and difficulty. It seems to us the time is opportune to bargain with Portugal for an exchange of territory, and even if we have to pay

for it, the advantages in the future are well worth it. Thus only is there hope for the Cinderella of Protectorate to enlarge herself and rise to greater importance, or to be absorbed by her neighbours. She is worthy of a better fate.[84]

This was not to be, but the question with which Hetherwick was wrestling continues to be a critical one more than 100 years later.

A Far Outlook

One feature that distinguished Alexander Hetherwick from the great majority of his fellow missionaries was the breadth of his outlook. Most of the others were concerned with their own particular sphere and the projects in which they were engaged. Hetherwick too was constantly absorbed by the minutiae of the management of the large enterprise that was Blantyre Mission during his time. Yet at the same time he was deeply informed about all aspects of the life of the Protectorate and had a clear vision as to its future direction. He was a churchman and a missionary to the core, but his interpretation of his vocation meant that he was concerned with the social, economic and political life around him as much as with the spiritual and ecclesiastical. He had a vision for the future of the country which to some extent was realised during his lifetime while at the same time he fought many a battle to resist influences that he believed would take Nyasaland in a direction that was not in its own interests.

When he reflected in 1904 on the Missionary Conference that was held at Blantyre that year, he observed that, 'We had a magnificent Conference here – it was an inspiration to us all who had the privilege of being at its meetings ... [Its resolutions] are far reaching in their aims – and God knows we need a far outlook in this land. The man who cannot see beyond his own nose is the enemy of the work here.'[85] He himself modelled the 'far outlook' that he was concerned to advocate. His broad view of the development of the country was grounded in a comprehensive theological vision. As he wrote in *Life and Work* in 1900:

> We watch the development of a new country. We have seen it from its commencement. And each year sees new fields occupied and new enterprises inaugurated. Every quota of truth and knowledge, skill and labour adds to the sum of a people's advancement. The interests of all both European and native are one and the same, and the welfare of the one is coincident with the welfare of the other. The Kingdom of God comes in many forms – but beneath all variety there lies the unity of the One Foundation on which all true progress must be built – the Son of Man.[86]

In this way he took into a new era the vision that had been cast at Blantyre Mission during its inspirational early decades.

Many years later, he evoked the far outlook in a poignant way in his final speech to the Legislative Council, on 7 April 1925. It was not normal for the language of love to feature in the proceedings of the Council, but it was adopted by Hetherwick when he spoke of Nyasaland in these terms: 'It has had my love all these years and it will have it still. I wish I could be spared another 40 years to see what will happen, but that is impossible, so I wish the country all the prosperity that one's heart can desire.'[87] Beneath all the fighting talk there was a soft side to Alexander Hetherwick after all! The vision that had guided his involvement in the public life of the country across five decades had been a matter of the heart.

Notes

1. See further Benedict Anderson, *Imagined Communities: Reflections on the Origin and Spread of Nationalism*, London: Verso, 1983.
2. Alexander Hetherwick, *The Romance of Blantyre: How Livingstone's Dream Came True*, London: James Clarke, n.d.
3. The Hon and Reverend Dr Hetherwick, Legco Files, MNA 11/AHE.
4. Summary of the Proceedings of the Legislative Council of Nyasaland, Thirtieth Session, 30 March and 7 April, 1925, Malawi National Archives.
5. *Life and Work in British Central Africa*, February 1904.
6. Ibid.
7. Summary of the Proceedings of the Third Session of the Legislative Council, Held at Zomba on 4–6 May, 1909, Malawi National Archives.
8. See Harry H. Johnston, *The British Central Africa*, New York: Edward Arnold, 1897.
9. *Life and Work in British Central Africa*, December 1900.
10. *Life and Work in Nyasaland*, January–March 1917.
11. *Life and Work in British Central Africa*, December 1902.
12. Blantyre Mission Council, 14 January 1903, MNA 50/BMC/1/1/1.
13. *Life and Work in British Central Africa*, February 1903.
14. Alexander Hetherwick to John McMurtrie, 13 January 1903, MNA 50/BMC/2/1/46.
15. Ibid.
16. *Life and Work in British Central Africa*, February 1903.
17. Ibid.
18. Alexander Hetherwick to John McMurtrie, 13 January 1903, MNA 50/BMC/2/1/46.
19. *Life and Work in British Central Africa*, February 1903.
20. Ibid.
21. See further Mapopa O. J. Chipeta, 'Labour in a Colonial Context: The Growth and Development of the Malawian Wage Labour Force during the Colonial Period', PhD, Dalhousie University, 1986.
22. Alexander Hetherwick to John McMurtrie, 13 January 1903, MNA 50/BMC/2/1/46.
23. The Committees of the Central African Missions of the Church of Scotland and the United Free Church of Scotland to The Marquess of Landsdowne,

HM Principal Secretary of State for Foreign Affairs, 16 March 1903, MNA 50/BMC/2/1/47.
24. Alexander Hetherwick to Dr James Robertson, 19 March 1903, MNA 50/BMC/2/1/47.
25. Ibid.
26. Ibid.
27. Ibid.
28. John McMurtrie to Alexander Hetherwick, 23 March 1903, MNA 50/BMC/2/1/47.
29. Alexander Hetherwick to John McMurtrie, 3 April 1903, MNA 50/BMC/2/1/47.
30. Alexander Hetherwick to John McMurtrie, 28 March 1904, MNA 50/BMC/2/1/53.
31. Alexander Hetherwick to John McMurtrie, 14 March 1904, MNA 50/BMC/2/1/53.
32. Alexander Hetherwick to The Hon, the Master of Polworth, Convener of African Sub-Committee, 11 April 1904, enclosing letter to *The Scotsman*.
33. Alexander Hetherwick to Sir Alfred Sharpe, 5 April 1904, MNA 50/BMC/2/1/53.
34. Ibid.
35. Alexander Hetherwick to John McMurtrie, 26 July 1904, MNA 50/BMC/2/1/56.
36. *Life and Work in British Central Africa*, March 1893.
37. Alexander Hetherwick to John McMurtrie, 28 March 1904, MNA 50/BMC/2/1/53.
38. Ibid.
39. Alexander Hetherwick to J. D. McCallum, 9 March 1910, MNA 50/BMC/2/1/103.
40. See further Robert B. Boeder, 'Malawians Abroad: The History of Labour Emigration from Malawi to Its Neighbors, 1890 to the Present', PhD, Michigan State University, 1974.
41. See John McCracken, *A History of Malawi 1859–1966*, Woodbridge: James Currey, 2012, repr. Woodbridge: James Currey and Mzuzu: Mzuni Press, 2021, 83–87.
42. Bridglal Pachai, *Malawi: The History of the Nation*, London: Longman, 1973, 126.
43. See B. S. Krishnamurthy, 'Economic Policy: Land and Labour in Nyasaland, 1890–1914', in Bridglal Pachai (ed.), *The Early History of Malawi*, London: Longman, 1972, 384–404.
44. Andrew C. Ross, *Blantyre Mission and the Making of Modern Malawi*, Blantyre: CLAIM-Kachere, 1996, repr. Mzuzu: Luviri Press, 2018, 173.
45. Alexander Hetherwick to Mr McCall (Government official), 5 May 1910, MNA BMC/50/2/1/107.
46. William Manning, H.M. Deputy Commissioner & Consul to Alexander Hetherwick, 8 April 1900, MNA 50/BMC/2/1/33.
47. Alexander Hetherwick to John McMurtrie, 19 March 1903, MNA 50/BMC/2/1/47.
48. *Life and Work in Nyasaland*, November-December 1909.
49. Alexander Hetherwick to Sir Alfred Sharpe, 16 January 1905, MNA 50/BMC/2/1/64.
50. Sir Alfred Sharpe to Alexander Hetherwick, 19 January 1905, MNA 50/BMC/2/1/64.

51. Bridglal Pachai, *Land and Politics in Malawi, 1875–1975*, Kingston: The Limestone Press, 1978, 98.
52. Alexander Hetherwick to J. D. McCallum, 5 February 1909, MNA 50/BMC/2/1/98.
53. Alexander Hetherwick to J. D. McCallum, 26 October 1909, MNA 50/BMC/2/1/102.
54. Summary of the Proceedings of the Fifth Session of the Legislative Council, Held at Zomba on 24–26 May 1910. See further Bridglal Pachai, *Land and Politics in Malawi, 1875–1975*, Kingston: The Limestone Press, 1978, 94–98.
55. Alexander Hetherwick to The Chief Secretary, Zomba, 17 June 1920, MNA BMC/50/2/1/178.
56. Ibid.
57. Alexander Hetherwick to Sir George Smith, 22 June 1920, MNA BMC/50/2/1/178.
58. Alexander Hetherwick to J. L. Ogilvie, 9 December 1920, MNA BMC/50/2/1/184.
59. Alexander Hetherwick, 'Blantyre Mission Annual Report, 1921', MNA BMC/50/2/1/194.
60. 'An Ordinance to Regulate the Position of Natives Residing on Private Estates', Supplement to The Nyasaland Government Gazette of 31 August, 1928. MNA BMC/50/2/1/256.
61. See further John McCracken, *A History of Malawi 1859–1966*, Woodbridge: James Currey, 2012, 169.
62. Bridglal Pachai, *Land and Politics in Malawi, 1875–1975*, 121.
63. Alexander Hetherwick, 'Nyasaland Today and Tomorrow', *Journal of the Royal African Society* 17 no. 65 (October 1917), 11–19, at 11.
64. Ibid.
65. *Life and Work in British Central Africa*, August 1898.
66. John McMurtrie to Alexander Hetherwick, 11 January 1901, MNA 50/BMC/2/1/36.
67. Ibid.
68. *Life and Work in British Central Africa*, August 1902.
69. Ibid.
70. Alexander Hetherwick to John McMurtrie, 30 December 1902, MNA 50/BMC/2/1/45.
71. Alexander Hetherwick, 'Nyasaland Today and Tomorrow', 12.
72. Alexander Hetherwick, 'Report for the Year 1908', MNA 50/BMC/2/1/96.
73. *Life and Work in British Central Africa*, August 1902.
74. Ibid.
75. Ibid.
76. Alexander Hetherwick, 'Notes for Report on Year 1912', MNA BMC/50/2/1/123.
77. Alexander Hetherwick, 'Nyasaland Today and Tomorrow', 17.
78. Ibid.
79. *Life and Work in Nyasaland*, January–March 1917.
80. Alexander Hetherwick, 'Nyasaland Today and Tomorrow', 18.
81. Ibid., 19.
82. Ibid.
83. *Life and Work in Nyasaland*, July 1918–June 1919.

84. Ibid.
85. Alexander Hetherwick to James Robertson, 6 November 1904, MNA 50/BMC/2/1/63.
86. *Life and Work in British Central Africa*, January 1900.
87. Summary of the Proceedings of the Legislative Council of Nyasaland, Thirtieth Session, 30 March and 7 April 1925, Malawi National Archives.

CHAPTER SEVEN

The Linguist and Bible Translator: Words Must Be Christianised

If Alexander Hetherwick had done nothing else, he would be remembered as a pioneer linguist and Bible translator in the Malawi context. To some extent his work on language flowed naturally out of his daily interaction with the people around him. When he went on *ulendo* (a trip) to 'Angoniland' (Ntcheu), for example, he could be in African company and communicating in the vernacular for up to three weeks at a time. Yet the disciplined work of Bible translation and production of other forms of literature often had to be conducted in a quiet hour or two at the end of a busy day or during school holidays when he could sometimes snatch some days for concentrated work. This language work was close to his heart and he frequently lamented his failure to give it the attention he felt it deserved.

Two major languages were spoken in the Blantyre Mission sphere during the 1880s: Mang'anja and Yao. The first missionaries had favoured Yao as the likely lingua franca but by the time Hetherwick arrived Clement Scott had adopted Mang'anja as the primary language at Blantyre. Strategically, however, since the plan was for Hetherwick to establish a new station to the north in a predominantly Yao-speaking area, he decided that this was the language he should learn. At Scott's suggestion he went to stay with John Buchanan, one of the first group of Blantyre missionaries who had become an independent planter.[1] He was by now based at Zomba and had become a fluent Yao speaker.[2] Hetherwick employed what later became known as the 'immersion method', devoting two months to daily conversation in a Yao-speaking community. Soon he was being introduced to Yao folklore, thereby becoming ever more skilled in idiomatic expression.[3] By 1885, according to his biographer, he could speak Yao as fluently as English.[4] For Hetherwick, Yao was a most beautiful language – 'the Italian of the Bantu languages'.[5] He regretted that it was being displaced by Mang'anja as the primary language of the Shire Highlands.[6] 'I am glad to learn of your intention to do something at Yao,' he wrote to a European with language-learning aspirations in 1910. 'It is a very neglected tongue I fear nowadays, but it is by far the finest of the languages hereabout.'[7]

Hetherwick's rapid progress in gaining a command of the Yao language did not go unnoticed. In 1888 he was recruited by the British and Foreign Bible Society as one of its translators.[8] He recalled that in that same year the Society 'published a tentative edition of the Gospels and the Acts of the Apostles in the Yao language for use in [Blantyre] Mission and among the Yao-speaking people between Lake Nyasa and the East Coast of Africa.'[9] Regarding Hetherwick's Yao Gospel of Mark, the Anglican UMCA missionary linguist Chauncy Maples remarked that 'this is a genuine triumph of translation, and I cannot refrain here expressing my admiration for this splendid achievement'.[10] When he published the revised edition in 1903, the *Central African Times* observed that 'Dr Hetherwick is the recognised and only local authority on the Yao language'.[11] (In giving this accolade, the settler newspaper, of course, overlooked the large numbers of mother-tongue Yao speakers in the country.) Over the subsequent years Hetherwick continued producing further portions of the New Testament in Yao until in 1907 the Bible Society was able to publish a complete Yao New Testament, which enjoyed wide circulation in Nyasaland and Yao-speaking parts of Portuguese East Africa.

Meanwhile Hetherwick was also developing his knowledge of Nyanja and embarking on a collaboration with Clement Scott in dictionary and translation work, which he would continue single-handed for many years after Scott's departure from Blantyre. His extended spells covering for Scott's absences at Blantyre gave him the opportunity to develop fluency in Nyanja. By the early 1890s he was equally comfortable in Yao and Nyanja. When he celebrated the semi-jubilee of his arrival in Blantyre in 1908, his colleagues in their address singled out his linguistic work:

> As a linguist your work has been of the greatest service to the Mission and to the country. You were among the first to study the Yao language, and your Handbook is the standard work of reference in its grammar and vocabulary. In Chinyanja, the most important and widespread language of this part of Central Africa, your Manual is recognized as the most complete and authoritative work. In translation work in the New Testament in the Yao language is the result of your own labours, and you have also borne a large share in the latest translation of the New Testament into Chinyanja.[12]

Considering that, having had a classical education, he was also competent in Latin, Greek and Hebrew, Hetherwick had extraordinary linguistic range, which he relished putting at the service of the Mission especially in translation work.

By the turn of the century a regular feature on the inside back cover of the *Life and Work* magazine was a list of the books the Mission made available in vernacular languages:

Books in Mang'anja

Mang'anja Dictionary (Scott)
XII Lessons

Unit of Thought
Mang'anja Manual (Hetherwick)
Pilgrim's Progress (Dr W. A. Scott)
Do. (for children) (Illustrated)
Kucha Kwa-Dzuwa (Peep of Day)
Gospels (bound together)
Matthew
Mark
Luke
John
Epistles Eph., Phil and Col.
Matt. (New Translation Committee)
Book of Yao and Mang'anja hymns
Mang'anja Primer
Second Mang'anja Reader
New Mang'anja Reader (Illustrated)
Catechism
Ntanu (Stories in Mang'anja)
School Management Mang'anja

Books in Yao

Yao Handbook and Grammar
Matthew Gospel
Mark
Luke
John
Acts
Romans
Corinthians I and II
Gal. to Phil.
Hebrews to James
St Peter to Revelation
Genesis Chap 1–25
Catechism
Chikulupi cha wa Kristu
1st Yao Reader
2nd Yao Reader (Illustrated)
1st Yao Primer
2nd Yao Primer
Pandanda (Bible stories)
Book of Yao stories
Aesop's Fables
East African Tales – Yao English
English Yao Vocabulary[13]

The Yao books were almost all Hetherwick's work while he had also had a large hand in the Mang'anja literature. He often made use of his furlough periods in Scotland, not to rest and relax, but to see the latest productions through the press.

The revision of Scott's monumental dictionary remained always on his mind. When he returned to Blantyre in 1919 after a long furlough at the end of the First World War, one of the first things he did was to write to his Committee Secretary to request a special grant for this purpose:

> I intend revising Dr Scott's Dictionary by adding to it from the additional knowledge of the language which we have acquired since his day. To this end I need a native clerk and typist whom I should pay the salary of £18 per annum . . . It is to be a big job and as I have to do it in such time as I can get snatched from other work I must have someone to do the mechanical part of the task.[14]

He circulated a memo to colleagues in various different missions asking them to

> assist him with contributions of words which they have found are not included in the Dictionary, or words which bear a different dialect meaning from that at present recorded. Sentences in Nyanja illustrative of the uses of a word make a valuable addition to the interpretation. Similarly with words dealing with matters of native life and custom, a brief explanation of the habit or rite will be welcomed.[15]

Despite good intentions it was not long before he was complaining of his overwhelming workload and resultant lack of opportunity to pursue language work. By 1921 he felt obliged to put the project on hold, writing to McLachlan: 'Do not send me any more money for the Dictionary Work – I have done only a couple of hours on the job within the last two years and I cannot get time to think of it now . . . I have loads of material but no time to work it up. So do not send more money in the meantime – I have all I need as it is accumulating here and not being used as I hoped when I asked for it.'[16] In the end he took the dictionary project with him into his retirement and finally published the revised version in 1930.[17]

Nyanja Bible Translation Board

As Blantyre Mission developed this prolific output in vernacular languages, Hetherwick was thinking strategically, particularly in relation to Bible translation. Missionaries from many of the other missions would often spend a night or two enjoying the renowned hospitality of the Blantyre manse as they passed through on their way north. Talk in the evening would often turn to the benefits of a common Nyanja translation of the Bible. For Hetherwick, this was an idea to conjure with:

The value of such a translation would be inestimable. We know how much the Authorized Version of our English Bible has accomplished in welding together the language. So long as that version holds its place in the affections of our English speaking nationalities, so long there will be a bond of sympathy and support that no considerations of self-interest will ever be able to sever. What a strength to native Christianity to find Mang'anja, Angoni, Maravi, Chipeta, Anyanja, Ambo, Ambewe, Asena, all with the same version of Holy Scripture in their hands.[18]

He recognised that there would be difficulties to be faced, especially since there was no standard version of a shared language. Yet he was confident that the difficulties could be overcome: 'No one doubts that there is dialectic variety in the language spoken over so large an area but the diversity is not such as to make the dialect of one district not understood by the inhabitants of another.'[19]

Plans took concrete shape when Andrew C. Murray, the Head of the Dutch Reformed Church Mission, stayed at the Blantyre manse in March 1900. They agreed that a first meeting of the Translation Committee be held at Fort Johnston (Mangochi) from 24 to 29 May 1900.[20] When the board met, Livingstonia Mission was represented by A. G. McAlpine, the Dutch Reformed Church Mission by Murray and Robert Blake, while Hetherwick represented Blantyre.[21] He was elected Chairman, an office he continued to hold for decades to come. It soon became clear that Livingstonia would not play an active role since Nyanja was little spoken in its sphere of influence in the north. The project was carried through as a joint effort of the Blantyre and Dutch Reformed Church Missions. Active collaboration was soon underway. A. C. Murray was writing to Hetherwick to ask: 'Do you have the word *sakasa* for seek? *mezetsana* for grafting (trees); *kudzininka*, to be conceited (cf give oneself airs)? *mpirimbedza* for an adder?'[22] The kind of consultation that was taking place is illustrated by another letter from Murray a few months later: 'In the text (Matt 11:28), "Come unto me all ye that labour etc", I had "*akulema ndi olemedwa ndi katundu*", which does not read well. Here they say "*otodwa ndi katundu*" for one overburdened with a load, is this known with you? *tobwa* is to be struck in the eye but *todwa* is to be overloaded and if known would I think do very well here in the above verse.'[23] Thus they compared notes about words and expressions that were in common use in their respective areas as they worked towards a translation that could find wide acceptance.

They threw themselves into their assignment, Murray writing to Hetherwick that, 'I hope to reach Blantyre by about the 12th. I think I shall be able to give you about a fortnight for revision work.'[24] Little did they know how many of such 'fortnights' lay ahead of their translation team. Meanwhile they got to work at Blantyre and could report that, '... it was finally decided to adopt *c* as the representative of the sound *ch* in church ... A word for *church* – the body of Christian believers, was also finally adopted – a word that is common to Yao, Tonga, Tumbuka as well as to Chinyanja. This word is *mpingo* which signifies a body of persons on the march, especially when associated under a single leader.'[25] These were decisions that would have far-reaching influence on life, faith and language in the Protectorate. The collaborative venture began buoyantly, and they could report that, 'The joint body of translators found a spirit of harmony and unity in their meetings which gave magnificent hopes for the result of their future labours.'[26] For his part, A. C. Murray wrote of Hetherwick that, 'with our mission he always worked very graciously together, and from him our mission always experienced the greatest kindness and hospitality'.[27]

Despite such a promising start, little progress was made during the first few years as all the leading participants were absorbed by the many and varied demands of missionary life. A breakthrough came in 1903 when the Dutch Reformed Church General Mission Committee took a strategic decision. A. C. Murray had been obliged to leave Malawi owing to the ill health of his wife and was succeeded as leader of the mission by his cousin W. H. Murray who also took his place on the Nyanja Bible Translation Committee. Now the decision was taken that Murray should be relieved of all other responsibilities so that he could devote himself exclusively to the translation of the Bible. Murray was reluctant at first but went on to devote the best years of his life to the task. He worked for a year and a half on the translation of the New Testament and then, his biographer recounts, 'went to Blantyre to discuss it once more with Dr. Hetherwick, who knew the language very well and who had also written a grammar which is still used today by new missionaries.'[28] At this decisive meeting they benefited immeasurably from the insights offered by a team of mother-tongue Nyanja speakers: Jonathan Sande of Blantyre, Ismael Mwale of Mlanda and Wilibes Chikuse of Mvera.

Their efforts met with success and Hetherwick could report that, 'In May and June of [1905] the Board – three out of its four available members in the country – met here at Blantyre and sat steadily for six weeks till the revision of the Tentative edition of the Testament was complete. It is done and soon will be in the hands of the printers. *Laus Deo* [Praise God].'[29] The Blantyre Mission Council could, 'record their satisfaction in the completion of the Nyanja Translation of the New Testament and congratulate the Translation Board on the success of their labours'.[30] It was agreed that it would be published by the National Bible Society of Scotland. At Hetherwick's suggestion, Murray travelled to Scotland to check the proofs and see it through the press, his six-month trip showing how committed they were to the task in hand.[31] At the same time, Hetherwick had completed the revision of the Yao New Testament so that it too was ready to go to the press. 'Thus,' he declared, 'the two important Versions, in the tongues of two tribes spoken and understood from the Zambesi to Angoniland and from the Loangwa to near the East Coast – many hundreds of miles in either direction, are soon to be placed in the hands of the people who are yearly being taught in their thousands to read them.'[32]

Hetherwick was able to report to the momentous Edinburgh 1910 World Missionary Conference, with its special interest in missionary cooperation, that the missions in Nyasaland had come together to form the Nyanja Bible Translation Board, which had '. . . produced the whole of the New Testament and are at present engaged on the Old Testament. Thus we have a common Nyanja Bible for the Nyanja speaking natives of the Protectorate, a matter of great utility and practical benefit to the work of the Church and the various Missions. They have also prepared translations of the Creed and the Ten Commandments which are used by us all.'[33] He spoke a little too soon of the common Nyanja Bible since the work on the Old Testament proved to be taxing and it would be another twelve years before it was finally published.

Hetherwick was the first to admit that his other responsibilities had hindered him from giving the translation work the attention that it required. The oft-lamented shortage of staff at Blantyre Mission meant that he was perennially over-stretched but when the appointment of Robert Napier in 1909 gave him some hope of relief, his immediate thought was that, 'This will let me get something done at translation which has been in abeyance for the past three or four years – and I have made myself responsible to the Translation Board for the completion of the Book of Genesis and the Prophet Isaiah. When I come home [in 1911] I hope to have the half of the Old Testament with me to put through the press.'[34] Napier more than fulfilled his hopes, proving to be a highly effective missionary to whom he could delegate many responsibilities. As a result, he could write that, 'I have been able this year to do a little of the translation of the Old Testament – I have managed my share of the tasks given out by the Translation Board two years ago – Genesis and Isaiah. But it was by a spurt at vacation time when there was not much to do in the School and things could slacken off a bit.'[35]

Early in 1911, as Hetherwick's furlough was approaching, Murray again came to Blantyre for an intensive spell of translation work. Their aim was to complete the translation of the Psalms so that Hetherwick could see to their publication while he was on furlough in Scotland. As he explained to readers of *Life and Work*: 'Although other parts of the Old Testament are nearly ready in manuscript their publication will be delayed till the entire canon is completed, but the Psalms will shortly appear by themselves and be sold at a low figure. Once again in history the heart songs of old Israel will speak to new hearts far distant from Zion and lead them nearer to Jehovah.'[36] The project was implemented successfully and, on his return to Blantyre, Hetherwick could report that, 'the psalms have been put into the hands of the Christian Church for the first time, and their daily use with us in Blantyre, only reveals to us how much the Church has missed in the past from being so long deprived of this magnificent aid to the praise and prayers of the people's devotions.'[37]

Meanwhile the Nyanja New Testament continued to be in high demand – 'twice we have been sold out and at present the store is empty. Another consignment is on the way.'[38] These were very encouraging developments but there was also a negative note to be struck at this time:

> Alas! The translation of the remainder of the Old Testament proceeds but slowly. The plea of every one to whom the task has been allotted is 'no time'. I sympathise with them for my own contribution to the year's quota of work in this direction has been only thirty-two chapters of Jeremiah, and since 7th August up till now my only plea for not adding a single verse to that small contribution is that of my fellow labourers, 'no time'.[39]

Once again, it was the commitment of the Dutch Reformed Church Mission to devote the entire time and energy of its leader W. H. Murray to translation work that made the decisive difference. He was given a house at Kaso, near Mvera, where he had peace and quiet to devote the years from 1915 to 1918 exclusively to the work of Bible translation. Other DRC and Blantyre missionaries took on specific assignments: another of the Murray family, Dr W. A. Murray, translated the First Book of Kings and part of the second, A. L. Hofmeyer translated the First Book of Samuel and part of the second, Robert Napier of Blantyre translated Proverbs and the Song of Solomon while Hetherwick was allocated the substantial books of Genesis, Isaiah and Jeremiah. The lion's share was undertaken, however, by W. H. Murray during his three years of dedicated work at Kaso.[40] From time to time he would make the trip to Blantyre so that he could consult with Hetherwick, staying at the Blantyre manse for weeks at a time. He recalled that, 'Dr Hetherwick's knowledge and his courtesy made it a happy partnership. If he was critical – and he was – he was also able to appreciate the viewpoint of the other. It was interesting but wearying work, though often enlivened by animated discussion between our Native assistants.'[41] These spirited discussions, Hetherwick wryly observed, were driven by 'the opinion held by each translator that his own is the best and only good version'.[42]

By early 1917 Hetherwick was sounding quite upbeat about completing the Old Testament:

> Six weeks of Mr Murray of the Dutch Reformed Church Mission – the Secretary and Translator of the Nyanja Translation Board – down here in Blantyre enabled us to get the Pentateuch revised and made ready for the press. A month of Mr Napier and Mr Murray at Mvera in Angoniland put the translation of Jeremiah into shape. Next year four months of Mr Murray and Mr Napier together should see most of the Old Testament fit for the press.[43]

A year later he was less sanguine: 'The war is likely to prevent the early publication of the Old Testament in Chinyanja. The work of translation is almost completed but the difficulty of printing and the enhanced cost of wages and material makes it imperative to delay matters until after the war.'[44] Returning to Blantyre at the end of the war he was able to finalise Isaiah and Jeremiah, his sense of relief palpable as he wrote to Murray, 'It was good to have the work done and I never enjoyed tying up a parcel in my life so much as I did tying up these three parcels of manuscripts.'[45]

However, it took until 1921 before they were ready to send the complete manuscript of the Old Testament to Scotland. There then followed a lengthy process of checking and revision as the proofs were sent, thirty pages each week, from Scotland to Nyasaland to be read first by Hetherwick at Blantyre and then by Murray at Mvera.[46] Finally in 1922 the complete Nyanja Bible was published, including a revised version of the New Testament. It was built on what Retief Müller describes as the 'intellectual collegiality' between the Blantyre and Dutch Reformed Church missionaries, Hetherwick and W. H. Murray in particular.[47]

Triumphantly Hetherwick wrote to a colleague: 'I have just finished the last page of the final proof of the Nyanja Bible! Laus Deo!! [Praise God.] It was begun in May of 1900, and I am the only one left of the original Board of Translators. So I have been singing Te Deum's for the past hour.'[48] The greatly longed-for day had arrived when they could 'put the whole of the Nyanja Bible into the hands of the Nyanja speaking peoples – numbering well nigh two millions. *Illa die laus Deo* [Praise be to God that day].'[49] By 1930, Hetherwick could record that they had sold 46,250 copies of the whole Bible, 67,721 copies of the New Testament and 93,980 portions.[50] Even then they were not yet finished and in 1936 produced a new edition with paragraph headings and text references. By this time Hetherwick had been working collaboratively on the Nyanja Bible translation for thirty-six years since his election as Chair of the Translation Board at Fort Johnston (Mangochi) in 1900.

Hymns and Hymnbooks

The life and worship of a church needs to be equipped not only with the Bible in the vernacular language, but also hymns through which the people can join their voices in the praise of God. This was particularly the case in the Malawi context where music and communal singing struck a chord in the hearts of the people like nothing else. When Andrew Ross was conducting his research on Blantyre Mission in the 1950s and 1960s, he noted that hymns played a particularly powerful role in the communication of the Christian message.[51] The first hymnbook at Blantyre Mission was published the year before Hetherwick arrived, in 1882. It was the work of David Clement Scott and, though it was only eight pages in length, it contained translations of such hymns as 'Lord, a little band and lowly' and 'When he cometh, when he cometh, to make up his jewels', that proved to be of enduring value.[52] When later editions of the hymnbook were published Hetherwick was able to add Yao translations as he introduced hymns to the life of the Domasi Mission. In some cases, the original European tune was adapted to African rhythm and melody while in others African tunes were adopted, including some that had originated as war songs.

In a parallel development to the Nyanja Bible Translation Board, when the Federated Board of Missions in Nyasaland was formed at the Mvera Missionary Conference in 1910 one of its first actions was to appoint a joint working group to compile a common hymnbook. Hetherwick hosted the first meeting of the working group at Blantyre and, with his musical ear, it was a pleasure for him to be involved in its work. Besides hymns that were already familiar at Blantyre he was introduced to the early hymnody of other missions in the Protectorate, including that compiled by Livingstonia Mission in its *Sumu za Ukristu*, which included hymns by talented composers among the first generation of Livingstonia Christians such as Charles Chinula, Peter Thole and Mawelera Tembo.[53]

When the joint hymnbook *Nyimbo za Mulungu* was published in 1914, it included translations of several of the Tumbuka hymns but omitted most of those that featured in the Blantyre collection. The reason for the omission is that there were objections from the Zambezi Industrial Mission and the South African General Mission who condemned them as *nyimbo za chamba* (dancing tunes or, more literally, marijuana songs).[54] This was a disappointment to Hetherwick who protested that: 'It means a great deal to the Christian Church when the old war chants are put to Christian use in the service of the Lord's house.'[55] Nevertheless he understood that in a shared project there is always need for compromise and he had to accept the omission from the hymnbook of hymns that were well known and well loved in the village congregations of Blantyre Mission. In return, there was the benefit of another unifying factor – a hymnbook for use in worship across the different bodies in membership of the Federated Board. He had no hesitation in recognising and welcoming it:

> The new Nyanja Hymnbook compiled by a Committee of the Federated Missions of Nyasaland has at last been completed and is now ready for the press. It consists of 310 hymns – many of them new, and others revised from those already in the collections of the various Nyanja-speaking Missions of the Protectorate. The collection embraces hymns dealing with most of the leading themes and phases of the Christian life and acts of Christian worship, and when printed will form a valuable contribution to the life of the native church.[56]

Hetherwick had a major hand in its preparation. It would be another vehicle through which his influence would continue to be felt in Malawi for many years to come.

Philosophy of Language

Having mastered two African languages and having laboured long and hard at translation work, Hetherwick did not lack opportunity to think about the nature of language and the challenges of translation. In February 1900, as he looked forward to the launch of the Nyanja Bible Translation Board, he wrote a major article in *Life and Work* in which he assessed the difficulties that would need to be overcome:

> There arises first, in all work of translation, the difficulty presented by the different idioms of two languages. Two such divergent types as Greek and Nyanja must of necessity run on lines that are widely separate. Greek thought flows in a wholly different groove from Mang'anja or Nyanja thought. The Greek mind is trained to deal with abstract ideas and subjective conceptions. Their thought flows in strict logical sequence – the one premise following the other – the subject being clearly differentiated from the object. Thought follows thought in manifest order and the train can be traced from the first premise to the conclusion. The African on the other hand deals with the concrete rather than the abstract. He prefers action to passivity. Hence his narrative is largely descriptive of the concrete reality that passes before his vision. Thought is always thought in action. Hence his predilection for the use of the demonstrative pronoun.[57]

For drawing this contrast Hetherwick has recently been taken to task by Harri Englund, who regards his approach as a drastic departure from the confidence in African vernacular languages that had characterised Clement Scott's work. In Englund's critique, 'Hetherwick was considerably less sanguine about the prospects of Chimang'anja/Chinyanja to offer appropriate concepts and idioms in the manner of English some centuries earlier. Because Chimang'anja/Chinyanja was a vehicle "almost entirely void of religious or theological phraseology", recourse had to be taken to more "civilized tongues".'[58] On this basis Englund makes the more far-reaching criticism that, 'In Scott's inspired celebration of African linguistic resources and Hetherwick's dour committee work lies a contrast that was to become all the more pronounced as the twentieth century dawned. It is a contrast between the ethos of attributing a basic unity to humankind and a paternalistic (and in some cases racist) division of humanity into civilized and uncivilized tongues and peoples.'[59]

In Hetherwick's *Life and Work* article, however, he reaches exactly the opposite conclusion to that attributed to him by Englund. 'It may be taken as an axiom,' he states, 'that a good translation contains as few transliterated terms as possible. Native words should be used except for very strong reasons to the contrary.'[60] Far from proposing that recourse be taken to so-called more civilised tongues, as Englund suggests he did, Hetherwick advocated precisely the opposite: 'When we come to the use of the Mang'anja language in translation, it will be found that after all very few foreign terms will have to be employed. The great verities of our faith "God", "heaven", "life", "death", "sin", "incarnation", "atonement", "resurrection", "judgement", can all be denoted by native expressions.'[61] Rather than concluding that Mang'anja would be a deficient language when it came to expressing the biblical faith, Hetherwick struck a note of confidence.

He informed the 1910 World Missionary Conference that, 'all instruction of Church members in the truths of our Faith would be in the vernacular tongue'.[62] Like Scott before him, he was excited by the prospects of the Christian faith coming to expression in African vernacular language. It can be valid to draw some contrast between the two since Hetherwick admittedly lacked the extraordinary qualities of imaginative sympathy that distinguished Scott's work, including his passionate embrace of the Mang'anja language. Scott, however, completed relatively little Bible translation and it was the allegedly 'dour' work of Hetherwick and his committee that saw through the ambitious exercise of rendering the entire Bible into the Nyanja language.

This meant that Hetherwick, to a much greater extent than his colleague and mentor Clement Scott, had to wrestle with the dilemmas and trade-offs of the work of translation. 'Vividness, action, present perception form leading characteristics of native speech,' he wrote. 'Hence the transference of thought from Greek into Mang'anja or Nyanja must also necessitate a transformation of idiom and speech into the active and present.'[63] This is not a matter of saying that Greek is a better or 'more civilised' language than Nyanja. It is simply appreciating that the two languages differ, as do their underlying cultures, so that to transfer meaning from one to the other involves a search for 'dynamic equivalence' rather than just a wooden translation of each word. 'Thus,' Hetherwick realised, 'the practical question that presents itself to every translator is, Am I to sacrifice Greek Idiom to Nyanja or vice versa? Shall I follow the Greek form of expression with its passive voice and its oblique constructions, or shall I transform them into the active and direct as a native would do in actual speech or conversation?'[64] This was neither a matter of denigrating the African language nor of extolling the Greek. It was simply recognising the difference between the two.

Even today, when many Malawians are bilingual, they will naturally turn to English for the expression of more abstract ideas while preferring their vernacular language when addressing the concrete realities of everyday life. It remains the case that, as Hetherwick recognised, 'all exact scientific teaching must be in English, for the native tongue contains no terms that are suitable and it is as easy to give the English equivalent as to make up a native one which may be misleading in the extreme'.[65] The translation challenge that Hetherwick identified has not gone away.

Given the relative lack of abstract terms in the Nyanja language to accommodate the intention of the Greek, Hetherwick concluded that, 'the translator must either introduce new terms from some cognate or foreign tongue, or endeavour by Christian usage to graft a new meaning on to the old stem'.[66] Again, this is a recognition of something that is a perennial reality – language is not constant but is subject to continual shift in meaning as new influences are brought to bear. The arrival of the Christian faith and the biblical text in the Malawi context was, on any reckoning, a major new influence that was sure to have its impact on the language. As Hetherwick wrote, 'In many cases the native meaning may have to be modified – but language being the vehicle of thought must submit to conversion as well as people. In our own tongue many words have been Christianised and have entirely lost their original heathen significance.'[67] The conversion metaphor was evidently a convincing one for Hetherwick since he had earlier stated it as an aphorism, 'Words have to be Christianised as well as lives'.[68]

This was intrinsic to the missionary calling – seeking to introduce a ferment of change that would be transformative at many different levels, including informing the meaning of language with a new understanding. Where Hetherwick might be open to criticism is that he showed little appreciation that this was a two-way process, since Christianity would be Africanised at the same time as Africa was Christianised. Clement Scott, with his speculative and adventurous approach to the missionary task, was perhaps more open to a new interpretation of Christianity emerging from the African reception of the faith. Hetherwick, with his more conservative cast of mind, seems to have had little expectation that the translation enterprise would shed new light on the meaning of Christianity. He was aware, however, that it was a dynamic field where profound transformation was taking place as the African language and the biblical faith were brought together. The historian of mission Andrew Walls has written that, 'The fundamental missionary experience, by which the endeavour stands or falls, is to live on the terms set by someone else'.[69] This is what Hetherwick was doing for half a century as he applied himself to understanding Yao and Nyanja.

A critical question, however, is how far Hetherwick's language ideology was governed by an accommodation with the colonial regime that came to dominate the landscape by the early twentieth century. On Harri Englund's analysis, 'he was to grow into an "establishment" figure quite unlike Scott ...'.[70] This is a somewhat anachronistic comparison since there was no 'establishment' for Scott to be part of during his time at Blantyre. It was only during Hetherwick's later years that the colonial society developed what might be termed an 'establishment' and he had to decide how to position himself in relation to it. Despite being critical of the direction Hetherwick took, Englund acknowledges that, 'his involvement in the Legislative Council and the Blantyre Chamber of Commerce often served a moderating purpose vis-à-vis settler and colonial interests'.[71] Nonetheless, Englund argues that, 'the paternalistic aspect of this moderate – as opposed to Scott's radical and visionary – liberalism can be detected in Hetherwick's language ideology'.[72]

In advancing this critique, Englund lays much weight on a passage where Hetherwick offers a vivid description of a typical scene in the Bible translation exercise:

> Within his tiny study he sits, a solitary white man, at a rough table on which lie small slips of paper to which he refers again and again. Round him are squatted half a dozen natives in garments of varied hue and odour with whom he is talking, asking them questions in turn, now referring to his slips, now to the human figures before him, sometimes getting an answer, sometimes meeting with silence, for the head of the questioned one has sunk lower and lower till chin rests on chest – the owner overpowered by the noontide heat ... The piles grow as the years pass, till the day comes when he makes all the contents of his slips into a Book.[73]

Admittedly, this is a paragraph that invites textual analysis in terms of how far it contains colonialist and racist tropes. The 'white man' *sits* while the 'natives' *squat*. The 'white man' is evidently masterful and purposeful while the 'natives' are described in derogatory terms as smelly and sleepy. Englund makes a fair point that such a description betrays a considerable degree of paternalism, with the racism that was inherent to such an outlook. At the same time, there are some mitigating factors to consider. Englund himself concedes that the text was written 'with some humorous intent'[74] and Hetherwick was poking fun at himself more than anyone else. It was also written for a European audience and it seems likely that Hetherwick is imagining how the scene would appear to them rather than reflecting his own experience as someone who spent long periods of time in entirely African company. Leon de Kock makes the point that, 'By the very nature of their vocation, missionaries were always under a duty to *report back* to their sponsoring bodies. They therefore provide a pre-eminent example of entrapment within a particular mode of expression.'[75] Hetherwick could be a case in point where there was a distance between his own experience of life and the terms in which he felt obliged to 'report back' to his supporting constituency at home in Scotland.

Taking this paragraph alone, it is fair enough for Englund to comment that, 'The *co-production* of linguistic knowledge as a relationship between people with different linguistic repertoires seems rather remote here'.[76] However, when Hetherwick departed from this semi-jocular and rather tongue-in-cheek tone to write in more sober terms, he struck a very different note. When he published his edited version of Clement Scott's magisterial *Encyclopaedic Dictionary of the Mang'anja Language* in 1930, in his preface he expressed the customary thanks to those who made the publication possible but then continued: 'Nor must he forget his obligations to the many Africans who in the course of his past years have helped in the collection and definition of the new words added to the original work. *In many cases these definitions are the very words employed by the natives to express the meaning.*⁷⁷ The co-production of linguistic knowledge, which Englund laments as being absent from the 'solitary white man' passage, is exactly what Hetherwick is at pains to acknowledge in this more serious text. Far from portraying the 'white man' as masterful and the 'natives' as feckless, as might be expected in a colonialist discourse, Hetherwick frankly acknowledges that he depended entirely on his African collaborators to arrive at the true meaning of a term, to the extent of adopting the exact words that they proposed.

He also departs from the stereotypes of colonialist discourse by naming one particular African to whose expertise he felt the dictionary was particularly heavily indebted: 'The Editor cannot close this brief Preface without recalling the memory of one to whom both the Author [Clement Scott] and himself owed much of their knowledge of the Nyanja tongue: Che Ndombo, Headman, Christian, Linguist, and Leper; on whose familiarity with various African tongues both were privileged to draw.'⁷⁸ It is a tantalisingly brief passage, leaving the reader wishing to know much more about the interaction of Scott, Hetherwick and Ndombo. But it is not a sentence that could have been written by someone who was easily conforming to colonialist and racist frames of thought. Though it is evidence that runs counter to his argument, in fairness Englund notes that Scott did not 'acknowledge any individual collaborators in his dictionary or published translations as contemporary linguists and translators would be expected to do', whereas it was Hetherwick who acknowledged their debt to Ndombo.⁷⁹

The hypothesis that there is a dramatic contrast between Scott and Hetherwick, with the former being pro-African and egalitarian and the latter colonialist and paternalist, does not seem to stand up to close examination. Hetherwick was certainly not immune to the influence of the cultural hubris, racism and paternalism that came to hold sway at the height of the colonial era. There were very few Europeans who could claim such immunity at the time. Whether joking or not, he could not have written the 'solitary white man' passage without colonialist stereotypes having made some impression on his mind. But there seems to be a lack of evidence that he departed altogether from Scott's understanding of shared humanity to let his linguistic work be governed instead by a codification of a sense of peoplehood where language, ethnicity and territory were supposed to coincide.⁸⁰ For one thing, he was relentlessly opposed all his life to the racial politics of South Africa where such ideas did take hold. For another, his vision for Nyanja was that it would be a unifying language, transcending ethnic and territorial differences. His publisher, the Bible Society, based its strategy on the assessment that, '. . . it seems to be at least probable that Chinyanja may become the sort of Lingua Franca in Central Africa'.⁸¹ Far from narrowing down the language to a particular ethnic or territorial unit, he believed he was involved with the emergence of a lingua franca that would transcend these differences.

It is often in 'throw-away' remarks that he reveals his underlying presuppositions. Englund fears that Hetherwick was privileging a 'civilised' language like English and denigrating the 'uncivilised' African languages with which he was concerned in his translation work. Once, however, when he was reflecting on vernacular exams that he had been marking, he drew a contrast that was completely the other way round:

> ... though grammarless in the sense that they know nought of these parts of speech, every native speaks correctly. There is no vulgar tongue among these peoples – nothing corresponding to the Dorset, Yorkshire, or the Cockney of our English language. Every native speaks 'like a gentleman.' He never drops his 'h's' or his 'g's' nor does he add an 'r' to the end of his words, making 'idea' into 'idear,' and 'Zomba' into 'Zombar.' These idiosyncracies are left to the vagaries of civilized and superior races. The native speaks his 'mother' tongue as his mother speaks it, and so he never has trouble over his verbs, regular or irregular – they are all regular to him.[82]

The point here is that he was mocking the idea that there are civilised races with superior languages, not adopting it.

Struggles and Achievement

Hetherwick's language and translation work did not go unrecognised. During his furlough in Scotland in 1901–2 he was awarded an honorary Doctor of Divinity degree by his alma mater Aberdeen University in recognition of his literary work. On his return, the Mission Council celebrated the award as meaning that, '... his many years of arduous and faithful labour in the translation of the New Testament and in other literary work, were thus fittingly recognized'.[83] In his own mind, however, far from feeling any sense of crowning achievement he was constantly disappointed that he was not making the progress for which he had hoped. In 1904 he confided to a friend that, 'My chief sorrow here is that I cannot get time to go on with my language work – it is practically at a standstill – and till I get help ... I see no prospect of doing anything more. I feel that if the coming year is as barren as the past, I must resign my position as Chairman of the Nyanja Bible Translation Board, which will be a great sorrow to me.'[84]

Despite his own sense of failure and under-achievement, however, the British and Foreign Bible Society regarded its collaboration with Hetherwick as a great success story. 'You will be interested to know,' wrote its Secretary Arthur Taylor in 1908, 'that the success of the Nyanja Testament has been very great. So much so that we are at present going to press with a second edition which will be composed of 10,000 Testaments and 10,000 copies of the combined Gospels. That it should have been necessary to reprint within the short space of time of about two years ... is a great proof of the social and educational and religious uplift which has been given ... by the work of the Missionaries.'[85] Recognition of such achievement came in the form that Taylor explained to Hetherwick in 1910: 'it is with great pleasure that I communicate to you the wish of the British and Foreign Bible Society Committee that you will accept from them the appointment of Honorary Governor of the Society for life'.[86] It was a rare distinction and it must have meant a lot to Hetherwick to accept it.[87]

In 1927, when he finally intimated his intention to retire from mission service, he added a postscript: 'I hope still to be able – if the way is open – to return to this country and finish my work on the native language which owing to the pressure of other duties has lain untouched for the past ten years.'[88] It was a hope that remained unfulfilled, though he did succeed in publishing the revised edition of Scott's dictionary that had for so long been on his mind. The fact that he contemplated returning to Nyasaland in his old age with the sole purpose of doing further work on Chinyanja demonstrates the extent to which the language had captured his imagination.

Notes

1. See John Buchanan, *The Shire Highlands*, Edinburgh and London: William Blackwood, 1885; repr. Blantyre: Blantyre Print and Publishing Company, 1982.
2. See Alexander Hetherwick, *Introductory Handbook of the Yao Language*, Aberdeen, n.p., 1899, repr. Andesite Press, 2017.
3. W. P. Livingstone, *A Prince of Missionaries: Alexander Hetherwick of Blantyre*, London: James Clarke, n.d., 30.
4. Ibid.
5. Stephen Green, 'Blantyre Mission', *The Nyasaland Journal* 10/2 (1957), 6–17, at 9.
6. Ibid., 31.
7. Alexander Hetherwick to Major Stevens, 23 December 1910, MNA BMC/50/2/1/111.
8. Alexander Hetherwick to J. D. McCallum, 11 February 1909, MNA 50/BMC/2/1/98.
9. Ibid.
10. Chauncy Maples, *Yao-English Vocabulary*, Zanzibar: Universities' Mission Press, 1888, 7, cit. Tobias J. Houston, 'Utenga Wambone – the "Good News": An Exploration of Historical Ciyawo Bible Translations and Linguistic Texts', *Studia Historiae Ecclesiasticae*, 2022, 18 pages, https://doi.org/10.25159/2412-4265/11186, 10.
11. *Central African Times*, 31 October 1903.
12. *Life and Work in Nyasaland*, July–August 1908.
13. See e.g. *Life and Work in British Central Africa*, September 1902.
14. Alexander Hetherwick to W.M. McLachlan, 2 April 1919, BMC/50/2/1/164.
15. Memo to the Members of the various Nyanja-speaking Missions in Nyasaland, July 1919, MNA BMC/50/2/1/167.

16. Alexander Hetherwick to W. M. McLachlan, 25 July 1921, MNA BMC/50/2/1/190.
17. D. C. Scott and Alexander Hetherwick, *Dictionary of the Nyanja Language*, London: Religious Tract Society, 1930.
18. *Life and Work in British Central Africa*, October 1898.
19. Ibid.
20. Andrew C. Murray to Alexander Hetherwick, 29 March 1900, MNA 50/BMC/2/1/32.
21. M. W. Retief, *William Murray of Nyasaland*, [Alice]: The Lovedale Press, 1958, 96.
22. Andrew C. Murray to Alexander Hetherwick, 11 June 1900, MNA 50/BMC/2/1/33.
23. Andrew C. Murray to Alexander Hetherwick, 7 November 1900, MNA 50/BMC/2/1/35.
24. Andrew C. Murray to Alexander Hetherwick, 21 November 1900, MNA 50/BMC/2/1/35.
25. *Life and Work in British Central Africa*, October and November 1900.
26. Ibid.
27. A. C. Murray, *Ons Nyasa-akker: Geskiedenis van die Nyasa sending van die Nederd. Geref. Kerk in Suid-Afrika*, Stellenbosch: Pro Ecclesia, 1931, 131, cit. Retief Müller, *The Scots Afrikaners: Identity Politics and Intertwined Religious Cultures in Southern and Central Africa*, Edinburgh: Edinburgh University Press, 2022, 100.
28. M. W. Retief, *William Murray of Nyasaland*, 98.
29. Alexander Hetherwick, 'Report for the Year 1905', 26 January 1906, MNA 50/BMC/2/1/72.
30. Mission Council meeting at Blantyre, 26 July 1905, MNA 50/BMC/1/1/1.
31. M. W. Retief, *William Murray of Nyasaland*, 99–100.
32. Alexander Hetherwick, 'Report for the Year 1905', 26 January 1906, MNA 50/BMC/2/1/72.
33. The Hon and Rev A. Hetherwick Central Africa, No. 83, World Missionary Conference, 1910, Correspondence of Commission VIII, Cooperation and the Promotion of Unity, 280.215 W893c VIII, Ecumenical Institute, Bossey, Switzerland.
34. Alexander Hetherwick to J. D. McCallum, 1 December 1909, MNA 50/BMC/2/1/103.
35. Alexander Hetherwick, 'Notes for Annual Report, 1910', MNA BMC/50/2/1/110.
36. *Life and Work in Nyasaland*, April–May 1911.
37. Alexander Hetherwick, 'Notes for Report on Year 1912', MNA BMC/50/2/1/123.
38. Ibid.
39. *Life and Work in Nyasaland*, January–February 1913.
40. M. W. Retief, *William Murray of Nyasaland*, 101.
41. Livingstone, *A Prince of Missionaries*, 160.
42. Alexander Hetherwick, cit. Livingstone, *A Prince of Missionaries*, 105.
43. *Life and Work in Nyasaland*, January–March 1917.
44. *Life and Work in Nyasaland*, April–June 1918.
45. Alexander Hetherwick to W. H. Murray, 2 December 1919, MNA BMC/50/2/1/172.

46. Retief, *William Murray of Nyasaland*, 102.
47. Retief Müller, *The Scots Afrikaners*, 103.
48. Alexander Hetherwick to Frederick Alexander, 22 March 1922, MNA BMC/50/2/1/197. The *Te Deum* is an ancient Latin Christian hymn of praise and thanksgiving.
49. *Life and Work in Nyasaland*, January–March 1917.
50. Alexander Hetherwick, *The Romance of Blantyre: How Livingstone's Dream Came True*, London: James Clarke, n.d., 239.
51. Andrew C. Ross, *Blantyre Mission and the Making of Modern Malawi*, Blantyre: CLAIM-Kachere, 1996, repr. Mzuzu: Luviri Press, 2018, 197–98, n21.
52. Alexander Hetherwick, *The Romance of Blantyre*, 204.
53. See Kenneth R. Ross (ed.), *Christianity in Malawi: A Sourcebook*, 2nd ed., Mzuzu: Mzuni Press, 2020, 64–85.
54. John Weller and Jane Linden, *Mainstream Christianity to 1980 in Malawi, Zambia and Zimbabwe*, Gweru: Mambo Press, 1984, 122.
55. Hetherwick to Morrison Bryce, 28 January 1914; cit. Andrew C. Ross, *Blantyre Mission and the Making of Modern Malawi*, 180.
56. *Life and Work in Nyasaland*, March–April 2014.
57. *Life and Work in British Central Africa*, February 1900.
58. Harri Englund, '"Africa Is an Education": Vernacular Language and the Missionary Encounter in Nineteenth-century Malawi', in Kenneth R. Ross and Wapulumuka O. Mulwafu (eds), *Politics, Christianity and Society in Malawi: Essays in Honour of John McCracken*, Mzuzu: Mzuni Press, 2020, 138–62, at 158.
59. Ibid., 141.
60. *Life and Work in British Central Africa*, February 1900.
61. Ibid.
62. World Missionary Conference, 1910, Correspondence of Commission III, Education, submission of The Hon and Rev A. Hetherwick D.D., Nyasaland, 280.215 W893c III, Ecumenical Institute, Bossey, Switzerland.
63. Ibid.
64. Ibid.
65. World Missionary Conference, 1910, Correspondence of Commission III, Education, submission of The Hon and Rev A. Hetherwick D.D., Nyasaland, 280.215 W893c III, Ecumenical Institute, Bossey, Switzerland.
66. Ibid.
67. Ibid.
68. *Life and Work in British Central Africa*, October 1898.
69. Andrew F. Walls, *The Missionary Movement in Christian History: Studies in the Transmission of Faith*, Maryknoll, NY: Orbis and Edinburgh: T. & T. Clark, 1996, xix.
70. Harri Englund, '"Africa Is an Education"', 155.
71. Ibid.
72. Ibid.
73. Cit. W. P. Livingstone, *A Prince of Missionaries*, 191–92.
74. Harri Englund, '"Africa Is an Education"', 155.
75. Leon de Kock, *Civilising Barbarians: Missionary Narrative and African Textual Response in Nineteenth-Century South Africa*, Johannesburg: Witwatersrand University Press and Lovedale Press, 1996, 82.
76. Harri Englund, '"Africa Is an Education"', 155.

77. David Clement Scott, *Dictionary of the Nyanja Language, Being the Encyclopaedic Dictionary of the Mang'anja Language*, edited and enlarged by Alexander Hetherwick, London: Lutterworth Press, 1930, repr. 1951, my italics.
78. Ibid.
79. Harri Englund, '"Africa is an Education"', 155.
80. See Harri Englund, '"Africa Is an Education"', 143.
81. R. H. Falconer, National Bible Society of Scotland to Revd Robert Macfarlane, 17 March 1911.
82. *Life and Work in Nyasaland*, July–August 1909.
83. Mission Council meeting at Blantyre, 6 May 1902, MNA 50/BMC/1/1/1.
84. Alexander Hetherwick to Revd W. S. Sutherland, 19 January 1904, MNA 50/BMC/2/1/52.
85. Arthur Taylor, Secretary, British and Foreign Bible Society, to Alexander Hetherwick, 15 May 1908, MNA 50/BMC/2/1/89.
86. Arthur Taylor, Secretary, British and Foreign Bible Society, to Alexander Hetherwick, 20 April 1910, MNA 50/BMC/2/1/106.
87. Alexander Hetherwick to Revd Arthur Taylor (BFBS), 7 June 1910, MNA BMC/50/2/1/107.
88. Alexander Hetherwick to W. M. McLachlan, 1 June 1927, MNA BMC/50/2/1/249.

CHAPTER EIGHT

The Mission Thinker: Priorities and Policy

Hetherwick led a very active life, his days and nights filled with meetings, events and travels. Yet he also had a strongly contemplative side and was given to reflecting on the nature and meaning of the missionary work in which he was engaged. On one occasion when there had been many visitors at the Blantyre manse he complained to fellow missionary Margaret Christie, 'So I have not had the chance of "thinking long".'[1] A capacity to take the long view was his hallmark. Often when engaged with a particular incident or episode, he would explain it in terms of how it exhibited a broader trend or illustrated a deeper principle. When these reflections are drawn together, a clear philosophy of mission is revealed. For example, he took a very wide view of the missionary calling. Rather than restricting the engagement of the Mission to any narrowly conceived religious sphere, in his view it ought to be concerned with every dimension of life.

This guided his policy as editor of *Life and Work*, the mission magazine that enjoyed a wide readership and often aroused controversy during the early years of the British Protectorate. As he once explained in an editorial:

> Nothing that in any way concerns or influences directly or indirectly the wellbeing of the country we consider out of our province. *Nihil Africanuum a me alienum puto* is our motto ['I regard nothing African as alien to me']. We hold that the missionary principle has room for all agencies that help on the true progress of the country and people, and therefore we deal with many questions that may seem outside the sphere of missionary operations.[2]

He was well aware that this policy was open to criticism: 'A candid friend once told us that we were not religious enough in our tone – not missionary enough, that we do not follow the common type of missionary magazines.'[3] Members of the oft-criticised British Administration had also made it clear that they wished that *Life and Work* would confine its attention to strictly religious matters. Alfred Sharpe had written to Scott some years earlier, 'Personally I have no objection to your using your newspaper for the purpose of sounding what you are pleased to call "Warning notes", though I think experience has shown that it would be far better if a Mission paper confined itself to its own sphere and left politics alone.'[4] Hetherwick would have none of it:

Our position is clear. Here in this land is the kingdom of God being founded. We missionaries are striving to obey our Blessed Lord's last command to preach the gospel to all nations. But we welcome every form of civilization that helps us to attain this great end. We welcome trade, planting, administration, scientific research as fellow workers. We believe all of them are meant to be sanctified to the use and service of God's kingdom in this land. Therefore we claim to deal in this magazine with everything that affects the state of the country and the people. Both in success and in failure we are tied in the same bundle of life.[5]

This broad understanding of mission applied, of course, not only to *Life and Work* the magazine but to all of Hetherwick's life and work in Malawi. Whether he was conducting Sunday worship in Blantyre or sitting the next day in the Legislative Council or the Chamber of Commerce, he regarded all of his wide-ranging involvement as the fulfilment of his missionary calling.

Another point to which Hetherwick often returned was the value of perseverance and consistency in mission work. Here he was a good foil for his long-time colleague Clement Scott. He could never match his friend and leader for brilliant and original ideas but when it came to taking up the ideas that gave Blantyre Mission its distinctive character and putting them into effect year after year, decade after decade, Hetherwick's gifts and temperament came into their own. He once remarked to his Committee Convener in Scotland, 'Our motto here in Blantyre is "adialeiptos"[6] – "unceasing" – but true and healthful'.[7] Keeping going through thick and thin, the dogged determination to persevere regardless of the odds – these were qualities on which Hetherwick set a premium. Reflecting on the death of Janet Beck in 1917 he observed that, 'Brilliant ideas do not count for much in Africa, if there is not the power and doggedness to carry them out. It is the constant grind that tells.'[8]

When he went to Livingstonia for the creation of the CCAP in 1924 he became aware of the tension there between Robert Laws, who had been leading the Mission for almost fifty years, and the brilliant rising star Donald Fraser. Hetherwick was not impressed with the latter: 'he is not a leader to carry on a settled policy. He is here today and there tomorrow.'[9] In Robert Laws, however, he recognised a kindred spirit – another mission leader for whom *adialeiptos* was a watchword. He was sometimes irked that his home constituency craved spectacular news when all he had to report was 'the dull routine of everyday work'. But he was convinced that it was the steady and usually unspectacular round of daily work that would yield lasting results.

Another lesson learned from experience was that the decisive factor in missionary work is 'the human element'.[10] A great deal of Hetherwick's time and much of his heart-searching was taken up with managing the human resources of the Mission. When he reflected on his experience with the 'impossible' missionary Elizabeth McGillivray, he wrote to his Committee Convener that, 'We must remember that the problem of missions is the problem of the European Missionary. The difficulties of the Mission Field are the difficulties of the European Staff. That is the result of my own past experience during all these years here.'[11]

Another book would need to be written to give an account of the many problems with which Hetherwick had to deal at the human level. Missionaries, in the nature of the case, tended to be strong characters and prone to clash with one another. Blantyre Mission had at least its fair share of such characters and more often than not there was some friction to address among the staff. How grateful Hetherwick was for those like John McIlwain or Janet Beck who were the exception to the rule. But he concluded sombrely: 'I have a saying which I fear I repeat to my friends too often when discussing points of mission policy and mission methods: "The problem of Missions is always the problem of the Missionary".'[12] This could also be stated in more positive terms, as Hetherwick did when he gave the closing address at the first united Missionary Conference held at Livingstonia in 1900, 'pointing out that the pre-eminent factor, the most potent influence in all their work, was personal touch, soul with soul, life with life'.[13] Perhaps it was his consciousness of the decisiveness of the human factor that brought him back time and again to the spiritual quality that was needed for missionary work.

The Spiritual Heart of Mission

While Hetherwick held a broad view of mission as encompassing the entire development of a people and nation, he never lost his sense of the centrality of the spiritual dimension. When Blantyre hosted the Missionary Conference in 1904, Hetherwick was invited to address the topic 'The missionary's temptations in his work'. He took the opportunity to remind his fellow missionaries that, 'We are here for our work's sake, not our work for ours. Therefore our work demands our whole soul thrown into it – all the force and energy of our character.'[14] He returned to the theme in 1908, writing in *Life and Work* that, '. . . the best gift that any one of us can give to the Mission is our own individual spirituality'.[15] There were always innumerable practical, financial and logistical issues that demanded attention when the staff came together but there were times when Hetherwick felt the need to bring them back to the spiritual dimension that he regarded as foundational. Late in 1909 for example, he spoke to them about 'the deeper things of our life here – it touches the spring of all our work – to remember what we are here for. This can be dealt with only from within and from beneath. We need our spiritual thought and consciences freshened.'[16]

A formative experience for Hetherwick was the religious revival within the Blantyre Mission that he dated from 1887. As he recounts in his history of the Mission:

> The religious awakening which had begun in 1887 grew in intensity. Many a quiet knock came to the manse study door at night, and in response to the invitation, 'Come in,' the door would be opened and a shy voice would plead, 'I want words.' And the words would be that a desire for more knowledge of higher things had come, and the speaker had many questions to ask. Not a few times the 'words' would be about a dream that had come once, twice, thrice, in the night, and whose interpretation the visitor greatly desired . . . An old man or woman, grey-haired and wrinkled, would follow the minister after Sunday morning service and say, 'I want God.' That was all they could say, just 'I want God.' Surely that was enough! 'They that seek shall find.' And so the number of those gathering in a little wattle and daub church on a communion Sunday gradually increased, till on occasions it could hold no more.[17]

Critics of Hetherwick who consider him to have been aloof and unapproachable in his attitude to the African community around him can be challenged to imagine the encounters and conversations that he evoked in this passage. In the nature of the case, these took place far from the public eye but there can be little question that Hetherwick was engaged in a very personal way with the people who formed the mission community out of which the church would grow. It is also clear that ministry at the spiritual level was integral to his daily life.

In terms of his theology and spirituality, Hetherwick was conservative. Here a contrast can be drawn with the speculative and adventurous theological approach of Clement Scott. To venture, as Scott did, the idea of Africa as a Christ figure – 'Africa bears the sins of the world's rulers' – was to stretch far beyond Hetherwick's theological range.[18] Likewise Scott's imagining of a language and people that would be 'broad enough for Mahomet and Christian Missionary, and with room for more . . .' is not a thought that would have occurred to Hetherwick.[19] He was more inclined to stick to the traditional Christian faith in which he had been formed as he grew up in Aberdeen.

Preparing lectures for the small theological class that he taught at Blantyre in 1907–8 exposed him to the higher criticism of the Bible that was provoking reassessment of traditional theology at the time. He was not impressed. He wrote to a friend that, 'I like to find some people who can place their faith in the old gospel and the old truths nowadays. My work with my classes in the Old Testament has made me look into the theories of the newer criticism – and I am not enamoured with the new knowledge as these higher critics give it out.'[20] On the other hand, he relished the devotional and evangelical writing of the celebrated Scottish preacher Alexander Whyte. Lending one of Whyte's books to fellow missionary Barbara Low, he wrote, 'If you get to love his writings as much as I do you will find in them as much blessing to the soul as I do. I read one of his chapters from one of his works every morning and have done so for over fifteen years since I discovered him.'[21]

In the divided ecclesiastical landscape of Scotland in Hetherwick's youth, the Church of Scotland (to which Blantyre Mission belonged) was generally regarded as the moderate 'folk church' while the Free Church and the United Presbyterian Church were more identified with evangelical and revival-orientated spirituality. Nevertheless, Hetherwick, through his teenage church involvement at the West Kirk in Aberdeen and participation in a student missionary society during his university years, came to hold a strongly evangelical faith. One of the high points of his Blantyre years was the visit in 1910 of Charles Inwood from the Keswick Convention with its emphasis on spiritual life and personal holiness. Hetherwick and Donald Fraser of Livingstonia invited Inwood to come on a tour of the different missions in Nyasaland. When the Committee in Scotland strongly urged Hetherwick to come on furlough so that he could attend the great Edinburgh 1910 World Missionary Conference, one of his reasons for refusing was that he did not want to miss the visit of Inwood, 'who comes to give the various Missions the help that such as he can alone give in stirring up our spiritual life and faith'.[22] So while the celebrated World Missionary Conference took place in Edinburgh, Hetherwick was in Blantyre translating for Inwood when he preached to the African congregation.

He must have felt his decision was vindicated when the Mission Council recorded that, 'the whole Mission and Church life has received a fresh spiritual impulse from Mr Inwood's services and message that will under the Divine blessing bear rich fruit in the years to come'.[23] Hetherwick wrote enthusiastically at the time about Inwood's ministry but, many years later, when he was looking for a visiting speaker for the Blantyre Mission Golden Jubilee in 1926, he remarked that, 'I should particularly like a man from our church because you know that he would not run off the rails in the matter of emotionalism which Inwood did on more than one occasion'.[24] After all, despite the warmth of the occasion at the time, he understood the Church of Scotland as keeping a certain distance from an overly 'emotional' approach.

Nonetheless, personal piety was a matter to which Hetherwick clearly attached the highest importance. His fellow missionary Dr Elizabeth McCurrach recalled that

> ... morning after morning at four o'clock when nature was quietest, the light from the study window appeared like a beacon in the darkness ... However hard the day before had been, however dispirited or weary he might be, that time of prayer and communion was never missed. In it lay the secret of his wonderful freshness of mind and his faith, and his ability to deal with the things of the spirit.[25]

Perhaps on the place of spirituality in the life of the Mission, the last word should go to Hetherwick himself. During Holy Week in 1905 he offered the following reflection:

> We never dare hide our eyes to the fact that the Cross enters every true missionary life – the crucifixion in self, of all prejudice, prepossession and prejudgement – the stooping down to learn how to meet and raise the vast multitude of human life around us. For this, one thing is needful – the realization by the souls of all the awful responsibilities we have voluntarily taken upon us, for the souls of those whom we have gathered round us and with whom our work brings us into touch day by day. 'Their blood will I require at thy hands' – yes, every soul we meet in Church, Hospital, School, Workshop and Field, will God require at our hands.[26]

On the twenty-fifth anniversary of his arrival in Blantyre in 1908 he reflected that, 'I sometimes think I am only beginning my real work in Blantyre – so much has the way been opened up lately towards the ideals I have been striving after for years and now hope to see fulfilled. Only we need more of the Spirit of the Crucified in the Mission amongst us all.'[27]

Mission Thrives on Expansion

Besides the cultivation of individual spirituality, Hetherwick was always aware that the Mission as a whole needed a fresh spiritual impulse if it was to maintain its integrity and vitality. As a young man, when he was establishing the new mission station at Domasi, Hetherwick contemplated the possibilities for mission work in Yao country and declared, 'I am sent not as a stationary but as a missionary'.[28] It was a phrase that he would often repeat and a conviction that remained with him. In later life he would say, 'A mission that ceases to expand will soon cease to live. We need advances to stimulate us and give fresh interest to our work.'[29] This was not an easy position to sustain, particularly since the Mission was constantly short-staffed and under-resourced. Most of the time it seemed like an unequal struggle just to keep the existing work going without thinking of adding to it.

Nevertheless, for Hetherwick there was a spiritual principle at stake. A mission needs to be advancing or it will begin to crumble. When he wrote the annual report for 1904, he indicated where he thought the next advances might be made: 'Chiromo lies still without the Gospel – a scandal at our Mission door; the great Mang'anja population of the West Shire District is still untouched by Missionary effort.'[30] At the same time, he was inspired by the new churches that were being founded through the influence of Blantyre Mission. These played a key role in his missionary strategy:

> These daughter churches, while they look to the mother Church of the 'diocese' for guidance and council will each form distinct self-propagating, self-supporting churches. This is my ideal for the Evangelization and Christianizing of Central Africa. I believe it to be the true ideal, and the one best adapted to the life and thought of the African race.[31]

This was a vision of an African-led missionary movement. The centralisation of the education and training function of the Mission at Blantyre was a major preoccupation for Hetherwick in the years after this policy was agreed by the Missionary Conference of 1904. Though it sounds paradoxical, the purpose of the centralisation was to release energy for expansion. With the role of the European missionaries concentrated on providing training and formation as well as overall supervision, the expansion and growth of the church would be led by its African leaders and members. In Hetherwick's mind this was the only way forward: 'A trained and well equipped native staff is now the sole agency left us for the extension of mission work in the country owing to the curtailment of home support. This staff can be supplied only from a well-staffed central training institution or college.'[32] This policy was crystallised at a meeting of the Mission Council in 1908 when it was agreed:

> That the future policy of the Mission with regard to extension be directed towards (1) the occupying of the whole country by planting native stations such as Panthumbi, Chiradzulo, etc., under trained native Evangelists, Teachers, Ministers, etc. (2) the better training and equipment of native workers for this work, and (3) the more effectual and regular supervision of these stations by the European Missionary from the various European centres of the districts.
>
> That the work of the present European stations be devoted more and more to the effective superintendence of the district work in their respective spheres, leaving the work of training Evangelists, Teachers etc more and more to the Central Institution at Blantyre.[33]

A clear strategy was now in place, and it was the one that guided the work of the Mission for the remainder of Hetherwick's leadership. Nonetheless he was always concerned lest it lose its outward-looking and pioneering spirit. As he wrote to his Committee Convener in 1909: 'I feel that in some of the Departments we are getting into a somewhat mechanical rut and have the danger before us of losing the forward impulses that keep our work alive and our own enthusiasm keen. There is a great danger here of settling down and letting things come to us instead of going out to meet and find new sources of work and advance.'[34]

This outward dynamic eventually found expression in a fresh drive to revive and expand the work of the Blantyre Mission beyond the borders of Nyasaland into Portuguese East Africa. This is something that had already begun in the 1890s but the early mission outposts in PEA had to be closed down because they were not approved by the Portuguese authorities. Now the Mission sensed that the time might be ripe for a fresh approach and it was an opportunity that caught the imagination of the Blantyre missionaries in the years before and after the First World War. As noted in Chapter Four, towards the end of 1910 they took the unusual step of making a formal statement, which all the missionaries signed, to appeal to their

Church at home in Scotland to sanction and support an expansion of the Mission's work into Portuguese East Africa.

Hetherwick followed up on this, early in 1911, with a lengthy memorandum in which he explained the thinking that lay behind the resolve of the missionaries.[35] He invoked the recommendation of the Missionary Conference of 1904 that all the missions should centralise their training work with a view to extension. At Blantyre the centralisation had been successfully implemented and this, he argued, should now lead to extension. He went on to point out that there were very few opportunities remaining for Blantyre Mission to extend its work within the Nyasaland Protectorate. There were only two districts in the Blantyre sphere and one in the Domasi sphere that lacked a Blantyre Mission presence, and he was confident that within two years these areas would be covered. In terms of geography there would then be nowhere left within Nyasaland where the Mission could start completely fresh pioneering work.

From Hetherwick's perspective this impending lack of opportunity for expansion posed a threat to the integrity and vitality of the Mission itself. 'Extension is vital to mission life,' he wrote, '– the moment we cease to extend into new work and new regions we cease to grow and that means stagnation which in this land of heathenism is fatal.'[36] He was confident that the Mission itself could mobilise resources for the extension, generating more funds locally so that existing funding could be redirected to support the new work. He argued that a unique moment of opportunity presented itself:

> There is now an open door into this Portuguese part of Africa ... The Jesuit Missions have been expelled from all Portuguese colonies – it is for us to take the speediest means of getting in and filling the room they have left. For now that they have gone there is not a single Christian missionary in the whole of this part of Portuguese East Africa which lies north of the Zambezi and eastward of Blantyre.[37]

There was a remarkable opportunity in front of the Mission but the argument on which Hetherwick placed greatest weight was that it needed a fresh challenge if it was to sustain its authentic missionary character. He wrote: 'It is needful to keep alive in ourselves the Missionary ideals. There is the temptation amongst us to forget the end and purpose for which we are here – and I say it frankly it is a growing temptation. We are tempted to settle down comfortably each in our own station or department of work, to discharge our day's task and be satisfied with that. Such a position is far from the life that our Lord calls us to in the missionary vocation.'[38] This would have come as no surprise to the Committee in Scotland since he had written two months earlier that, 'The whole tone and attitude of our Mission both European and Native demand the fresh impulse and uplifting which only an advance into new fields will give us. It is absolutely essential if we are to be saved from *settling down* into our present posts which is deadly and fatal to all the higher spirit of Missionary life and work in the Kingdom of God.'[39] Hetherwick has sometimes been portrayed as a missionary who settled comfortably into the colonial establishment in Nyasaland. In fact, his driving passion was to extend beyond it to embark on pioneering missionary work in new areas.

Education as Mission

Meanwhile there was a certain 'establishment' in terms of the everyday institutional life of the Mission. When it came to the everyday life and daily routine of Blantyre Mission, a great deal of it revolved around the life of the schools.[40] Blantyre itself was a thriving educational centre and the hub for a network of village schools in the Mission's sphere of influence that numbered 239 in 1915.[41] By the time he had completed two decades of service Hetherwick was thoroughly convinced that this vast educational enterprise was the key to the fulfilment of the Mission's purpose. 'Without doubt,' he wrote, 'one of the best and surest ways to reach the hearts of the people among whom it is our lot to labour is through the school. Looking back over past years we find that to our schools we must look in great measure, for success in our mission work.'[42] Towards the end of his life he remained convinced that, 'Out of the schools in Africa has sprung the Christian church'.[43] It was a point that he made very often and elaborated most systematically when he responded at length to the questionnaire that he received from Commission III of the 1910 World Missionary Conference, which was responsible to consider the educational dimension of the missionary enterprise.[44]

When asked about the purpose of education, Hetherwick was emphatic that, 'The first and main purpose of all education in the work of Christian missions is to impart a knowledge of the true God'.[45] He resisted the idea that education might be secular in character: 'In education it is fatal to distinguish between the sacred and the secular, especially in work among the heathen. All true education is religious, for it is meant to explain the world and you cannot explain the world without God.'[46] This was an absolutely essential point for Hetherwick. He had struggled long and hard to secure financial support from the government for the educational work of the missions. But he was emphatic that,

> I would accept the Government grant only on the same conditions as at present are in vogue – that as regards our religious education we are to be free to follow such a system as pleases each mission to adopt. On no account would I allow the receipt of any Government grant to interfere with our position as a mission to the heathen or allow it to absorb too much of our energies in such subjects as will secure to us a share of the grant.[47]

From Hetherwick's perspective, the school was an essential part of the work of the Mission and integrally connected to the emergence of the church. As he explained: 'In Central Africa, Primary Education has been wholly religious and the Church and school have gone hand in hand in their aims to reach the people. In almost every instance in our mission, the Church has grown out of the school. The teacher has been the evangelist and preacher and has been the means of gathering the first fruits of the Church for Christ.'[48] He was pleased to receive financial support for the schools from the government but not if it were to carry any risk of compromising their core purpose as he understood it.

Until 1926 when the government first established a Department of Education, all formal education in Nyasaland was delivered by the Christian missions.[49] Only after intensive campaigning led by Hetherwick did the government begin in 1907 to give 'grants-in-aid' to support the educational programmes of the missions. Even then, the total annual grant was only £1,000. As Hetherwick pointed out, this amounted to 2 pence per pupil compared with 15 shillings and 6 pence in South Africa, 10 shillings in Bechuanaland and 13 shillings and 5 pence in Basutoland.[50] 'Certainly,' he concluded, 'the Nyasaland Government cannot be accused of extravagance in their expenditure on native education.'[51] A sore point for Hetherwick was that, 'This parsimony is all the more apparent when we consider the saving effected to the cost of administration by the employment of trained and educated natives whom the Government employ as clerks, printers, artisans, overseers, interpreters, etc., etc., in place of more highly paid Europeans or Indians.'[52]

It was a matter of pride to Hetherwick that those who graduated from the Blantyre Mission schools were in high demand as both the government and the private sector sought to recruit well-qualified staff. He was constantly receiving requests to recommend someone suitable to fill a vacant position. The fact that, by and large, graduates of the Blantyre Mission educational system had acquitted themselves well in their employment was a sufficient reply, in Hetherwick's view, to those who were inclined to criticise the provision of educational opportunity for Africans. As was his wont, he drew the contrast between the situation prevailing in South Africa and that in Nyasaland: 'In South Africa among the run of colonists, the opinion is freely expressed that education makes a man a worse worker and turns him against all forms of manual labour as degrading and beneath his dignity as an educated man. We have not the same attitude here among the Europeans of Nyasaland, where there is demand for the trained native . . .'[53]

The resistance to the development of high-quality education for African communities in South Africa, in Hetherwick's view, was attributable to three reasons:

1. The white man dreads the competition of the native in the labour market and in the commercial market. 2. The increased self-respect which education gives to the native is resented by the average white

man of the colony, as it makes the native refuse to submit to the position of a chattel or serf to become the drudge of the white man. 3. Because the educated native will demand rights which will make him a power in the political or commercial world and thus an antagonist or rival of the white man.[54]

He had no time for such attitudes and was confident that Nyasaland was taking a very different direction.

Far from seeing the development of education in the African community as a threat, Hetherwick regarded it as entirely positive and transformative. From his experience, 'The difference between the village where there is a school built by the people themselves and for their own use and their children, and a village where there is no such educational movement is manifest to the visitor at once.' Much of this difference could be attributed in Hetherwick's view to the cultivation of a work ethic: 'You cannot leave the native in the lazy habits of his village life and expect him to remain long a true Christian. He must be taught the place and value of labour as an element in Christian life. His time must be filled in somehow or other and there is no better means than that of educating him to work.'[55] Coming from a Scottish, Calvinist and industrial background, everything in Hetherwick's formation put a premium on hard work, thrift and the entrepreneurial spirit – perhaps to a fault. In practice, this meant that the Mission emphasised not only book learning but the acquisition of skills that was often termed 'industrial education'. 'For the African race,' wrote Hetherwick, 'a system of industrial or technical education is essential to the development of his full manhood. He must be taught habits of industry and the skill to apply himself to the labour of his two hands.'[56]

This did not mean, however, that the objective was to limit the educational opportunity so that Africans would be trained only for manual roles. Hetherwick argued on the contrary that, 'In African educational work wherever possible industrial training should be combined with literary instruction'.[57] The Mission was also committed to offering 'higher education', which he saw as 'essential for all true leadership in the Church or in Education'.[58] Special emphasis was placed on the training of teachers: 'We need a teaching profession – a class of trained workers who will be available for the education of the people of the country – a class with an *esprit de corps*. This can only be done by putting a high standard of training before the students and keeping the end of their profession always before them.'[59] This was what was being attempted at the centralised institution at Blantyre, which Hetherwick regarded as 'the embryo of our Nyasaland University'.[60] He observed that, 'The training we have hitherto given our teachers has been in most instances a path to a better education and to entrance on other occupations'.[61] When he gave evidence to the Phelps-Stokes Commission in 1924 he could proudly claim: 'We have supplied this growing civilized community with trained artisans, clerks, educated native overseers of plantations, etc . . . who are taking no small part in the development of their country. We have saved the country from requiring Indian or Chinese skilled labour and in its place we have trained our own natives to do the job.'[62]

Much of the educational enterprise was a matter of using Western methods and exposing the students to Western ways. Hetherwick saw the value of this in terms of equipping the next generation of Africans to meet the very different world that now confronted them. Yet he also had misgivings about an educational system that revolved entirely around methods and ideas that came with the Europeans and had little, if any, place for African inspiration. He recognised that it was 'unavoidable that much of our education is to graft on western ideas and ideals, and often in too great a measure to expect western results. I do not see how it is possible to do otherwise, but we must take care and leave room for the African to develop his own ideals in his own way and in his own time.'[63]

He saw that the system in place in his time was temporary and provisional. He understood the project in which the Mission was engaged as one that would, one day, overcome the foreign and alienating character of the educational system. 'The difficulty of the race problem meets us here,' he remarked, 'and till we have a Native Church with a native ministry and native leadership, we cannot secure the indigenous elements that lie at the root of the African mind and character. At present he is acquiring our ideals which we are giving him and this is not seldom to his loss.'[64] He pinned great hopes on what would be achieved when an African church with African leadership would become the driving force.

One of the questions asked by the World Missionary Conference questionnaire was about the rise of nationalism. Hetherwick's response was that, 'I cannot say I have discerned any tokens of a movement towards a national spirit among the people round us. We look for it, however, and hope to meet it to some extent by striving to impress on the young Church of this land the ideal of a self-supporting, self-extending, self-governing Native Church.'[65] This was not someone who viewed education as a means of entrenching the colonial system or denigrating African life and values. On the contrary, he looked at the educational programmes of the Mission as paving the way for an African leadership in the church and, ultimately, in the nation. This aspiration provokes wider questions about the place of African beliefs and values in the church and community emerging through the work of the Mission.

Continuity and Discontinuity

At the core of the missionary project was the aim and hope that it would result in people coming to faith in Jesus Christ. A key question that invariably presented itself, however, is the relation of this new faith to all that had gone before in the life of the people now receiving the Christian message. Their culture, their beliefs, their traditions – were these to be abandoned and replaced by something entirely new? Or would there be some element of continuity through which what had gone before would be integrated with the newfound Christian faith. Like many missionaries, Hetherwick had to face these questions and he came to a clear view: 'The missionary of these new days has abandoned the old attitude to the faiths of the heathen world, which looked upon them as wholly erroneous and must therefore be denounced and set aside. He is taught rather to look for elements of truth among these non-Christian faiths and to utilize them as foundation-stones on which to build up the fabric of truth he has come to teach.'[66] This orientation had far-reaching significance, perhaps more than Hetherwick realised at the time, in terms of taking a fundamentally affirmative approach to the African traditional beliefs and values of the people to whom the Mission brought its message.

Both Scott and Hetherwick were fond of reminding their compatriots that there was a time when it was the Britons who were considered to be heathen and savages and who were on the receiving end of Christian missionary efforts. Hetherwick invoked Pope Gregory and the strategy he advised for the evangelisation of Britain at the end of the sixth century. This entailed preserving as far as possible elements of pre-Christian religion so that temples would become churches, traditional feasts would become Christian festivals, and so on.[67] Applying this strategy to the African context, Hetherwick concluded:

> All heathen customs cannot be classed among these which the missionary is called on to condemn. Very many are part of the racial, tribal, or national life of the people, and the wise missionary will do well to endeavour to conserve as many of these as are not antagonistic to the Christian life and faith. Thus he will preserve such features of their character as may make valuable contributions to the life and history of the human race, and at the same time build up their Christian life on a foundation that will make it the natural expression of their tribal or racial character.[68]

Englund's critique of Hetherwick's approach suggests that he departed from the 'universal' range of Clement Scott's thinking to adopt a missionary approach that prioritised the ethnic and territorial identity of the people.[69] For Hetherwick, however, these were not opposing approaches to the indigenisation of the Christian faith in Malawi. His vision was for a Christianity that would *both* reflect the distinctive character of the Malawian people *and* allow them to contribute to 'the life and history of the human race'.[70] The particular and the universal, for him, were not in opposition to one another but rather complementary.

He was aware, however, that a demanding process lay ahead as decisions would need to be taken as to how to relate the Christian faith and the inherited African tradition to one another. He realised his own limitations in this regard but placed his confidence in the emerging African church: 'The question of how far some of these native customs can be Christianized – baptized as it were into Christian use and practice – as Pope Gregory suggested – is one that the Native Church itself will be better able to afford an answer.'[71] Meanwhile he himself was able to discern some obvious points of continuity. He noticed that there was a highly enthusiastic response to Harvest Thanksgiving services held in church and could see that this was motivated by a line of continuity that stretched back into the African tradition. He could see that these services were, 'entirely in the line of native religious thought and feeling, which in the old days, by offerings at the village shrine or grave of dead chief or headman, expressed thanksgiving for the bounty vouchsafed by the Unseen Spirit'.[72] So, he explained to his readers, '. . . on this Thanksgiving Sunday the members are encouraged to bring offerings of the fruits of the earth, a link with their pre-Christian religion-practice which it was thought well to keep unbroken'.[73] Hetherwick clearly affirmed and valued the continuity that he detected between the Christian worship and the traditional African religious practice that had preceded it.

Rather than looking on African religious belief as something to be swept away and replaced by the Christian faith, Hetherwick saw the former as a foundation on which the latter could be built. 'Far from being a materialist,' he wrote of the African, 'the largest and most powerful realities in his life are those of the spirit. The Bantu world is therefore full of the things that are spirit – a world surely in which the Gospel that deals with things spiritual and eternal will find a ready home.'[74] The fundamentally religious worldview that he found among the peoples of the Shire Highlands he regarded as offering hospitable conditions for the proclamation of the Christian message: 'The cardinal truths of belief in spirit, in a spirit world, in a Supreme Spirit in some form or another, in communion with the spirit world through prayer and sacrifice, these the messenger of the Gospel finds ready to his hand – to make the path of the preacher easier to the heart and conscience of the African tribesman.'[75]

He established the fundamental point that the God whom the missionaries came to proclaim was not a new or different God from the God already known and acknowledged in the African tradition. He wrote:

> The early missionaries were happy in finding, ready as it were to hand, this word [Mulungu] which they could use in application to the Christian God of Whom their Evangel spake. It was ready to form a foundation on which the preacher of the Gospel could build the fabric of its faith in the soul of men and women whom he was sent to seek and to save. The seed of the Evangel thus finds soil, ready prepared, for the seed he is to sow.[76]

For the missionaries, as Hetherwick understood it, this meant that they were not preaching their message into a void but rather must seek to answer the questions and meet the longings that were in the minds and hearts of the people with whom they were working. In the language of his time he wrote, 'A Gospel, that is to be indeed a Gospel to the heathen, must be the response to his cry after truth and light, and must solve all those problems of life's mystery which he himself had in the past failed to unravel, and satisfy that hunger of the soul which his heathen faith is utterly unable to meet'.[77]

This meant that the missionary must address matters that loomed large in the consciousness of the people, such as the spirit world and communion with the dead, the reality of the mystic spirit indwelling all the phenomena of the natural world, and belief in the solidarity of clan and family life.[78] At the same time, the missionary task was not only to affirm positive values but to turn them in a new direction and open up new possibilities. 'The conception of the Christian Church,' observed Hetherwick, 'will bring him a wider and fuller sense of unity than he has ever hitherto conceived of in his village, clan and tribal institutions. By his membership in the Church he is brought into a new relationship with peoples and races, with tribes and tongues living far away from the villages on the Shire Highlands or along the shores of Lake Nyasa.'[79] Thus there was both continuity and discontinuity in the relationship between the old and the new, both the particular and the universal as points of reference, both an affirmation and a transformation of traditional life and culture.

A Broad Basis

A key principle for Hetherwick was that, 'The Christianity of Africa must be built in a broad basis. We must touch the native character on all its sides, social and physical as well as spiritual and moral.'[80] A good example is the institution of marriage, which was a constant preoccupation for Hetherwick, presenting itself not only in general terms but in the pastoral reality of couples who sought Christian marriage and the many who experienced marital difficulties of one kind or another. This experience led Hetherwick to the conclusion that, 'So large a proportion of native thought, native custom and habit, and native social life is built upon the native conception of the marriage relationship, that to accept the Christian principle of marriage means a complete revolution in native social habits and family life.'[81] He regarded it as one of the main achievements of his term on the Legislative Council that it passed the Native Marriage Ordinance of 1912, which for the first time allowed for African Christian marriages to be recognised in law.[82] The impact of Blantyre Mission on the understanding and practice of marriage would require a book of its own.[83] Likewise many other social issues could be considered, such as Hetherwick's campaign in 1909 to ban the sale and consumption of beer in Blantyre and Limbe.[84] Such was the range of Hetherwick's interest and involvement that it is necessary to be selective and this chapter has attempted to set out his most characteristic concerns when he was thinking about the meaning of mission.

Notes

1. Alexander Hetherwick to Margaret Christie, 24 June 1920, MNA BMC/50/2/1/178.
2. *Life and Work in British Central Africa*, December 1900.
3. Ibid.
4. Alfred Sharpe to D. C. Scott, 30 October 1894, MNA 50/BMC/2/1/10.
5. Ibid.
6. *Adialeiptos* is a biblical word, used for example by Paul to describe his 'unceasing' prayers in Romans 1:9.
7. Alexander Hetherwick to J. D. McCallum, 23 November 1910, MNA BMC/50/2/1/111.
8. *Life and Work in Nyasaland*, April–December 1917.
9. Alexander Hetherwick to John McIlwain, 8 October 1924, BMC/50/2/1/224.
10. Alexander Hetherwick to W. M. McLachlan, 15 January 1913, MNA BMC/50/2/1/124.
11. Alexander Hetherwick to J. D. McCallum, 8 June 1910, MNA BMC/50/2/1/107.
12. Alexander Hetherwick to W. M. McLachlan, 15 January 1913, MNA BMC/50/2/1/124.
13. W. P. Livingstone, *A Prince of Missionaries: Alexander Hetherwick of Blantyre*, London: James Clarke, n.d., 114.
14. *Life and Work in British Central Africa*, October–November 1904.
15. *Life and Work in Nyasaland*, July–August 1908.
16. Alexander Hetherwick to J. D. McCallum, 1 December 1909, MNA 50/BMC/2/1/103.
17. Alexander Hetherwick, *Romance of Blantyre: How Livingstone's Dream Came True*, London: James Clarke, n.d., 72–73.
18. *Life and Work in British Central Africa*, August–December 1897, cit. Andrew C. Ross, *Blantyre Mission and the Making of Modern Malawi*, Blantyre: CLAIM-Kachere, 1996, repr. Mzuzu: Luviri Press, 2018, 170.
19. *Life and Work in British Central Africa*, April 1897, cit. Harri Englund, '"Africa Is an Education": Vernacular Language and the Missionary Encounter in Nineteenth-century Malawi', in Kenneth R. Ross and Wapulumuka O. Mulwafu (eds), *Politics, Christianity and Society in Malawi: Essays in Honour of John McCracken*, Mzuzu: Mzuni Press, 2020, 138–62, at 145.
20. Alexander Hetherwick to James Paterson (Hon Treasurer FMC), 12 August 1907, MNA 50/BMC/2/1/82.
21. Alexander Hetherwick to Barbara Low, 5 June 1924, MNA BMC/50/2/1/220.
22. Alexander Hetherwick to J. N. Ogilvie, 11 September 1909, MNA 50/BMC/2/1/101.
23. Mission Council meeting at Blantyre, 13 July 1910, MNA 50/BMC/1/1/1.
24. Alexander Hetherwick to W. M. McLachlan, 28 April 1925, MNA BMC/3/1/11.
25. Cit. W. P. Livingstone, *A Prince of Missionaries*, 193.
26. *Life and Work in British Central Africa*, April 1905.
27. Alexander Hetherwick to Dr Caverhill, 27 August 1908, MNA 50/BMC/2/1/92.
28. Livingstone, *A Prince of Missionaries*, 37.
29. Cit. Livingstone, *A Prince of Missionaries*, 177.
30. Alexander Hetherwick, Report of the Blantyre Mission for the Year 1904, MNA 50/BMC/2/1/63.

31. Ibid.
32. *Life and Work in British Central Africa*, December 1904
33. Mission Council meeting at Blantyre, 15 January 1908, MNA 50/BMC/1/1/1.
34. Alexander Hetherwick to J. D. McCallum, 1 December 1909, MNA 50/BMC/2/1/103.
35. Alexander Hetherwick, 'Notes on the Scheme of Readjustment of Mission Methods to Allow of the Extension Into the New Territories of Portuguese East Africa', Blantyre, 28 January 1911, MNA 50/BMC/3/18/2.
36. Ibid.
37. Ibid.
38. Ibid.
39. Alexander Hetherwick to W. M. McLachlan, 22 November 1910, MNA BMC/50/2/1/111.
40. See Gilbert Davison Foster Phiri, 'A History of Education in Blantyre Synod (1876–2018)', PhD, Mzuzu University, 2020; Kelvin N. Banda, *A Brief History of Education in Malawi*, Blantyre: Dzuka, 1982.
41. John McCracken, *A History of Malawi 1859–1966*, Woodbridge: James Currey, 2012, 115.
42. *Life and Work in British Central Africa*, November 1902.
43. Alexander Hetherwick, *The Gospel and the African: the Croall Lectures for 1930–31*, Edinburgh: T. & T. Clark, 1932, 142.
44. World Missionary Conference, 1910, Correspondence of Commission III, Education, submission of The Hon and Rev A. Hetherwick D.D., Nyasaland, 280.215 W893c III, Ecumenical Institute, Bossey, Switzerland.
45. Ibid.
46. Ibid.
47. Ibid.
48. Ibid.
49. See R. J. Macdonald, 'A History of African Education in Nyasaland, 1875–1945', PhD, University of Edinburgh, 1969.
50. Alexander Hetherwick, *The Romance of Blantyre: How Livingstone's Dream Came True*, London: James Clarke, n.d., 230.
51. Alexander Hetherwick, 'Nyasaland Today and Tomorrow', *Journal of the Royal African Society* 17 no. 65 (October 1917), 11–19, at 16.
52. Ibid.
53. World Missionary Conference, 1910, Correspondence of Commission III, Education, submission of The Hon and Rev A. Hetherwick.
54. Ibid.
55. Ibid.
56. Ibid.
57. Ibid.
58. Ibid.
59. Ibid.
60. Alexander Hetherwick to Alexander Mauchline, 1 August 1921, MNA BMC/50/2/1/191.
61. World Missionary Conference, 1910, Correspondence of Commission III, Education, submission of The Hon and Rev A. Hetherwick.
62. Bridglal Pachai, 'A History of Colonial Education for Africans in Malawi', in A. T. Mugomba and M. Nyaggah (eds), *Independence without Freedom: Colonial*

Education in Southern Africa, Oxford: Clio Press, 1980, 133, cit. Gilbert Phiri, 'A History of Education in Blantyre Synod', 63.

63. World Missionary Conference, 1910, Correspondence of Commission III, Education, submission of The Hon and Rev A. Hetherwick.
64. Ibid.
65. Ibid.
66. Alexander Hetherwick, *The Gospel and the African*, 100–1.
67. Ibid., 154–55.
68. Ibid., 155–56.
69. Harri Englund, '"Africa is an Education"', 143.
70. Alexander Hetherwick, *The Gospel and the African*, 156.
71. Ibid., 163
72. Alexander Hetherwick, *The Romance of Blantyre*, 149.
73. Ibid.
74. Alexander Hetherwick, *The Gospel and the African*, 72.
75. Ibid., 109.
76. Ibid., 70–71.
77. Ibid., 101.
78. Ibid., 142–43.
79. Ibid., 144.
80. *Life and Work in British Central Africa*, October 1902.
81. *Life and Work in British Central Africa*, 1899, cit. W. P. Livingstone, *A Prince of Missionaries*, 101.
82. Alexander Hetherwick, 'Notes for Report on Year 1912', MNA BMC/50/2/1/123.
83. Dr Gift Kayira and Dr Hendrina Kachipila have, in fact, initiated a book project on the institution of marriage in the early colonial period, which promises to be a valuable addition to the literature.
84. Summary of the Proceedings of the Fourth Session of the Legislative Council, Held at Zomba on 2–4 November, 1909; see further Joey Power, 'Individual Enterprise and Enterprising Individuals: African Entrepreneurship in Blantyre and Limbe, 1907–1953', PhD, Dalhousie University, 1990.

CHAPTER NINE

The Church Leader: Imagination and Reality

During Hetherwick's later years in Blantyre he was not only Head of the Mission but increasingly had a significant role as a church leader. He had seen the early beginnings of what would become the Blantyre Synod of the Church of Central Africa Presbyterian (CCAP) but at first it was a matter of just a few dozen who had been baptised. By the turn of the century, it was a few hundred and by 1914 had increased to 11,630.[1] In the organisation and development of this emerging church community Hetherwick had a leading role to play. At the same time, he was much occupied with the question of how this young church would be related to the other churches that were emerging in other parts of the Protectorate, particularly those originating from the Livingstonia Mission in the north and the Dutch Reformed Church Mission in the central part of the country. What sort of connection these might have with one another and what kind of church might result from their interaction were questions that loomed large in his mind from the early 1900s onwards.

For his final sixteen years, from 1912 to 1928, Hetherwick lived alone in Blantyre. When he and Elizabeth went on furlough in 1911, they took the decision that Elizabeth and the children, Clement and May, would remain in Scotland while Alexander returned to Blantyre by himself.[2] It was a common dilemma in those days for missionary families – they wanted their children to have the opportunity to be educated in their homeland and either had to leave them in the care of relatives or the mother had to remain at home while the father continued his service overseas. The dilemma was particularly acute for the Hetherwicks, as Alexander later explained to a colleague, 'I think the holiday time is more important for the girls than the school time. It was holiday time that made Mrs Hetherwick stay at home with May – had we had anyone to take her for the holidays it would have been different – but neither of us have any relations and one does not like to entrust one's girl at a most impressionable age with strangers.'[3] In Elizabeth's case, she had lost both the children of her first marriage when they died at an early age in Blantyre so it can well be imagined that the surviving children were very precious and she did not want to be separated from them. Still, she had spent her entire adult life in Blantyre and it must have been quite an adjustment to start a new life in Scotland at the age of fifty. Though it was nothing very unusual at the time, their decision seems to have come as something of a shock to their colleagues in Blantyre. They were quick to express their sympathy, John McIlwain writing to Hetherwick that, 'You will be a lonely man and I am sorry for you'.[4]

Hetherwick seems to have been pragmatic about the situation and always fully absorbed by the many different dimensions of his work in Blantyre. Only occasionally did he reveal some of the feelings he must have had as a result of being separated from his family. When the First World War broke out, his son Clement (aged nineteen) was enlisted in the army like so many of his age-mates, many of whom would not return from the battlefields. Hetherwick wrote poignantly to the Africa Committee Convener that, 'I would not recognize my son now if I met him in his uniform – he is in the RAMC at Stirling and waiting for the call to go to the front.'[5] Even then, he showed the 'stiff upper lip' that was expected at the time, writing to a government official whose son had also gone to the battlefront, 'I hope both our lads may be spared through all this to come home to us again. They are both in the path of duty and we are proud of them.'[6] In the event Clement did survive and the whole family came through their lengthy separation during the war years. Later when he met Dorothy Kidney, a contemporary of May's and saw that she was 'quite a grown up young lady', he reflected, 'I am wondering what like I shall find May when I see her next at home'.[7]

Only periodically were they reunited when Hetherwick returned to Scotland for furloughs in 1917–19 and 1923–24. By the mid-1920s the children had grown up and the family began to think it could be possible for Elizabeth to come back to Blantyre.[8] Returning from furlough in 1924 Alexander wrote to Barbara Low that, 'I am glad to be "home again". I hope Mrs Hetherwick will be able to come out in the end of next year when May has got her training finished.'[9] They made their plans accordingly, but it was not to be. Early in 1926 Hetherwick informed his colleagues, 'I had a wire last night from home – the Doctors have told my wife that it would be unwise of her to come out again – so my bachelor days are still to go on.'[10]

They did not go on, however, for very much longer. By 1928 it was time for Hetherwick to retire to Scotland, allowing the two of them to be reunited for the final decade of his life. They made their home in Aberdeen and joined the parish church to which Alexander had belonged in his youth where he resumed the role of Sunday School Superintendent, which he had relinquished half a century earlier. The year after he returned to Scotland the great church union of 1929 took place, bringing together the Church of Scotland and the United Free Church, which had been separated since 1843. This meant that Blantyre and Livingstonia Missions both now came under the direction of the same Foreign Mission Committee. Hetherwick and Robert Laws, also now retired to Scotland, were both made members of the Committee. They sat together at the back, saying very little. Nevertheless, in W. P. Livingstone's observation, they were 'a strangely arresting pair: Dr Laws with rugged weathered features, white beard and hair, and eyes in which humour gleamed like autumn sunshine;

Dr Hetherwick with round, darkly-tanned face crowned with white and a smile as spontaneous and naïve as a boy's.'[11]

After Alexander's death in 1939, Elizabeth moved to Edinburgh to be near Clement and his family until her own death in 1945, by which time she was the last remaining member of the missionary group that had started Blantyre Mission in the 1870s.

An African Church: Vision and Achievement

From their early days the Blantyre missionaries had imagined the emergence of an African church in response to their work. Unlike at many other missions of the time, the ideas cultivated at Blantyre were not confined to envisaging a replication of the missionaries' home church on African soil. In fact, this was something actively resisted by David Clement Scott, an approach that landed both him and Hetherwick in trouble both with settler opinion and with their own colleagues who were more conservative in their Scottish Presbyterianism. Just before his life was struck by tragic family bereavements, in March 1895 Clement Scott wrote in *Life and Work*: 'When will the larger and wider unity be possible of an African Church, built on the foundations of the Prophets and Apostles, not after the inanity of undenominationalism but after the Catholicity of Primitive Christianity? Why should the sin of home schism be laid on Africa? "Lo we have sinned and done wickedly: but these sheep what have they done?"'[12] This was the vision that had guided the construction of the remarkable St Michael and All Angels Church in Blantyre. It bears no resemblance to an average Scottish parish church but was designed rather, with its Moorish towers and Byzantine domes, to evoke the entire heritage of the universal church on which Scott imagined the African church would draw as it forged its own identity.

As Scott departed Blantyre, bereaved and broken, Hetherwick took up where his colleague had left off, writing in the very next issue of *Life and Work*:

> The African has a part yet to play in the Church of Christ Universal. His character and his influence have still to be reckoned with. In the early days of Christianity the African was a leader in Christian life and thought; while the Church of North Africa sent its representatives to take part in the Great Church Councils. We Christian nations of Europe are the heirs of those ages and of the labours of those men. Our debt has consequently yet to be paid back to the newborn African races of today.[13]

Such thinking was being cultivated by Hetherwick not only as a general notion but in terms of practical proposals for how the worship of the church might develop at Blantyre. Infrequent communion was one of the hallmarks of Scottish Presbyterian churches, with communion being celebrated in some churches only once each year. In Blantyre, Hetherwick envisaged moving in a very different direction: 'The end we look to is a return to the primitive and certainly Apostolic custom of a Weekly Communion. We could not have higher sanction than that of our Lord's own Apostles who on the First day of the week met together for "the breaking of the Bread".'[14] There was no shortage of biblical and ecumenical precedent on which Hetherwick could draw but this was just the kind of proposal that set red lights flashing among diehard Scottish Presbyterians who sensed 'ritualism', 'Anglicanism', 'Romanism' and a departure from what they regarded as the true faith.

Hetherwick himself was conservatively inclined. Had he remained in Aberdeen he might well have been comfortable all his life upholding a traditional Presbyterianism. In fact, however, he had been exposed to the wide spaces of Africa, glimpsed the potential of the people around him and, especially, come under the influence of his theologically adventurous leader Clement Scott. By 1895 he had a much more open outlook as he imagined what an African church might be like:

> We must beware of woodenness in our development of African Life. To attempt to force on Africa the details of Church life and organisation at home is we believe fatal to true growth. African life must be met in it is own way, and it will grow on its own lines. No one who understands the problem before him would dream for a moment of employing the same evangelistic methods in this country as one would do at home. We have said it again and again, and we repeat it doubtless *ad nauseam* that the African has got his own gift of Life and Work to present to the Church Catholic.[15]

This was the kind of open and creative space that Scott and Hetherwick had cultivated at Blantyre, one that was geared to foster the emergence of a truly African church. The snag for them was that they were out of step with their supporting constituency of conservative Scottish Presbyterians who expected to see a church shaped in their own image.

Tension around this issue built up steadily during the 1890s until it came to a head explosively in the Commission of Inquiry into Scott and Hetherwick's leadership that sat in Edinburgh during the early months of 1897. Its conclusion – 'not guilty, but don't do it again' – proved so devastating for Scott that he never recovered and Hetherwick too had hovered on the brink of resignation.[16] The complaints raised against the two of them were most likely driven mainly by differences of outlook on racial matters. The non-racial church that they had been fostering at Blantyre was increasingly at odds with an expectation in the emerging colonial society that church life, like every other aspect of life, should be divided on racial lines. However, their critics accurately sensed that the point at which they were most vulnerable was over the alleged 'ritualism' which touched such a raw nerve in Scotland. The upshot was that the church being formed through the work of the Blantyre Mission was required to, 'develop according to the Constitution of the Church of Scotland'.[17] From that point onwards, the challenge for Hetherwick was how he could keep alive the vision of a truly African church while working within the constraints imposed by his bosses in Scotland. He also had to reckon with the reality that the life and worship of the church had become a battleground on which opposing views of racial issues would fight it out. The race question and the church question had become inextricably intertwined at Blantyre.

One way of making virtue out of necessity was to use the Presbyterian structures that were now being required by Edinburgh to create a vehicle through which the emerging church could come to expression and find its life. When the Mission Council met at Blantyre in mid-1898, with Hetherwick in the chair, it agreed that,

> in view of the future development and extension of the Mission and the growth of the native Church, the Council consider that the spiritual interests of the Mission and the native Church would be advanced by the formation of a Presbytery, and hereby request the Foreign Mission Committee to take such steps as are necessary by application to next General Assembly towards the formation of such a Presbyterial body in connection with the Church of Scotland in British Central Africa.[18]

Not so fast, was the response from Edinburgh as Africa Convener Archibald Scott wrote to say, 'I don't think you are ready for such a step for as far as I know, you have no Kirk Session at any Station, and the Assembly will expect that these foundations be laid before they initiate a Presbytery among you.'[19] The Presbyterian system works through a fourfold hierarchy of courts, with the Kirk Session being the lowest court and operating at local level, the Presbytery bringing together a number of local churches in a particular district, with a Synod bringing together a number of Presbyteries in a particular region, and the General Assembly being the court that operates at national level and has final decision-making authority. Archibald Scott's point was that the new church structure being created at Blantyre had to start at the lowest level and build from there. Hetherwick was to become much accustomed to the slow and cautious instincts of Edinburgh church officials in the years to come.

Meanwhile, the Mission Council in Blantyre had to do what it was told and duly set about establishing Kirk Sessions. What complicated matters was that the issues to be navigated were not only ecclesiastical but also racial. A Kirk Session comprises a minister and a number of elders. The next step was therefore the ordination of the elders who would form the first Kirk Session. Since the General Assembly had already granted authority to European missionaries in East Africa to ordain elders as necessity arose, there was nothing to stop this being done. The snag was that the church congregation at Blantyre was racially mixed, including both Europeans and Africans. In terms of church law there was no need to make any distinction between the elders on racial grounds but there were evidently other forces at work in Blantyre.

As a result, when Hetherwick brought his proposal for the formation of a Kirk Session to the Mission Council in July 1900 it was for a single Kirk Session but with an arrangement whereby the distinct racial communities were recognised. The proposal was couched in the following terms:

1. That a Session be formed consisting of three Europeans to represent the European part of the congregation and five natives meanwhile to represent the native part of the congregation.
2. That all matters of discipline in native cases be referred to the native part of the Session, sitting as a Committee of the whole Session, with a reference and report to the whole Session.
3. That European cases be similarly referred to the European Committee.[20]

The view of the Council was that this arrangement was 'fitted to meet the difficulty of united European and native congregations'.[21] In earlier times Scott and Hetherwick had rejoiced in the worship of a single congregation that transcended racial differences. Now this was regarded as a 'difficulty'. It soon became apparent that this was the thin end of a wedge that would bring an end to the days of Europeans and Africans coming together to worship as one. Meanwhile Henry Scott told the meeting that he planned to form Kirk Sessions on a similar basis at Domasi and Zomba.[22]

Hetherwick did not easily give up the old ideal, writing to Robert Laws in 1904 that, 'I want to see ONE church in Central Africa. I have fought for this in Blantyre here – latterly it has become more difficult with the greater variety of European elements in the country ... still we are one, and if the church is from the beginning laid down on true lines, I think the race feeling in church affairs will not prevail as they have done in the south.'[23] However, there was also a resigned acceptance on Hetherwick's part that notwithstanding the commitment of the Mission to the oneness of the church transcending racial boundaries, in practice even the Blantyre church itself ended up with two congregations during the colonial period: one for Europeans and the other for Africans. 'Theoretically,' observed Hetherwick, 'the two congregations at Blantyre are one, with one session and one session minute book, but in actual practice they are two separate congregations and sessions.'[24] The earlier determination of the Mission to witness to the oneness of the church across the racial divide had not been forgotten by Hetherwick but he had to acknowledge that in practice the Mission had yielded to the expectations of a colonial society by organising separate congregations for Europeans and for Africans. By 1929 he was looking at the appointment of a chaplain to minister exclusively to the Blantyre-based Scots as an unobjectionable development.[25]

Pugnacious though he was, Hetherwick realised that he had to pick his battles. Reluctantly he concluded that it would be a losing battle to attempt to sustain at Blantyre a congregation united across the racial divide. Racist sentiment among the European settlers had fuelled the Commission of Inquiry that had almost finished Hetherwick. If he was to continue with the work to which he was called, he concluded that he would have to go along with the divided worship that was against his better judgement. He hoped it would be a strategic retreat for he had not abandoned his view of what ought to be the case:

> The ideal in the life of the Church in such circumstances would be that of one Church – white and black working together for the kingdom of God and worshipping together side by side in the Lord's House on the Lord's Day – an ideal, however, which nowhere in Central Africa has yet been attained. In the early days of Blantyre, when the number of Church members – both European and Native, was small, and when the sympathies of the few Scottish settlers were entirely with the missionaries in their attitude towards native Christianity, an attempt was made to secure this ideal in the Church there. At the European service, such of our native Christians as understood English attended and took part in the English service. Together they partook of the Holy Communion at the one Holy Table. It was an ideal spectacle, and as one looked at it one hoped that the problem of the one Church was being solved, in Blantyre at least, and the reproach of a divided Christianity taken away.[26]

It was not willingly that Hetherwick departed from the arrangement that he continued to regard as 'ideal'. Many years later, when the Blantyre Mission was preparing to celebrate its golden jubilee in 1926, Hetherwick was determined that the celebration service would be a united event that would bring together Europeans and Africans, English and Chinyanja. He was still inspired by the old ideal and he was still met with objection. This came from one of his closest colleagues on the Mission staff, Frederick Alexander, the minister at Zomba, who wrote to say: 'I think it is a great mistake to mix it – half English, half Chinyanja is bound to mean a mongrel kind of service, lacking in dignity and failing to impress either race. It would have been better to have two separate services.'[27] Hetherwick was unmoved: 'I am sorry you do not like the Mixed Language Service – but we must bring the Natives into it as the fruits of our fifty years work.'[28] This was at the core of Hetherwick's understanding of his vocation and remained always close to his heart.

The circumstances that faced him in Blantyre at the turn of the century, however, particularly with the growth of a European settler population that was determined to hold itself apart from the African community around it, let him to conclude, mournfully, that he would have to conduct separate services for two congregations divided on racial lines:

As the number of European settlers increased, the atmosphere in both Church and social life gradually changed. The sympathies of the outside community towards both Natives and missions gradually cooled, and the breach between colour and colour grew until it became apparent that common worship on the Lord's Day was impossible. Now in Blantyre, as elsewhere in Africa, the two races have each their own service of worship – and each congregation has its own session for the management of its own congregation's affairs. In Presbytery, however, and also in Synod, both races meet and take part, and there at least the Church is one; but alas, only there.[29]

Rhodian Munyenyembe aptly explains Hetherwick's approach: 'As a member of Scott's inner circle, Hetherwick did not completely break with Scott's views though it was very difficult for him to continue with the way Scott was doing it. It became obvious to Hetherwick that in some situations he just had to bow down to the inevitable.'[30] For all his remaining years in Blantyre Hetherwick had to endure what to him was the anomaly of a European congregation worshipping separately Sunday by Sunday. It was the price he felt he had to pay to continue, without undue disturbance, the work with the emerging African church where he found his true purpose and fulfilment.

He did not make any secret of the fact that this was the primary focus of the Blantyre Mission: 'The Native Church. This is the end and aim of all that we are planning and building, and merits the first place in our notice of the work at Blantyre. The African Church – not a mere mission, or an appendage of the home Church – but the body of our Blessed Lord living and growing in the life of the African – that is what we wish to see, with the eye of faith if not with the eye of sight.'[31] The next step towards the fulfilment of this dream was the formation of a Presbytery.

When the Mission Council met early in 1902 it was ready to move forward with this, on the following basis:

1. The Presbytery shall consist of (1) all European Ordained Missionaries; (2) All European Elders; (3) All native ordained Ministers; (4) One representative native Elder from each Session, chosen annually.
2. The Moderator of the Presbytery shall always be one of the ordained European Ministers, who shall be elected annually, the office falling in rotation to the various ministers according to the dates of their ordination, commencing with the senior ordained minister.
3. The Presbytery shall be the final court of appeal in all matters relative to the native church – pending the formation of a Synod or Assembly of the African Church.
4. The Presbytery shall have power to license and ordain native candidates for the ministry, for work in Africa only, on complying with the courses of study sanctioned by the General Assembly, and to exer-

cise discipline over its own licentiates according to the laws of the Church.[32]

Racial identity was also written into the constitution of the Presbytery but, while it accorded certain privilege to its European members, it also looked forward to the day when there would be African ministers and an African Church that would form the supreme court of appeal.

Hetherwick made the best of it and when the Presbytery was duly formed in 1903, he celebrated by interpreting the initiative in terms that recalled the dreams that he and Scott had cherished:

> It means the organisation and development of the native church life as apart from the Mission that was the means of giving it birth. It means that the Church life here can take on a stamp that is its own and not a mere wooden reproduction of the life and character of the home church and home Christianity. The Church must be native and not exotic – and the freest scope must be given to native character in the development of its work and organisation.[33]

This guiding vision ran in uneasy tension with the racism that was intruding into the life of the church during the early twentieth century. Unlike their fiery Livingstonia counterparts in the north, the African Christians at Blantyre were not often provoked to react to racist and colonialist attitudes but even they were moved to object to the way in which the racial division was becoming definitive in the life of the church. Early in 1906 the Blantyre Kirk Session questioned a decision of the Presbytery, 'that it is unconstitutional for a European to hold office in the native eldership and any such ordination is invalid'. They asked, '(1) Why should a European not hold the office of an elder together with native elders? (2) Why is it that such an ordination is unconstitutional and invalid, when the office of the eldership is of the *same Church*?'[34] Good question! In reality it reflected the uneasy compromise by which the Blantyre church of Hetherwick's time accommodated the racist assumptions prevailing in the colonial society of which it was part while still nurturing the vision of a truly African church with its own African government and leadership that had inspired the Mission from its early days.

A high-water mark for Hetherwick, and indeed for all who were involved with Blantyre Mission, was the ordination in 1911 of its first African ministers, Harry Kambwiri Matecheta and Stephen Kundecha. Hetherwick had known them both since they were schoolboys, the former at Blantyre and the latter at Domasi. He had always been there for them, their mentor as they cut their teeth in mission work as evangelists and teachers. For two years he had been their theological tutor, preparing them for ordination. Now he saw them step forward to constitute the start of an African ministry within the life of the Presbytery, Matecheta at Blantyre on 9 March 1911 and Kundecha at Zomba a few days later. On the day after Matecheta's ordination he wrote to his Committee Convener in Scotland: 'Yesterday's Ordination was a day of days in all our lives and brought back the old days when I called Harry then a little urchin with four inches of calico on him to come to the Mission to the school.'[35] He had a keen sense of the historic significance of what was occurring:

> These ordinations mark a new advance in the work on the field. They carry us back to the time centuries ago when foreigners came to the rugged, untamed isle of Britain, some to the Hebrides, some to Galloway, some to Kent, and there, after spreading the Gospel themselves, set apart natives of that island to the work of ministry. First comes the foreigner and the foreign religion. Then comes its adoption by the people as something partly theirs and partly a strange importation. Finally it is their own, an eternal Word for all races and the property of none. A native ministry in part marks the time when that last step has been taken. From that point onward the Church is native and national.[36]

Despite being constrained by the imposition of a Presbyterian structure and despite the colonialist and racist attitudes of the European community having infiltrated the life of the church, nonetheless Hetherwick could glimpse his dream of a truly African church coming to fulfilment. His own attitude to the oneness of the church across racial boundaries was revealed some years later when he was preparing to make a Sunday visit to Domasi and wrote to Barbara Low, the missionary there: 'Please tell Stephen [Kundecha] that I shall be glad to preach on Sunday but I should like him to take the Communion Service – tell him that I have never had Communion from him and it will be something to think of when I recall the way in which Stephen was "called" to the Mission forty years ago.'[37] His wish was fulfilled and he wrote afterwards, 'I was much touched by the Communion Service when Stephen gave me the Communion'.[38]

Meanwhile a memorable week late in 1916 saw another three men ordained to the ministry: Thomas Maseya at Blantyre, Joseph Kaunde at Mulanje and Harry Mtuwa at Zomba. With satisfaction Hetherwick could write to his Committee Secretary: 'Now the native church of Blantyre Presbytery has five native ministers all of them to be supported by the native church'.[39] For him these were very personal occasions that stirred his memory: 'Thomas Maseya! The name brought back old days in Blantyre – three and thirty years ago – when David Clement Scott took the present writer one night down to the dingy brick dormitory to see the Makololo boys – the chiefs' sons sent up from the River to school, and among them this Maseya's son, a little boy of ten or twelve with a piece of calico round his shoulders and another round his waist, and an ivory bracelet on his arm as became a chief's son.'[40] He remembered Harry Mtuwa as 'a scholar in Domasi twenty five years ago – then a round faced little lad, earnest and thoughtful. He is now an earnest and thoughtful man who will draw others

Figure 9.1 The Wedding of Lewis and Grace Bandawe, conducted by Alexander Hetherwick, Blantyre Mission, 1913

to him by his strength – not clever or brilliant but strong.'[41] It was through such men that he saw dreams beome reality.

Here there was a clear parting of the ways between the Blantyre Mission and the colonial government. One of the provisions of the 1912 Native Marriage Ordinance was that the government would license clergy who were authorised to conduct marriages. Hetherwick sent in the names of the ministers who were serving with Blantyre Mission at the time: himself, Smith, Anderson, Alexander, Napier, Bowman, Matecheta and Kundecha. The response of the government was to send licenses for all the European ministers but not for Matecheta and Kundecha. The only explanation was a terse note to the effect that, 'His Excellency does not propose to licence any native ministers of any mission at present'.[42] The confidence Blantyre Mission had shown in its African ministers was clearly not shared by the government. Hetherwick, of course, was undeterred.

When he returned to Blantyre in 1919, after a long furlough at the end of the First World War, he was scathing in his assessment of the demoralisation he witnessed in the European community but struck a very different note in regard to the African church: 'One thing has cheered me on my return and that is that the Native Ministry and the Native Church have come well through the trying ordeal. They have had trying times and hard work for the European help in the native churches has had to be very small. But they have all done well.'[43] It was in the ministers, elders and members of the African church that his hopes for the future were invested.

Hetherwick, though not without his own patriarchal instincts, was also ahead of his time in regard to the role of women in church and society. In the mid-1920s, the Blantyre Mission hospital was running highly effectively under the direction of Dr Elizabeth McCurrach. When the Committee in Scotland proposed that a new male doctor should, on arrival, be put in charge of the hospital, displacing McCurrach, Hetherwick was appalled. He wrote:

> She is a very capable woman of great tact and great thoughtfulness together with a power of management that has freed her from the many difficulties that usually beset a newcomer into this country . . . To set her aside from the charge of the Hospital to which she was appointed or in any way to lead her to believe that things were not efficiently carried on would be such a slight on her as would lead to unpleasant complications . . . She is a thorough missionary in all her work and outlook. Her linguistic powers are very high. Indeed, in every way she is an asset to the mission and to the Hospital which we should be thankful for.[44]

Besides the particular case of the Blantyre hospital, Hetherwick put the issue in broader perspective: '. . . to set her aside because "she is a woman" would cast a slight on the women of our staff which they would I feel sure most certainly and justly resent. We shall have to depend more and more on women for the future staffing of the mission, and any step such as you propose would not advance our cause.'[45] It was a theme to which he often returned in his later years, expressing his confidence that women would have a growing role in the leadership of the Mission in years to come.

So far as the African community was concerned, girls' education had been prominent from an early stage, particularly through the remarkable pioneering work of Janet Beck at Blantyre and Margaret Christie at Domasi and Zomba. In his submission to the 1910 World Missionary Conference, Hetherwick stated that, 'We aim in our work at a higher ideal of the life and influence of African womanhood. There is a long lee-way to be made up in this direction by the African woman. In her heathen state she was a beast of burden, a slave, a chattel. Christianity has given her a place and freedom. Now she has to be taught to realise that freedom and to use it right.'[46] He looked forward to the educational advancement of women: 'As yet we have done little or nothing in the way of training women teachers, but now we intend to use the services of the younger ones who are through the lower standards of the school and who are going on to the higher standards as teachers in the junior Department of the school.'[47] These hopes came to fruition as commitment to the development of girls' education became a marked feature of the work of Blantyre Mission during the 1920s, 1930s and beyond.[48]

Architect of Church Union

When Scott and Hetherwick, in the heyday of their partnership, had been able to let their imagination run free as regards what kind of church might emerge from the work of the Mission, the question of church union loomed large in their thinking. The question of union was closely integrated with the question of enabling a truly African church to emerge. They could see no good reason for all the denominational divisions of European Christianity to be imported into Africa. 'Could not the various Missions,' asked Hetherwick in 1896, 'send their representatives to a Council, held say in Blantyre township or in the Mission, and see how far Catholic Christianity could come to agreement respecting Orders, Sacraments, Church doctrine and founding for the Native Church of Africa?'[49] It was an ambitious ecumenical vision, which would never be fulfilled as he first imagined. Nevertheless, it remained a guiding light for Hetherwick and inspired his work in bringing the missions and churches into closer relations with one another. This bore fruit first in the creation of the Federated Board of Missions in Nyasaland in 1910 and later in the formation of the Church of Central Africa Presbyterian in 1924.

The Federated Board was the institutional outcome of a growing cooperation among the main Protestant missions in the Protectorate, which found expression in periodic conferences. Hetherwick wrote at length to Commission VIII of the Edinburgh 1910 World Missionary Conference, which was concerned with cooperation and the promotion of unity.[50] He explained that representatives of all Protestant missions in Nyasaland had gathered first at Livingstonia in 1900 and then at Blantyre in 1904. Those represented were the Livingstonia Mission of the United Free Church of Scotland, the Blantyre Mission of the Church of Scotland, the Dutch Reformed Church of South Africa, the London Missionary Society, the Zambesi Industrial Mission, the Nyasaland Industrial Mission, the Scottish Baptist Mission, the South Africa General Mission, the Berlin Mission in German East Africa and the Moravian Mission in German East Africa.[51] He noted that the Universities Mission to Central Africa and the various Roman Catholic Societies 'stand aloof from these Conferences entirely'.[52] In his estimation the conferences had been successful in deciding on lines of General Mission policy, in creating and fostering a mutual sympathy and co-operation between the various missions at work in the country, and in paving the way for a closer federation of both the missions and the native church represented.[53]

A major achievement has been the adoption of a common Educational Code in 1900 and the appointment of a permanent Board of Education in 1904. On this basis the missions had been able to reach an agreement with the government under which they received grants-in-aid to help support their educational work.[54] They also reached important agreements on ecclesiastical matters, such as not 'encroaching' on one another's territory and acceptance of one another's certificates of membership when a church member moved to a new area.[55] This collaboration was set on a permanent basis a few months after the Edinburgh 1910 World Missionary Conference when Nyasaland's third major Missionary Conference was held at Mvera where Hetherwick was elected President and the Federated Board of Missions was formed. The message of Edinburgh 1910 that greater cooperation among the missions would strengthen their evangelistic work found a ready response among the Protestant missions of Nyasaland.

The Edinburgh 1910 World Missionary Conference had excluded ecclesiastical questions from its consideration since these were thought to be divisive whereas the participants found unity in their common commitment to the missionary task. A surprising outcome, however, was that the achievement of unity for the sake of mission stimulated the idea of working for church unity in many different parts of the world. Nyasaland was a case in point. No sooner had the Presbytery been formed at Blantyre than Hetherwick was thinking that it was just a first step on the further journey that would lead to a wider church union: 'This is another step in the foundation of the Church of Central Africa. The final step is, we hope, not far distant when we will join with the other Presbyteries in a General Synod of all the churches who acknowledge the Presbyterian form of church government.'[56] Hetherwick saw the way ahead very clearly and he was a man in a hurry:

> A union of two Presbyteries would give us a court of final appeal in all matters affecting the comity of the native churches and strengthen the hands of each in dealing with the many problems that arise in the organisation of native Christianity. We cannot come together too soon, so that the lines of policy and method may be laid down while the churches are yet young.[57]

Meanwhile the series of Missionary Conferences that led to the creation of the Federated Board of Missions in 1910 stimulated at the same time the idea of church union. Young African churches were being born through the work of all the different missions. Might they form one church instead of many different ones? Such an idea caught the imagination of missionaries such as Donald Fraser of Livingstonia and Hetherwick of Blantyre. They imagined the possibility of one African church resulting from the work of all the missions represented in the Federated Board. Failing that, the next best thing would be that at least the Presbyterian or Reformed missions, which already had so much in common, might combine to create a united church. At each of the Missionary Conferences, additional sessions were organised to allow representatives of Livingstonia, Blantyre and the Dutch Reformed Church Mission to explore this possibility.

To set this movement on a formal basis, shortly before the 1904 Missionary Conference, Hetherwick brought a motion to the Presbytery of Blantyre at its meeting on 11 May 1904, 'that the Presbytery appoint a committee for the purpose of taking steps to join with the Presbytery of North Livingstonia in the formation and constitution of a synod of the Church of Central Africa Presbyterian'.[58] The motion was unanimously agreed and this enabled representatives of the Presbytery to meet with their Livingstonia counterparts during the 1904 Missionary Conference. History was being made. Though it would be twenty years before the Church of Central Africa Presbyterian came into being, its origins can be traced back to Hetherwick's motion. When the Blantyre committee met with its counterpart from Livingstonia, with observers present also from the Dutch Reformed Church Mission, Hetherwick moved that Robert Laws take the chair while he found himself becoming heavily involved in the work of the sub-committees on the creed and constitution of the new church.[59]

Having launched the process with much energy and enthusiasm, it rather stalled over the next few years as attention turned to matters of detail. By 1909 Donald Fraser was writing impatiently to Hetherwick:

> It is a deplorable fact that we are getting no nearer either to federation or union. The various churches have gone no further yet with the discussion of federation, though the Dutch brethren have written to say they are still keeping it in mind. Now even if all the missions are only prepared to go the length of Federation, it seems to me that we of the Livingstonia and Blantyre and Mvera Missions must not stop short of Union.[60]

By the time they met at Mvera the following year, they were ready to take firm steps:

> It was unanimously agreed that in the opinion of the joint Committee appointed by the Blantyre and North Livingstonia Presbyteries it will make for the extension of the Kingdom of God and the glory of the Lord Jesus Christ that the Presbyteries should now be united in one Synod of a common Church.
>
> It was agreed that the name of the Church be 'The Church of Central Africa, Presbyterian'.
>
> That the creedal basis of the Church be the Apostles' Creed for members and the Nicene Creed for office-bearers, and that the worship and order of the Church be Presbyterian.
>
> That the government of the Church be on the Presbyterian basis, by sessions, presbyteries and synods.
>
> That each presbytery shall meantime retain its present constitution.
>
> That the synod shall consist of all the ordained ministers, with an equal number of elders chosen by the presbyteries.
>
> That the synod shall meet every three years.
>
> That European members of Presbytery shall continue in their present relations to the home Churches.[61]

This agreement was enthusiastically adopted by the church courts both at Livingstonia and Blantyre so that by February 1912 Hetherwick was in a position to write to Edinburgh to request the approval of the General Assembly. Since moves were already being made in Scotland for a reunion of Blantyre and Livingstonia's two mother churches, the Church of Scotland and the United Free Church, his request was well received.

Meanwhile in Nyasaland, two issues had required much discussion. The first was the question of what the name of the church should be. The joint committee of the two mother churches in Scotland had recommended 'The Presbyterian Church in Africa' but this was regarded as emphasising the non-African, Presbyterian element too much. 'The Church of Central Africa', Donald Fraser's preference, was viewed as ignoring the Presbyterian element entirely. Hetherwick, still moved by the old ideals he had shared with Clement Scott, explained that 'Central Africa' was stressed because 'we mean it to be the Church of the land and people'.[62] His point was taken but the term 'Presbyterian' was added at the end rather than at the beginning as was more common with Presbyterian churches. Tension remained about whether the new church's identity was a matter of the 'land and people' or of its Presbyterian character. It was a tension that was left to be resolved by history. More than 100 years later the name agreed at Mvera in 1910 is still in place.[63]

The second major decision was that European missionaries would continue to be subject to the courts of their home churches, rather than to those of the new church coming into being. Hetherwick's starting point on this issue had been very different. He wrote to Robert Laws in 1904 to insist that, 'Missionaries who come out from the Home Church must throw in their lot with the church they are sent to here, and put themselves under the jurisdiction of the local church courts. There can be no half measures in the matter: the Home Church must learn to trust the good sense of their daughters in the foreign field ... the local church must be independent of the Home Church, that is my point.'[64] This proved to be another losing battle in the racialised atmosphere of the time. When Hetherwick reported to the Edinburgh 1910 Commission in 1909, he had to concede that 'the position of the European Missionary in the Constitution of the United Synod' had proved to be a 'difficulty'.[65] The fact that the European ministers and elders did not become part of the new church was presented as an opportunity for a truly African church to come into being, unconstrained by the European way of doing things. However, it also gave rise to a church that was divided on racial lines and could be seen as a failure to witness to oneness in Christ. Once again, racial attitudes subverted sound ecclesiology. It took the crisis of the Federation years in the 1950s to demonstrate that this division was unsustainable and in 1959 Church of Scotland ministers entered fully into the structures of the CCAP.

Meanwhile the Missionary Conference that had been planned for Livingstonia in 1914, where it was hoped to bring the united church into being, had to be postponed indefinitely because of the outbreak of the First World War. It was not until 1924 that it was possible to convene the

Conference. After it concluded, the ministers and elders of Blantyre and Livingstonia met together and formally constituted the Church of Central Africa Presbyterian. It might not have been all that Scott and Hetherwick had hoped for in terms of a truly African church that was unencumbered by the ecclesiastical divisions imposed by European history. Nevertheless, after twenty years of patiently working towards this union, it was a day of no small achievement for Hetherwick when it became a reality.

An Indigenous Church

Whether in the week-by-week development of the young churches emerging from the work of the Blantyre Mission or in the patient work across decades to bring the nationwide Church of Central Africa Presbyterian into being, the driving passion of Hetherwick's life was that a truly African church might be the end result: 'We must keep a Native church in view, a Church that will be in line with native life and thought and not an exotic fed on artificial philosophy.'[66] This was the idea, suggests his biographer, 'which was to dominate all his thoughts and energies'.[67] It made him rather self-critical. Late in life he reflected on the pattern of worship that had developed in the Blantyre Mission congregations and noted the contrast with traditional African worship, which featured clapping of hands, swinging of the body, ululation and dancing. This prompted the question in his mind:

> Do we Scots missionaries do right by our converts in imposing on them our own quiet, solemn and expressionless form of worship . . . Have we, Scots folk, by the sombreness of our forms of worship which we have imposed on him, given the African an equivalent for that visible and physical expression of his feelings which his old form of worship afforded him?[68]

Little did Hetherwick know that he was anticipating the pentecostalisation of worship that would be such a marked feature of Malawian Christianity in the early twenty-first century.[69]

He could not know what lay ahead but he did know where the answer to his questions would come from: 'On this subject, as on so many others that the would-be reformer of the African peoples is faced with every day, the African himself will in his own time give his own opinions in his own way.'[70] At the height of the colonial era, most Europeans regarded the African as a 'child rather than a man', to borrow the language of Andrew Ross.[71] Much as Hetherwick could lapse into a paternalistic attitude at times, his fundamental confidence in the Africans with whom he was working, and their potential to shape the future, never wavered. Though it would be another generation before Malawians would take over full responsibility for the leadership of their churches, Hetherwick in 1930 was already looking forward to that day: 'The young African Church has as yet much to learn, especially in the matter of the management of its finances. But assuredly the day will come – sooner perhaps than we at present dream, when the Native Church will ask to be set free to order its own life in its own way.'[72]

Such was the force of racist and colonialist thinking during the early decades of the twentieth century that it could appear as if the dreams of an indigenous church that Scott and Hetherwick cherished had come to nothing. Hetherwick felt he had no choice but to accommodate the expectations of a colonial society but he worked within it towards the creation of the indigenous church that would outlast it. The dreams of Scott and Hetherwick were never completely extinguished. Just a few months after he retired and left Blantyre for the last time, a newly arrived missionary Patrick Borrowman wrote to his successor James Reid: 'I entirely agree that we are not bound to uphold here the Presbyterian System in its entirety as it exists at home. We have to evolve an indigenous Presbyterianism, and not transplant a Western System readymade.'[73] The spirit of Scott and Hetherwick lived on.

Notes

1. *Reports of the Schemes of the Church of Scotland 1915*, Edinburgh: William Blackwood, 1915, 297–98.
2. See John McCracken, 'Class, Violence and Gender in Early Colonial Malawi: The Curious Case of Elizabeth Pithie', *Society of Malawi Journal* 64/2 (2011), 12.
3. Alexander Hetherwick to A. Melville Anderson, 22 April 1919, MNA BMC/50/2/1/164.
4. John McIlwain to Alexander Hetherwick, 22 February 1911, MNA 50/BMC/3/18/2.
5. Alexander Hetherwick to J. D. McCallum, 16 August 1915, MNA 50/BMC/2/2/8.
6. Alexander Hetherwick to W. Wheeler, HM Admin, 7 December 2016, MNA 50/BMC/2/2/9.
7. Alexander Hetherwick to J. F. Alexander, 15 June 1922, MNA BMC/50/2/1/200.
8. J. Sabiston to Alexander Hetherwick, 12 August 1925, MNA 50/BMC/2/2/16.
9. Alexander Hetherwick to Barbara Low, 14 March 1924, MNA BMC/50/2/1/217.
10. Alexander Hetherwick to J. F. Alexander, 11 February 1926, MNA BMC/50 2/2/16.
11. W. P. Livingstone, *A Prince of Missionaries*, London: James Clarke, n.d., 203.
12. *Life and Work in British Central Africa*, March 1895.
13. *Life and Work in British Central Africa*, April 1895.
14. *Life and Work in British Central Africa*, May 1895.
15. *Life and Work in British Central Africa*, September 1895.
16. See Chapter Three above.
17. Archibald Scott to Alexander Hetherwick, 30 November 1898, NLS 7537/47–49.
18. Mission Council, meeting at Blantyre, 6 July 1898, MNA 50/BMC/1/1/1.
19. Archibald Scott to Alexander Hetherwick 30 November 1898, NLS 7537/47–49.

20. Mission Council meeting at Blantyre, 11 July 1900, MNA 50/BMC/1/1/1.
21. Ibid.
22. Ibid.
23. Alexander Hetherwick to Robert Laws, 9 August 1904, cit. Andrew Ross, *Blantyre Mission and the Making of Modern Malawi*, Blantyre: CLAIM-Kachere, 1996, repr. Mzuzu: Luviri Press, 2018, 233.
24. Alexander Hetherwick, *Romance of Blantyre: How Livingstone's Dream Came True*, London: James Clarke, n.d., 126.
25. Ibid., 257.
26. Alexander Hetherwick, *The Gospel and the African: the Croall Lectures for 1930–31*, Edinburgh: T. & T. Clark, 1932, 172–73.
27. J. F. Alexander to Alexander Hetherwick, 6 Sept 1926, MNA 50/BMC/2/2/23.
28. Alexander Hetherwick to J. F. Alexander, 6 Sept 1926, MNA 50/BMC/2/2/23.
29. Alexander Hetherwick, *The Gospel and the African*, 173.
30. Rhodian Munyenyembe, *Pursuing an Elusive Unity: A History of the Church of Central Africa Presbyterian as a Federative Denomination (1924–2018)*, London: Langham, 2019, 71.
31. *Life and Work in British Central Africa*, January 1903.
32. Mission Council meeting at Blantyre, 11 February 1902, MNA 50/BMC/1/1/1.
33. *Life and Work in British Central Africa*, January 1903.
34. Letter from the Blantyre Mission Native Session to the Presbytery, 6 January 1906, signed Cedric R. Masangano, Clerk, MNA 50/BMC/2/1/72, italics original.
35. Alexander Hetherwick to W. M. McLachlan, 10 March 1911, MNA BMC/50/2/1/114.
36. *Life and Work in Nyasaland*, April–May 1911.
37. Alexander Hetherwick to Barbara Low, 16 June 1924, MNA BMC/50/2/1/220.
38. Alexander Hetherwick to Barbara Low, 10 July 1924, MNA BMC/50/2/1/221.
39. Alexander Hetherwick to W. M. McLachlan, 6 November 2016, BMC/50/2/1/146.
40. Alexander Hetherwick, 'Three Ordinations in Nyasaland', MNA BMC/50/2/1/147.
41. Ibid.
42. Government Secretary's Office to Head of the Blantyre Mission, 10 May 1913, MNA BMC/50/2/1/127.
43. Alexander Hetherwick to J. L. Ogilvie, 31 March 1919, MNA BMC/50/2/1/163.
44. Alexander Hetherwick to W. M. McLachlan 5 August 1924 NLS 7608/113.
45. Ibid.
46. World Missionary Conference, 1910, Correspondence of Commission III, Education, submission of The Hon and Rev A. Hetherwick D.D., Nyasaland, 280.215 W893c III, Ecumenical Institute, Bossey, Switzerland.
47. Ibid.
48. See Gilbert Davison Foster Phiri, 'A History of Education in Blantyre Synod (1876–2018)', PhD, Mzuzu University, 2020, especially 157–60.
49. *Life and Work in British Central Africa*, September 1896.
50. World Missionary Conference, 1910, Correspondence of Commission VIII, Cooperation and the Promotion of Unity, 280.215 W893c VIII, Ecumenical Institute, Bossey, Switzerland, The Hon and Rev A. Hetherwick Central Africa, No. 83.

51. Ibid.
52. Ibid.
53. Ibid.
54. Ibid.
55. Ibid.
56. *Life and Work in British Central Africa*, September 1902.
57. Ibid.
58. Blantyre Presbytery meeting, 11 May 1904, Presbytery of Blantyre, 'History of the Movement for Union between the Presbyteries of Blantyre and Livingstonia', 5 February 1912, MNA 50/BMC/3/2/1.
59. Committee of North Livingstonia and Blantyre Presbyteries, meeting at Blantyre on 19 October 1904, Blantyre Presbytery files, MNA 50/BMC/3/2/1.
60. Donald Fraser to Alexander Hetherwick, 20 December 1909, MNA 50/BMC/3/2/1.
61. Presbytery of Blantyre, 'History of the Movement for Union between the Presbyteries of Blantyre and Livingstonia', 5 February 1912, MNA 50/BMC/3/2/1.
62. Alexander Hetherwick, cit. John McCracken, *Politics and Christianity in Malawi 1875–1940: The Impact of the Livingstonia Mission in the Northern Province*, Cambridge: Cambridge University Press, 1977; 2nd ed., Blantyre: CLAIM, 2000, 294.
63. See further Rhodian Munyenyembe, *Pursuing an Elusive Unity*.
64. Alexander Hetherwick to Robert Laws, 9 August 1904, cit. Andrew Ross, *Blantyre Mission and the Making of Modern Malawi*, 232.
65. World Missionary Conference, 1910, Correspondence of Commission VIII, Cooperation and the Promotion of Unity, 280.215 W893c VIII, Ecumenical Institute, Bossey, Switzerland, The Hon and Rev A. Hetherwick Central Africa, No. 83.
66. Cit. Livingstone, *A Prince of Missionaries*, 44–45.
67. Ibid., 45.
68. Alexander Hetherwick, *The Gospel and the African*, 63–64.
69. See Kenneth R. Ross and Klaus Fiedler, *A Malawi Church History 1860–2020*, Mzuzu: Mzuni Press, 2020, 362–77.
70. Alexander Hetherwick, *The Gospel and the African*, 64.
71. Andrew C. Ross, 'The African – A Child or a Man: the Quarrel between the Blantyre Mission of the Church of Scotland and the British Central Africa Administration, 1890–1905', in Eric Stokes and Richard Brown (eds), *The Zambesian Past: Studies in Central African History*, Manchester: Manchester University Press, 1966, 332–51.
72. Alexander Hetherwick, *The Gospel and the African*, 149–50.
73. P. H. Borrowman to James Reid, 14 August 1928, MNA 50/BMC/2/2/30.

CHAPTER TEN

Missionary *and* Empire Builder?
Tensions and Contradictions

After Hetherwick's death a plaque was erected in his memory in his home church, the West Church of St Nicholas in Aberdeen. On it he is remembered as, 'PIONEER MISSIONARY AND EMPIRE BUILDER'. Though he cannot be held responsible for the epithet, he might not have been entirely uncomfortable with it. At the time, Mission and Empire were widely assumed to be very closely related and Hetherwick was an exemplar. Though there was never any doubt that his missionary calling was the primary one, he had also played his part in the building of the Empire. He had campaigned successfully for the establishment of the British Protectorate in Nyasaland, and he had become one of its most prominent civic figures, serving terms on the Legislative Council, being one of the first members of Blantyre Town Council, playing a leading role in the Chamber of Commerce and developing a high profile as an activist and campaigner on a wide range of social, economic and political issues. Admittedly he was a 'critical friend' and often a thorn in the side of the British Administration, but he identified strongly with the British Empire, which he viewed as, on the whole, a benign influence.

From the late nineteenth century, it was widely assumed that the Christian missionary enterprise and European colonial rule were close allies, even if there might occasionally be tensions between them. When J. D. McCallum was covering for Hetherwick during his furlough in 1906 he caught the spirit of the times when he gave his assessment of Hetherwick's status:

> It has been the good fortune of the Church of Scotland to have had located here one so scholarly, so practical, so capable an organiser and administrator, so whole-heartedly missionary. In the development of this land, and alike to the advantage of European and native, the Mission has played a great and honourable part, and when the history of the makers of this new portion of His Majesty's Dominions comes to be written, a very high place in it will be occupied by Dr Hetherwick.[1]

Such words were written out of a complacent assumption that the dual role of missionary and 'empire builder' was an admirable one. There was little expectation at this time that imperialism and colonialism would come to be discredited and the reputation of missionaries such as Hetherwick would suffer severely because of their supposed complicity with it. Our examination of his career, however, suggests that perhaps a more nuanced consideration is needed. He cuts something of a contradictory figure, on the one hand a prominent figure in the advent of British colonial rule in Malawi yet, on the other hand, so strongly identified with the African community that he regularly took a line that was subversive of colonial assumptions. What are we to make of the tensions and contradictions that we have identified in Hetherwick's life?

Hetherwick and the Empire

There is no doubt that Blantyre Mission was loyal to the British Empire. While Hetherwick could be sharply critical of specific policy decisions, he took the view that British rule was beneficial overall and identified himself with it. After all, it was the Blantyre Mission that had campaigned for the imposition of British rule in the late 1880s when it looked likely that the Shire Highlands would fall to Portugal as the 'scramble for Africa' took effect. Hetherwick always looked back on this as a close shave, when everything he had been working for in the Shire Highlands was in jeopardy. He was forever grateful that, 'just in time the British Government stepped in – just in the nick of time, for the Christian side in the struggle had practically reached the limit of its resources ... The situation in a few more months would have been impossible, and the forces of Christianity and civilization would have been compelled to withdraw. The gate that Livingstone opened and which he asked the Cambridge students not to allow to be shut again, would have been closed in our face and on a slave-driven people with none to befriend them.'[2] The conclusion he drew was that, 'For the action taken by the British Government at that time, as well as for the *Pax Britannica* that followed, the cause of missionary enterprise in Central Africa cannot voice a too grateful meed of praise.'[3]

As time went on and colonial rule became the established order, Hetherwick in common with the vast majority of missionaries accepted it as the best available option. Indeed, the Mission played an active role in promoting the compliance of African communities with the imperial order. Revealingly, Hetherwick liked to recall that David Livingstone, while he was a missionary par excellence, was also, during the travels that brought him to Malawi, British Consul for the Region of the Central African Lakes and thus an official representative of the British government.[4] It seems that in Hetherwick's mind this recollection operated as a justification for viewing his own missionary vocation as also being closely connected with British imperial rule. When Nyasaland became a Crown Colony in 1907, he was unequivocal in his affirmation: 'Those who remember the early struggles to secure the establishment of a Protectorate over this part of Africa cannot but feel that this is the goal of their efforts and rejoice to see the just and firm rule of the British Crown thus confirmed over the tribes and peoples among whom our Mission was first founded thirty two years ago. *Laus Deo* [Praise God].'[5]

Another incident that demonstrated the identification of Blantyre Mission with British colonial rule was the coronation of King Edward VII in 1902. The Zomba and Domasi Missions organised a letter of congratulation to be sent on behalf of the people of Nyasaland. No doubt with coaching from Henry Scott, the resident missionary, the letter was expressed in the following terms: 'To our Great Chief. The chiefs and people of this land rejoice that you are being crowned to be our Great Chief. We grieved when our Queen whom we much loved died, now God has given us you that you may rule over us your loyal children.'[6]

The way in which Hetherwick introduces this incident in his account of Blantyre Mission history is revealing. He recalls how in 1900 word reached Blantyre of a famine in many parts of India and of how moved he was that the congregations at Blantyre and other stations of the Mission took the initiative to raise funds to send assistance to their needy fellow Christians in India. This evoked for Hetherwick the collections organised by Paul in New Testament times when his recently founded congregations generously contributed to the relief of the church at Jerusalem during a time of famine. From this he moves seamlessly to the message sent to King Edward in 1902, which he describes as, '*a similar instance* of the new realization by the native of a wider community . . .'[7] The two incidents might be considered 'similar' in terms of Africans in Malawi gaining greater awareness of the wider world beyond their own continent. Nonetheless it is striking that a sense of belonging to the universal church could be associated in Hetherwick's mind with a sense of belonging to the British Empire without any sense of incongruity.

He also took it for granted that it was reasonable and acceptable for Africans in Nyasaland to be recruited into the imperial army and to put their lives at risk in combat.[8] There is a poignant passage in his memoir where he reflects on the 'price of Empire' being 'paid even by lonely dwellers in remote native villages among the hills of Yaoland and the lake shore of Nyasa'.[9] He recounts an incident when a battalion of the King's African Rifles returned to Zomba after a tour of duty in Somaliland. Among the welcoming crowd was a woman who had travelled eighty miles to welcome her six soldier sons who had been among the troops. On enquiry, she discovered that all six had been killed. Hetherwick clearly had human feeling for the devastating bereavement that the woman had suffered but his concluding reflection is simply that she 'had paid her share in full of the "price of Empire"' as if this were somehow defensible and indicative of some moral virtue.[10]

The commitment of the Mission to the cause of the Empire was particularly strongly apparent during the First World War. There was no hesitation on the part of the Mission in making available its personnel and resources to assist the British forces. Hetherwick could be sure of full support from his Committee in Scotland for any sacrifices made in the interests of the war effort. Its Convener J. N. Ogilvie wrote, 'I was delighted to hear of the substantial help the Mission staff have been able to give to the expeditionary force, and though the temporary loss of valuable members of staff is sure to check some useful work, I quite agree with your council in heartily recognizing the greater need. The FMC [Foreign Mission Committee] will to a man, share the feeling.'[11] The role of the Mission included playing a key role in the mobilisation of the large numbers of *tengatenga* (carriers) who were needed to support the war effort and who suffered grievously as a result.[12]

It took John Chilembwe to point out the injustice and tragedy of Malawians being mobilised to suffer and die in a war that was not of their making nor in any way being fought in their interest.[13] There was no such compunction on the part of Hetherwick or the Blantyre Mission. In fact, Robert Napier, the rising star among Blantyre missionaries, was a key player in mobilising Malawians to participate in a war that in the end would claim his own life as well as many of theirs. When Hetherwick later recalled the heavy losses suffered at the Battle of Karonga in 1914, after an encomium to the handful of British soldiers who were killed, he describes the far greater number of African troops who died as 'the pioneers of the thousands and thousands of native soldiers and native carriers who were to fall in that long wide front in East Africa . . .'[14] – as if this was simply something to be naturally expected in the line of duty. Even here, however, when Hetherwick is apparently most identified with the imperial cause, he reveals an awareness that there could be another side to the story: '. . . the African rarely reveals his mind. All that the war years taught him and revealed to him will come out some day.'[15] Here is a humility and a sensitivity to the experience of the African community that would not be found with someone who was a straightforward imperialist.

He also stood out from the prevailing European attitude by protesting about the imbalance that provided for European soldiers who were killed to be remembered with honour while no such recognition was given to the African troops who fell. After honouring the Europeans who fell at the Battle of Karonga in 1914, he went on: 'Of the native soldiers who died by their side we have no record; but their service was the same. Like their brothers who were killed in Ashanti and Somaliland, they laid down their lives in the service to the King and in defence of the Empire which has given their country the richest blessings which any nation or people can receive, the blessings of freedom and peace.'[16]

This was an issue that gained public attention in 2019 when Channel 4 in the UK broadcast a programme titled *Unremembered: Britain's Forgotten War Heroes*, presented by black Labour MP David Lammy.[17] It revealed how more than 100,000 Africans who died fighting for Britain during the First World War were denied an individual grave while the Imperial War Graves Commission took great pains to ensure that such recognition was given to all European soldiers who lost their lives. This prompted an official inquiry by the Commonwealth War Graves Commission, which reported in 2021 and concluded that there had indeed been inequality in the commemoration of the dead, with discrimination on racial grounds.[18]

Hetherwick was among the few who recognised at the time the discrepancy between the honours bestowed on the British heroes of the war and African troops who were killed. He also lamented the lack of recognition that followed for the *tengatenga* (carriers) who had borne the greatest suffering and without whom the war would never have been won:

> But the native carriers, the 'tenga-tenga' as they are called in the native tongue, the men who in their tens and tens of thousands fell on the line of communications, stricken down by hardships and disease – the men of whom General Northey said, 'the tenga-tenga won the war' – those of them who survived, battered broken and maimed for life many of them, crept home to their villages, unpensioned, unmedalled, undecorated, uncheered, the heroes of the war, the saviours of the Empire in Africa.[19]

Hetherwick could see that there was a poignant incongruity in the lack of recognition experienced by the carriers who had played such a vital role and at such great cost to themselves.[20] He could not see, as Chilembwe did, that this bitter experience called the whole imperial project into question.

The Mission and the Settlers: Keeping a Distance

At one level Hetherwick was highly integrated into the European order that now began to hold sway in Nyasaland. He was among its best-known public figures, prominent in the affairs of the Legislative Council and the Chamber of Commerce. He became a close friend of the Governor, Sir Alfred Sharpe, despite their having crossed swords on several occasions.[21] Yet at another level he kept his distance out of a keen appreciation that the purpose of the Mission was very different from that of the emerging European community in Nyasaland. At a time in 1896 when the Foreign Mission Committee in Scotland was proposing to curtail the expenditure of the Blantyre Mission because of financial pressures, Hetherwick resisted the proposal not because of the need for mission in the African community but rather because of the need to counter the influence of the European community. With typical vigour he wrote:

> This is not the time for curtailment or retrenchment in British Central Africa. The forces of the world, the flesh, the devil are pouring into the country, and are settling round and near Blantyre especially. The settlement here seems fated to become the centre of a European civilisation and life that is totally irreligious, anti-native, anti-mission, anti-Christian. In such a community the Mission must always be a

conscience, and the present necessity of a strong Mission becomes at once apparent.[22]

This hardly sounds like someone who is going to blend easily into the emerging colonial society. He maintained this sense of suspicion and hostility towards the European presence, even as he himself became, to some degree, part of it.

One telling episode was the debate within the Blantyre Mission in 1902 about the competing claims of the well-established mission station at Domasi and the expanding town of Zomba where the colonial administration was headquartered. While Hetherwick had been on leave in Scotland, the decision had been taken that the minister, Dr Henry Scott, should relocate from Domasi to Zomba. Hetherwick made it clear that, had he been present, he would have opposed this move 'on the ground that it was tantamount to the setting aside of Domasi as the Head station of the district and putting Zomba in its place'.[23] Of course, as the founder of Domasi Mission he could be expected to be its champion but amongst its virtues he emphasised particularly that it, 'is at a distance from the European centre at Zomba and so there are not the temptations and distractions of European society . . .'[24] By the time he got back to Blantyre preparations to implement the new arrangements at Zomba were advancing. When they were approved by the Foreign Mission Committee in Edinburgh he wrote to its Convener in uncompromising terms:

> The only European interests at Zomba are the Administration and by moving round to Zomba Dr Scott makes himself an appendage of the Government in the eyes of the natives. The mission at the door of the Government will see things only through Government eyes and that will be fatal to our duty to the people . . . Domasi occupied a magnificently independent position and could make itself a power that a mission at the door of the Administration never can do. Remember that our battles in the past for the good of the natives have all been with the Government . . . For Dr [Henry] Scott to go round and settle himself alongside the Government is to sap his whole power and influence on the side of the native.[25]

It was another of Hetherwick's losing battles but, though he might have lost the battle, he remained determined to win the war.

When discussing the appointment of a new missionary with his Africa Committee Convener the following year, he returned to the dangers posed by the European community:

> There are many temptations nowadays that we never saw here before – the growing life and society of the European element in the district is a continued temptation under which a weak man will go to the wall, and become a hanger on of those whose aims and interests are not for the cause of the mission or the Church in this land. We are saved

from much here [in Blantyre] by the mile that lies between us and the European quarter – at Zomba the temptation is at the door – and it will need strong grace in the heart of the man or woman who is located there to withstand it.[26]

It was a theme to which he would often return. When he gave his presidential address to the Missionary Conference hosted at Mvera in 1910, he struck a warning note on this very point: 'A Europeanised atmosphere is not conducive to missionary sympathies ... it is hostile in its background and fatal to that intercourse between the native and the European missionary which is essential to all true mission life and work.'[27]

However much Hetherwick adapted to the conditions of colonial rule and actively played his part in its social and institutional life, in his own mind he always kept a distance from it. He never forgot the missionary purpose that had originally inspired him and was alert to the danger of the Mission losing its identity and cutting edge if it settled too comfortably into the colonial society around it. This was part of the reason why he strongly championed the initiative for Blantyre Mission to extend its operations into Portuguese East Africa (Mozambique). In his view, this was desirable not only to fulfil the missionary ambition to reach new areas but also to sustain the missionary character of Blantyre Mission at a time when it could have been tempted to make itself comfortable in the colonial conditions of Nyasaland. As he observed in an influential memorandum:

> It is needful to keep alive in ourselves the Missionary ideals ... the atmosphere round us in the Shire Highlands grows year by year more Europeanised, and with the increasing number of European settlers and planters in the districts round the Mission stations, together with the consequent social attractions of such a European community, the dangers to the Mission life are very largely increased. I dread this as I cannot but foresee it to be a serious hindrance to the missionary position of the staff in the future. We must guard against it – we must fight against it ... .[28]

In seeking to resist what Hetherwick regarded as a threatening European influence, his concern for the integrity and vitality of the Mission was combined with his sense of solidarity with the African community. He saw the need to be alert, 'lest the "world be too much with us" and the Cross and Kingdom of Christ be too seldom before our eyes'.[29] But in the next breath he was equally alert to the dangers posed to the welfare and prosperity of the African community: 'I see there is still the natives' battle to be fought with the European settlers ... Land, taxation, labour are all problems which are full of difficulties and which if not handled wisely may bring dire disaster on the country and its people.'[30] In 1920, when the government introduced a Bill under which 'natives' would be required to carry a 'pass', a measure somewhat reminiscent of the notorious South African pass laws,

Hetherwick knew that he had a fight on his hands. He reported to his colleagues James Reid that, 'I had a battle royal at the Chamber on Tuesday. I was the only one who opposed the Bill.'[31] Far from his membership of the Chamber of Commerce aligning him with settler interests, he used his position to champion the interests of the African community, even if he sometimes had to stand alone to do so.

There was also the question of racial attitudes where he was all too aware of the difference between those that prevailed in the European community and those that he championed in the life of the Mission. As early as 1892, with the British administration just starting to make its presence felt, Hetherwick could see that there was need for a clear parting of the ways and that it was based on differing racial attitudes:

> We have been compelled to separate ourselves from the Administration, and to frankly tell the natives that we cannot and do not approve of what goes on ... The European camp here is divided up. The old unity is gone. There are those whose attitude is 'only a nigger' and there are those – alas, very few – who view the natives as rational beings who have some claim for freedom to exist and who have rights of their own. I am sorry to say that the Administration officers belong to the former class – at least their actions would lead one to such belief and their actions bear out their openly expressed opinions.[32]

Matters did not improve with the passing of the years. As colonial rule became established as the order of the day, it entrenched racist attitudes that privileged Europeans while promoting active discrimination against Africans.

Hetherwick had felt obliged to distance himself from the European community as early as 1892 because he could not accept such attitudes. He could not cease to be a European himself nor could he excuse himself from playing a prominent role in the colonial society coming into place in Nyasaland, but he knew that he had to keep a distance from it – both to be true to his missionary calling and because of his identification with the African community whose interests were very much at stake in the new social and political situation. As time went on, he became ever more concerned, writing to his Committee Convener in 1915: 'I do not think you realise how much the mission is changing these past ten or twelve years – becoming more and more assimilated to the outside commercial and Government concerns in the country. The old missionary spirit which led the mission life and policy at the beginning is fast disappearing.'[33] Hetherwick could recognise that times were changing but he was far from complacent when it came to sustaining the ideals with which the Mission had begun.

Paternalism and Stadialism

If Hetherwick kept his distance from the European community in Nyasaland and especially the crass racism that was found within it, this does not necessarily mean that he was free himself of a 'milder' form of imperialism and racism. The ideology that upheld the British Empire took a variety of forms. At its most extreme it regarded indigenous people as sub-human creatures who could justifiably be used as slave labour or even exterminated in the interests of progress. A milder strand in the ideology of Empire was stadialist in nature. On the basis of a racially defined hierarchy, it categorised humanity into different stages, from the most primitive to the most civilised. Europeans, of course, were considered to belong to the latter category, Africans to the former. This form of racism and imperialism had a more 'benign' character in that it included the possibility that those races and peoples currently found at a low level of 'civilisation' could in future advance through the different stages until, at least in theory, they could reach the highest level. It became a popular way of understanding and justifying the British Empire that it was helping primitive peoples to gradually advance and become more civilised. This served to mask the oppressive, violent and exploitative nature of the Empire by presenting it as a benign institution that was gradually enabling its subjects to advance through the different stages that would ultimately allow them to become fully civilised.

It was inviting for the missionary movement to position itself in this script, defining its project in terms of raising primitive people to higher levels of civilisation. It became the mainstream view in British society, not least in the churches that supported the missionary enterprise. Hetherwick's biographer, the influential journalist and editor William Pringle Livingstone, has recently been singled out as a prime example of stadialism.[34] Archibald Scott, the leading champion and fundraiser for Blantyre Mission during the time of Clement Scott and during the early years of Hetherwick's leadership, once explained its purpose in these terms: 'The Churches must not haul down the flag of defending the rights of the natives, for the natives have been given to the Churches not only to be defended, but to be converted and educated and *brought up to the same level as ourselves.*'[35] It was a pro-African standpoint but cast in a stadialist framework.

With stadialism came paternalism since the role of both imperialist and missionary was understood in terms of raising children. This had the effect of belittling or infantilising the 'primitive' peoples since the racial hierarchy placed them at the lowest level of 'civilisation'. There was a certain benign aspect to this in that 'children' can grow up and become adults. Well-meaning imperial officials and missionaries imagined that their role was a paternal one, bringing up the 'children' so that at some time in the future they would be equipped for 'adult' life. No matter if they were well intentioned, this was nonetheless a form of racism and imperialism. It was this form to which missionaries like Hetherwick were most vulnerable.

For all that the Blantyre Mission was pro-African in outlook and Hetherwick was a vigorous champion of African interests all his days, he was not without at least some element of stadialism and paternalism. As a young missionary in 1888 he made a revealing comment: 'What now does Africa need? . . . she could not tell you; she does not know her needs . . . It is only the missionary who knows Africa's needs.'[36] Young as he was, he had no hesitation in positioning himself as the all-knowing parent and 'Africa' as the helpless child. Likewise, his colleague and contemporary William Affleck Scott, David Clement's brother, advocated a paternalistic approach. 'We know as well as anyone,' he wrote in 1891, 'that government of natives is not like government at home. One man, one vote would never do here. I fully believe we have the right to decide what is best for the natives, and to tell them what to do, and they will obey. But the moment you appeal to such a paternal government, we ask, "Where is the *paternal feeling*, which is the only justification of paternal government?"'[37] His quarrel with the incoming British Administration was that they were not being properly paternal. Paternalism itself he believed to be the correct approach.

Clement Scott himself, who has been favourably compared with Hetherwick as regards social and racial attitudes, also had a distinct streak of paternalism that ran through his pro-African approach. This is apparent even in his celebrated statement that, 'Africa for the Africans has been our policy from the first, and we believe that God has given this country into our hands that we may train its peoples how to develop its marvellous resources for themselves.'[38] The pro-African vision is clear but so is the conviction that 'training' of the people of Africa is required and that this is the vocation of Europeans, particularly missionaries like himself. This was described by George Shepperson and Thomas Price as 'progressive paternalism'.[39] Scott also conflated the work of the Mission with that of the Empire when he set out his vision of 'Africa developed for and by the African under the guidance and training of old Mother Britannia'.[40] Again the pro-African stance is clear but so is the need for the paternal (or maternal!) influence of the British Empire. As Scott and Hetherwick felt their way through a period of rapid change during the last two decades of the nineteenth century they had to define their project with reference to the interplay of mission, race and colonialism that was shaping Malawi's history at that time. While they put up stiff resistance to crass forms of racism and exploitative forms of colonialism, they were hospitable to the idea that colonial rule, understood paternalistically, could be their ally in the achievement of the vision they had for Malawi.

After Scott's final departure from Blantyre in 1898 it fell to Hetherwick to defend their vision, now in face of the growing likelihood that Malawi would be targeted by labour recruiters from South Africa. 'Let us make the position clear,' he wrote, 'Central Africa in no way can be regarded as a dwelling place for the white races; it is the home of the black man and the black man alone. He alone can develop its resources under the guidance of the European. This is his place and sphere. Ours is to govern and teach him till he sees that his lot lies in his own home and on its soil and not in the mines of Kimberley.'[41] The pro-African, indeed pro-Malawian, note is just as strong and it is just as much allied with the paternalistic streak that viewed the African as being in need of European guidance and training.

Like Scott, Hetherwick also tended to conflate the presence of the Mission with that of the colonial regime. After the unsavoury incident in 1902 in which government troops and police abused the local population in villages near Blantyre, Hetherwick wrote in terms that express the paternalistic vision of colonial rule in classical terms: 'We have taken these people under our care, and we have replaced the old native jurisdiction by a system of our own. It is our solemn duty not to rest content till we have made that system a pledge of the peace of the country and its good government. It was for this end that the flag was hoisted over these highlands, and it is only a part of the "white man's burden" which *we* have undertaken to carry.'[42]

If the question is asked who are the 'we' of whom he speaks, it seems clear that it covers the entire European presence, government, settlers and missionaries, as a collective unit. The same 'we' appears in a reflection he offered the following year, that is cast in explicitly paternalistic terms:

> We took over the country from the native, we have revolutionised his whole life – we have given him peace, freedom and justice, the great factors in the progress of a nation. We have imposed laws on him which we believe are for his good. He is in the position of a child, a 'ward in Chancery' and it behoves us to act for his best interests both material and moral. We must see that his rights are secured – the rights to live, and grow and expand himself and his fortunes – and discharge his duties to the land that is his home.[43]

It is a clearly pro-African standpoint but equally clearly it assigns a paternalistic role to the European.

In Hetherwick's outlook, paternalism combined neatly with stadialism: 'While the great human world outside was gradually, generation after generation, discovering and developing the resources of science and industry, thus enriching its life with its knowledge and skill, the African race stood still. They have gone little beyond the Stone Age which the white man passed through two thousand and more years ago.'[44] Though he was an admirer and defender of the African community in which he lived his life, in Hetherwick's understanding of the relation of European and African, the European was far more advanced and he saw his own role as being a matter of enabling Africans to advance towards greater 'civilisation'.

This attitude was often revealed in throwaway remarks. When discussing building work, for example, he remarked, 'The native has *not yet* risen to the properties of a right angle'.⁴⁵ Here is a stadialist point of view: Africans have *not yet* reached this stage, but one day they will! At one and the same time this affirmed the potential of Africans and confirmed their inferiority. This was the tension that ran through Hetherwick's thought and was never completely resolved. When his biographer W. P. Livingstone was visiting the manse in Blantyre, he noticed a cupboard door open and Hetherwick remarked, 'You cannot get an African to shut a door'.⁴⁶ He was by no means free of the cultural hubris and racial stereotyping that marked European attitudes in his time.

Another trope favoured by Hetherwick that revealed a stadialist outlook was to compare conditions in Britain at the time of the Roman Empire with those found in Malawi in his own time. Irked by the racist attitudes of the European community now forming in Nyasaland, Hetherwick included a barbed comment in the March 1896 issue of *Life and Work*: 'It was good old Dion Cassius, we believe, who once described a certain race as "an idle, indolent, thievish, lying lot of scoundrels". We have heard and read almost the same words used to describe certain tribes of our Protectorate. The Latin historian's strong epithets referred however to the English.'⁴⁷ To underline his point, in the December 1898 issue Hetherwick included an article titled 'The People and Climate of Early Britain'.⁴⁸ Why was such an article included in a magazine concerned with Christian mission in Africa at the end of the nineteenth century?

Hetherwick's idea was that, 'When we attempt to picture to ourselves the future of Central Africa the question naturally arises in our minds: what sort of a place was Britain at a corresponding early stage of its development?'⁴⁹ This was, in its primary thrust, a positive and affirmative view of the indigenous people of Central Africa. They were of the same human stock as the people of Britain but at an earlier stage in their development. And there was nothing to stop them, in their turn, from advancing to the same high level of civilisation that the British had reached, especially if they enjoyed the benign guidance of the Scottish mission and the British Empire!

Hetherwick was altogether positive about the potential of the 'natives' to achieve such advancement: 'The limit of their [the Natives'] acquirement is the limit of our knowledge to teach; you can take them as far as you can. In some things they are ahead of the Europeans . . . I have often been in a tight corner but my Natives have never failed me.'⁵⁰ There is a tension in Hetherwick's thought as he buys into the stadialist and paternalist framework, yet his appreciation of the qualities of African communities seems to challenge it. It is a tension that has been described in another context as 'othering and brothering'. In the racist thinking of the time, an African was always 'other' to a European and Hetherwick, like almost everyone else, was influenced by this. Yet there is much in his writing that suggests he looked on his African companions more as 'brother' (and sister) than 'other'.⁵¹

In the introduction to his biography of Hetherwick, W. P. Livingstone frames his subject's life in a racially defined, stereotypical and stadialist way:

'The European and the Native were in contact, the one enterprising and aggressive, the other only half-awake and bewildered by the new conditions . . .'⁵² His assessment of Hetherwick's role in this situation reveals both his genius and his limitations: 'He knew the European and he knew the Native and, sympathising with both, he believed their interests to be identical.'⁵³ It is fair comment on Hetherwick that he had an unusual degree of sympathy with the perspectives of both Europeans and Africans but his genuine – and oft-repeated – belief that their interests were identical reveals a naïve confidence in the beneficence of colonial rule that would not stand the test of time.

He wrote in a Blantyre Mission Sunday School Letter in 1925, 'Africa is a grand country and its people are a grand people. But they need to be taught to use it and develop it and make it a land of which they will be proud. And you are helping us to teach them.'⁵⁴ At one and the same time he demonstrated his pro-African outlook while revealing the paternalism that assumed the superiority of Europeans in general and missionaries in particular. Hetherwick had no inkling that the stadialism and paternalism that guided his thinking were part of a colonialist discourse that disempowered and demoralised the people of Africa so that it was something they would need to overcome in order to advance. Nor did he have any idea that a time would come when the so-called progress of the white man would be identified as the cause of the climate change that puts the future of the earth in jeopardy and the imperative requirement is to learn from the sustainable approach to the natural environment that marked the life of indigenous communities.

Confronting Race Issues

However much Hetherwick's inclination towards paternalism and stadialism led him to take a generally positive view of the British Empire, he did not hesitate to confront the Administration in Nyasaland, particularly in regard to issues that revealed racist attitudes that he found unacceptable. There is a striking contrast between, on the one hand, his everyday work amongst the African community, which seems to have gone on steadily and methodically with rarely a word spoken in anger and, on the other hand, his relations with the colonial administration and the European community which were marked by a continuous succession of confrontations and controversy. His temperament was such that he never shrank from such controversy. In fact, he was rather in his element when there was a battle to be fought. When W. H. Murray of the Dutch Reformed Church was summoned to appear as a witness at the Commission of Inquiry into the Chilembwe Rising, he complained to Hetherwick, 'I hate all this controversy with the Government.' 'Hate it?' replied Hetherwick, '*I love it.* I know far more about this business than they do and I shall speak out and tell them what I think whether they like it or not.'⁵⁵ Such was his customary style.

When it came to issues of race, shortly after he succeeded Scott as Head of the Mission, he set out his stall in two issues of *Life and Work*. In February 1899 he seized upon a statement by the British general and statesman Lord Kitchener that England believes in 'educating the native'.[56] This he took as an affirmation of the Blantyre Mission educational enterprise that was already coming under attack from the colonial society emerging in Nyasaland. If Kitchener had ventured his statement in Nyasaland, Hetherwick suggested that 'he would have been howled down or else sneered at as an enthusiast of unparalleled foolishness'.[57]

He characterised the attitude he was up against in the following terms:

> Education of the native from the Colonial point of view is a profound mistake . . . It will make the native think he is as good as the white man. It will end in subverting the authority of the white race . . . The only safety lies in repression and keeping him in his present ignorance; and this belief is conjoined with another, namely that the native has not in his nature enough possibility of good to allow him to be trusted with education. This is briefly expressed in the common formula, 'Teach a native to write and he will forge your cheques'.

This, in Hetherwick's judgement demonstrated that his compatriots in Nyasaland were behind the times: 'Colonials are today expressing in a rather intenser form the sentiments of our great-grandfathers, who in their hearts thought the "blacks" were not really human . . .'[58] No wonder they were bewildered by the educated Africans who were already emerging to play their part in social and economic development:

> When the true Colonial arrives in British Central Africa and finds natives in places of responsibility, who can write and yet don't forge cheques he can only explain the mystery by saying 'Ah, you seem to have a different kind of native'. Are our natives so much the *crème de la crème* of savagery that they can be treated as no other savages can? Are the Maoris or the Zulus not as fine races? No! It is not a difference of raw native, it is a difference of treatment . . . If we do justly and love mercy, if we educate the native and not repress him, we will have a crop of the loyalist British subjects that ever grew up in the wide Empire.[59]

Thus he confronted and lampooned the racist sentiment that he detected in colonial society with the argument that his progressive educational policy was what would ensure loyalty to the Empire.

A year later he published another signature piece in which he contrasted the direction being taken by South Africa with what he understood to be the basis on which the Protectorate was developing. He observed that 'Entrance into the Protectorate of the British South Africa Administration has brought us into close contact with a system of ideas on things African and native that are entirely foreign to the original foundations of our community. The native has not failed to perceive the changed tone, and has speedily adapted to suit. The seeds of race feeling that has worked such dire harm both to African and European in the South have begun to be sown here.'[60] The big question, he suggested, that the Protectorate had to face was: 'Are we to develop on the lines of South Africa where the European element and the native have grown mutually aloof, or are we to proceed on the lines laid down by our first founders in the Missionary pioneer days, and hold that the prosperity of the country depends on keeping the two races in harmony?'[61] It was a question to which he would return time and again. He was clear in his answer:

> We have always held that the prosperity of the European will proceed on even terms with the prosperity of the native ... If our aim is to utilise either for our own enrichment or our own advancement we shall both fail of our aim and be faithless in our duty. Our prosperity and success as a community depend on our keeping together be we European or native, be we Government or Mission, trader or planter.[62]

He liked to make the claim that in Nyasaland, 'the two races live together on the best of terms and there is no race problem'.[63] If this seems naïve in historical perspective, nonetheless there was some degree of truth to it. Race issues played out very differently in Nyasaland from South Africa and, when the Federation of Rhodesia and Nyasaland imposed a more racist system in the 1950s, it was a great shock to the African population, which swiftly set about resisting the Federation and attaining independence. Meanwhile, in his time, Hetherwick stoutly defended what he believed to be the non-racist ethos prevailing in Nyasaland and did not hesitate to call out the government when it displayed what he considered to be unacceptable racist attitudes.

For example, in 1907 when the government was setting up the scheme to provide grant-in-aid to mission schools, Major Pearce, the Acting Commissioner, wrote to tell Hetherwick that he did not wish to distribute according to student numbers since he was suspicious of district schools under 'native capitaos'. He proposed instead that, '... all native schools should be under close European supervision, which I consider to be an exceedingly necessary and beneficial policy ... My own idea is that the disbursement of the grant should be in proportion to the number of Europeans engaged on the staff of each mission.'[64] Hetherwick was having none of it: 'I am strongly of the opinion that the grant should be per scholar or per certificated native teacher.'[65] This might sound like a procedural and technical wrangle but it revealed not only differences in regard to how education might best be delivered but also in regard to the underlying racial attitudes.

A sensitive point in a racist and colonialist frame of thought is sexual behaviour and sexual morality. Not only is there a concern that the races be kept apart sexually but there is always an aspersion that the 'lower race' lacks sound sexual morality and presents a threat at the sexual level. Hetherwick was outraged when Sir Harry Johnston's book on British Central Africa was published because it took a very dim view of the level of marital fidelity in the African community.[66] In high indignation he wrote, 'Those of us who have lived any length of time in the country and who have been in close contact with native life in all its phases, must often have been struck with the high tone of native morality amid their social surroundings, and bear testimony to the fidelity of the native women to their husbands . . .'[67] He went on to give a remarkable testimony: 'We claim to speak from some experience of native life in these parts about Blantyre and Domasi, and during the period of wellnigh twenty years we have never seen an immodest action on the part of any native woman nor heard an immodest word.'[68] It would not be the last time that he rose to the defence of the African community when its sexual morality was being called into question.

An issue arose with the government in 1913 that would be comical if it were not evidence of the tragic contortions to which racism leads. Hector Duff, the Acting Government Secretary, wrote to Hetherwick confidentially about a matter that was of grave concern to the Governor. It had come to his notice that there were some 'male natives' in the Protectorate who were corresponding with schoolgirls in the United Kingdom, having been given their addresses by Missionary Societies. While he had no reason to suppose that the letters contained 'anything intrinsically objectionable', the correspondence had nevertheless set off alarm bells in Government House. As Duff explained:

> The unhappy experience of so many other States and Colonies as to the question of colour in its relation to sex is too well known to need any comment. In Nyasaland there has fortunately been no need hitherto of the severe legislation which has elsewhere become necessary to protect the women of the ruling race, and His Excellency feels that if this desirable state of affairs is to continue too much care cannot be taken to preserve to white women in this Protectorate the absolute and unquestioning respect with which natives have been taught to regard them.[69]

Hetherwick responded that he was not aware of any such correspondence and thought it was unlikely to occur. However, he was not going to leave Duff's assumptions unchallenged: 'Let me say that I do not believe the results of such correspondence would be those you seem to dread. The natives of this Protectorate will continue to respect white women so long as they continue to deserve their respect.'[70] As was his wont, Hetherwick turned the tables by pointing out that there were two sides to the relationship – so long as white women played their part in a mutually respectful relationship, he was confident that the 'natives' would play theirs. It was the breaking down of such respect in South Africa that posed the greatest threat to inter-racial relations in Nyasaland, Hetherwick suggested. Warming to another of his favourite themes, he urged the government to continue discouraging labour migration to the south. 'Meanwhile,' he concluded, 'there is no danger. One cannot but admire the respect and courtesy of all natives towards white women in this country, and one can only hope that the day is yet as far distant when that attitude of respect will be changed.'[71]

Duff persisted, however, and revealed that he had conducted a test case by examining one particular example of the correspondence that had given rise to the government's concern. John Williard M. Kalungwe had supplied a signed statement confirming that he had been corresponding with Miss Elsie Kydd in Scotland, having been given the girl's address by Hamilton Currie of the Blantyre Mission.[72] Duff sounded rather triumphant that he had caught Hetherwick 'red-handed'. On investigation, however, it turned out that the correspondence had begun when Kalungwe was a pupil at the school at Blantyre Mission and had written a letter to the Sunday School in Scotland which was sending support to the school. 'The correspondence,' concluded Hetherwick, 'is an absolutely innocent one, and I am unable to conceive of any evil results accruing from it to either party . . . I fail to see that letters of that kind will ever cause the native to lose his respect for the white woman or to do her less honour than it has hitherto done. In fact, I can see how it is possible for it to have an opposite effect.'[73] The incident reveals the paranoia that could afflict a colonial government when it feared that race and sex were combining in a way that might pose a threat to the colonial order. It also reveals that Hetherwick did not share such fears. On the contrary, he treated them with disdain and had absolute confidence in the moral integrity of the African community.

Having been stung by such indignant responses from Hetherwick, the government might have known what to expect when he was called to testify before the Commission of Inquiry into the Chilembwe Rising of 1915. As discussed in Chapter Five, the Rising was a very uncomfortable episode for Hetherwick. It cut against his whole understanding of the way Nyasaland worked and the harmonious relationship between the races of which he was so proud. He therefore tended to play it down as a local and inconsequential affair. In the aftermath he was very much on the defensive as the settlers and government jumped to the conclusion that it was mission education that was the underlying cause of the Rising. Since Blantyre Mission was the leading provider of education in the area where the Rising occurred, it was widely perceived as a culprit, much to Hetherwick's chagrin. He recalled that, 'For four and a half hours I myself was under examination and cross-examination and during the whole of that time not a single friendly question was put to me either by the Government representatives or the Planters representative.'[74] However, when he was questioned by two Government officials, Aubrey Turnbull, Assistant Chief Secretary, and Joseph Casson, Superintendent of Native Affairs, he was ready for them.

The Questions and Answers appear on the official record as follows:

CASSON: Do you think the native, educated or otherwise, is capable of understanding the Holy Scriptures?
HETHERWICK: Yes, as capable as any ordinary Christian.
CASSON: But you may misguide him by giving him the whole Bible!
HETHERWICK: I don't think you can.
CASSON: For example, Isaiah. – is it easy for the native?
HETHERWICK: I don't say so; but I would not withhold the Bible from anyone.
CASSON: Do you think the Bible in Chinyanja is clear and understood?
HETHERWICK: Undoubtedly.
TURNBULL: If a teacher selects an isolated portion or a verse, may he misapply it?
HETHERWICK: Yes, as a European might.
TURNBULL: We have it on evidence that native teachers do sometimes discuss among themselves texts of the Bible!
HETHERWICK: And why not?
TURNBULL: A village headman went round the country interpreting a certain text.
HETHERWICK: But that is not a reason why the Bible should be withheld, and no man will hinder the missions from putting it into the hands of the natives. We are Protestants, but not the Roman Catholic Church.
CASSON: Can the native interpret it correctly to others?
HETHERWICK: The native is as able to interpret the Bible as you are.[75]

The questioning then turned to the sensitive question of the level of responsibility that was entrusted to Africans and their role in the government of the church.

Q: Will there be a native ministry in the future?
A: That is entirely in the hands of the native.
Q: You don't expect the place of the European to be fully supplied?
A: Not meanwhile, but I have no objections.
Q: In the governing body has the native an equal vote?
A: Yes.
Q: You say there may be 12 Europeans and 10 natives, soon the native vote may have the majority. Are you prepared for the Church of Scotland practically to be governed by a native majority?
A: It may be.
Q: Is there not a danger in giving the native so soon such powers?
A: We have seen nothing of danger as yet and I fear none.[76]

A final set of questions concerned inter-racial relations and the lack of respect from Africans that many Europeans claimed that they were experiencing.

Q: Do you think the result of mission education is for natives to lose a sense of respect for Europeans, have you found this?
A: I have had respect from every native I met.
Q: Of course, natives get swollen head!
A: As Europeans do.
Q: We have met some (laughter).[77]

Hetherwick then made the point that in order to conduct the trials of those accused of participating in the Rising, the court had required the services of an interpreter, Ralph Maunde, and the conduct of the cases depended entirely on the accuracy and effectiveness of his work. John Gray Kufa, allegedly Chilembwe's second-in-command, had been cited as an example of what could result from mission education. 'Well sir,' stated Hetherwick, 'we have had John Gray held up as an example on the one side. I put Ralph Maunde on the other side. That account is now squared. I think when you can get education to produce one so trustworthy as that, you see the effect of education.'[78]

He was not yet finished. There was one final question, and he did not miss his chance to point out that Europeans had questions to answer as well as Africans.

TURNBULL: In regard to lack of respect. I believe certain natives refuse to take off their hats to Europeans?
HETHERWICK: I give no ruling to the natives. I think that the native should take off his hat, and I think that if a ruling should be made, that, wherever a native salutes the European, the European should make some acknowledgement of the salute. I have seen many Europeans absolutely ignore a boy's salutation. You know that the smallest drummer boy in the British army if he salutes Lord Kitchener, receives a salute in return. If a native salutes a European there will be no difficulty if the European makes acknowledgement. It indicates that there are two gentlemen and not only one.[79]

This is an oft-quoted passage and deservedly so since it captured at a decisive moment the difference in outlook between Hetherwick and the wider European community in Nyasaland.[80] Reciprocity of greeting is a fundamental cultural value in Malawi even to this day. Through his immersion in local culture, this was obvious to Hetherwick, but apparently not to many of his compatriots. The differences, however, went much deeper. In the highly charged atmosphere of the Rising's aftermath, the colonial establishment responded to an unprecedented challenge by blaming the attitude of educated Africans. The prevailing attitude of the European community in the Shire Highlands was that there would have been no problem if all Africans remained unskilled labourers accepting their lowly position in the European-dominated economy and society that was emerging. They noted that the Africans who led the Rising came from among those who had advanced in education through attending mission schools. They jumped on this as vindication of their view that mission education was 'spoiling the natives' and should be regarded as a menace.

No wonder that Hetherwick wrote anxiously to his Committee Secretary in Scotland '. . . there is a widely expressed opinion that this whole matter is the work of the whole of the Missions in Nyasaland and is the result of the educating and Christianising of the natives. Our Governor openly in his speech to the Legislative Council gave expression to this opinion!'[81] The entire project of Blantyre Mission for forty years had been to foster the emergence of a skilled and educated African elite equipped for leadership roles in church and society. This was now seen by most Europeans, from the Governor downwards, as a threat to the peace and stability of the country. As John McCracken explains, 'the all-too-visible presence of the first generation of literate Blantyre-educated Christians was an intolerable affront to settler sensibilities, challenging the assumption that Africans were morally and intellectually inferior to Europeans'.[82] The heat in the issue about removal of hats arose from fears that well-dressed Africans were, 'striking at the very roots of the colonial social order'.[83] Hetherwick was therefore pushed on to the defensive and was in fighting mood when he appeared before the Commission. This sets the context in which he turned the tables and made his point that racist and colonialist attitudes on the part of the European community were the underlying cause of the problem.

A further aspect of the wider context is that Hetherwick's application of the term 'gentleman' to members of the African community was a regular part of his discourse. For example, when he was critical of unsatisfactory members of his own European staff (a not infrequent occurrence) he often complained that they lacked 'gentlemanly' qualities and therefore were not well received within the African community. When he was telling the Committee Secretary in Scotland what kind of person he needed to fill a vacancy, he wrote that, 'he should be a young enthusiastic Christian gentleman – a gentleman in education and feeling for only such commend themselves to the African'.[84] In colonialist discourse the term 'gentleman' was reserved for Europeans but Hetherwick regularly subverted this convention by pointing out the gentlemanly qualities that he found within the African community. This, in fact, was part of his stock-in-trade.

During the early 1920s, when the *chotsa chipewa* (remove the hat) issue was still rumbling in Zomba, he responded to a request for advice by using almost the same words with which he had challenged the 1915 Commission of Inquiry:

> If only the Europeans were the Gentlemen that the native is and return the salute – the whole matter would be at an end. It is the non-acknowledgement of the salute that fires the hearts of the educated boys who are better mannered in this matter than their 'superiors'. I

preach this to all and every Mzungu [white person] whom I talk to on this matter. It is what the oldest Field Marshall in the British army does to the youngest drummer boy who salutes him.[85]

By his own admission this a point that he was frequently repeating, and bears witness to how consistently he was challenging the colonialist and racist tropes of the time. By putting quotation marks around the word 'superiors' and by implying that Africans met the expected standards of gentlemanly behaviour while Europeans failed to do so, he subverted racist and colonialist assumptions that were normally unquestioned in colonial society.

Another significant feature of the wider context is that Hetherwick's taking the European community to task at the Commission of Inquiry was of a piece with his attitude to the Rising, which was entirely different from that of most of his fellow Europeans. He had no sympathy for Chilembwe and felt sorry for people he knew, particularly John Gray Kufa, who were caught up in the Rising. He visited Kufa several times in a pastoral capacity while he was in prison awaiting execution and remained baffled as to how someone of such high character and reputation had become involved: 'his case is beyond any explanation of mine'.[86] He attributed the bloodshed to a combination of what he regarded as misguided 'Ethiopianism' on the part of Chilembwe and the harsh conditions imposed on labour on the Bruce Estates. 'The Magomero murders on the Bruce Estates,' he explained to the Committee in Scotland, 'were purely in revenge for bad treatment – a paying off of old scores at the first opportunity.'[87] He regarded the Rising as rather a pitiful affair since it had so small a chance of success and he was rather scathing about the motivation and rationale behind it. However, it was the response of the European community that really stirred his indignation.

This began with his dismay when all Europeans were called into the *laager* ('protective enclosure') at Mandala's headquarters, which Hetherwick considered a completely unnecessary panic: 'the saddest thing in the whole affair is the "funk" that the Europeans got into! I am ashamed of my countrymen!'[88] He was damning in his criticism: 'The Government and the European community have come out of this matter worse than anyone. The Government bungled the concentration business and the Europeans sought first to save their own skins – leaving the whole of the property of the Protectorate exposed to any native band of plunderers.'[89] Nor did matters improve, in his estimation, thereafter. He was scathing in his assessment of the government's handling of the affair: '[The Governor, Sir George Smith] is the last man to deal with such a situation as this is and he has as his Chief Secretary [Hector Duff] a swollenheaded fool whose one aim and end is to get promotion for himself. We are badly served here just now.'[90]

His dismay only deepened when he witnessed the relish with which the European community attended the public hangings of the 'rebels' who had been condemned to death: 'I found Zomba thirsting for revenge – the spirit of my countrymen and worse of my countrywomen made me thoroughly ashamed of them ... Six people were executed on Monday and the Zomba people were there with a dozen cameras.'[91] By contrast he himself was appalled and traumatised by the hangings: 'It is a degrading and barbarous procedure'.[92] For Hetherwick the episode revealed not anything wrong with the African community but much that was wrong with the European one: 'The way the ladies of Zomba crowded the court to see and hear these deluded wretches sentenced to be hanged, and the rush of Zomba men with cameras to the hangings only shows how little we are under the rule of the higher humanities'.[93]

A Person of his Time

'It is thirty years since I wrote my first report from Blantyre to the Foreign Mission Committee,' wrote Hetherwick in 1914.

> There was not much to write of then – no Domasi, no Zomba, no Mlanje, no native church, not a single baptized native Christian at Blantyre, no village schools anywhere in the country, not a halfpenny of contributions to the Mission from native sources ... Now I am sitting down to write about churches and native congregations, church building, Christian liberality, Christian Native Marriage Ordinances, Church Union, Mission extension, not to speak of railway competition and motor cycles – these last to prove themselves a most valuable agent in missionary expansion.[94]

He had indeed witnessed remarkable changes both within the life of the Mission and in the wider society within which it was set.

Besides material changes he had to navigate the advent of colonial rule and the European settler society that came with it while continuing the close relations with African communities that he had been cultivating for years before the declaration of the Protectorate in 1891. He sought to remain true to the mutually respectful friendships that formed the basis of the work of the Mission and to champion the interests of the African communities in the new world that was breaking in upon them. At the same time, he had had a hand in bringing British colonial rule to the territory and he continued to believe that it was the best available option. He was, after all, a person of his time and it came naturally to him to assume that European 'civilisation' was far superior to traditional African life and that ancillary to the evangelical work of the Mission was a responsibility to introduce its African protégés to the benefits of such civilisation. He was moulded by the prevailing framework of stadialism and paternalism that provided a justification and rationale for both Empire and Mission. This, however, did not stop him from recognising and celebrating the many positive qualities he recognised in African life and culture.

In the intellectual climate of the early twentieth century, the idea of a hierarchy of civilisations, generally understood in racial terms, was almost universally accepted. Only from a more distant historical perspective did it become apparent how far this was an ideological prop to support imperial rule. In Hetherwick's time, in the context of a British Protectorate in southern Africa, the prevailing assumption was that Africans occupied the lowest level in the hierarchy of civilisations. What was at issue was whether they should be consigned to a position of permanent inferiority or whether, with education and opportunity, they could ascend to higher levels, ultimately reaching the level of the Europeans (always assumed to be the highest). On this issue there is no doubt about where Alexander Hetherwick stood, his position frequently setting him at odds with his compatriots in the Administration and among the settlers.

Above all, he maintained all along his firm belief in the equality of all humanity and the dignity of the people of Africa. This belief was sometimes thrown into relief by his feisty confrontations with the colonial government when he detected racist attitudes or exposed unjust actions. It also came to light at other times when he was addressing a different issue but unconsciously revealed his underlying assumptions on matters of race. For example, when he was complaining on one occasion about the lack of generosity in the offerings of church members, he remarked, 'The same coldness creeps into the membership of the church here as at home – the same growing power of worldliness. Who dare say that humanity – black and white – are not of one stock? Let him just come out here and see the faults and failures of the home church reproduced here at Blantyre.'[95] It was a rather negative way of making a positive point – that human beings and church members are fundamentally the same wherever they are.

When he wrote to Robert Napier about the latter's intention to work for a year in a Scottish parish before embarking on his missionary career at Blantyre, he remarked that, 'Human nature is the same here as at home and experience at home is invaluable – especially experience of the lower strata of home society, for it makes one value the rich material we have to work on here as compared with the fallen and degraded of our own civilised life.'[96] This was going beyond equality to suggest that, contrary to colonialist thinking, the human material found in the African context was 'richer' than what Napier might be encountering in the 'civilised' world.

His confidence in the 'rich material' with which he was working found expression above all in the life of the church. At the end of his career, he was well aware that many vital questions remained unanswered. Answers would be found, he believed not from the supposedly superior Europeans but from the African church that was increasingly coming into its own. He looked forward to the day when Europeans would step back and African leadership would take the church forward. Early in 1914 he wrote to his Africa Committee Convener, 'I am more and more driven to the conclusion that we need an entire change of organization and policy if we are to get room for the full development of the native element in the work – and the replacement of the European by the native in the future of the African Church.'[97] A few weeks later he followed up with the conviction that, 'We must throw out our European forces into new fields of heathenism and let the native church develop the church already planted here.'[98]

At a time when most Europeans expected that it would be many generations before Africans would be able to occupy positions of senior responsibility, Hetherwick imagined a much shorter horizon. In 1922, as he argued for more missionary staff to be appointed, he wrote to Africa Committee Convener J. D. McCallum, 'I entirely agree with you in desiring the full utilisation of the native for the ministry of the church and we are pressing this on as fast as is prudent and wise, but we cannot do without European leadership for forty years yet.'[99] He was remarkably prescient in 1922 when he estimated 'forty years' since it was in 1962 that Malawi won self-government and in the same year Blantyre Synod appointed its first African General Secretary, Jonathan Sangaya.[100] This was the outcome that had been viewed with horror by the Commission of Inquiry into the 1915 Rising but that was regarded by Hetherwick as the objective towards which he was working.

Such confidence in African potential and African leadership set him at odds with his compatriots in the colonial government and the settler community, as was dramatically demonstrated by his encounter with the Commission of Inquiry. Though he remained convinced that the British Empire was a force for good and viewed it through the same stadialist and paternalistic lens that guided many imperialists, he was distinguished by a commitment to the African community that would ultimately bring colonial rule to an end. Andrew Ross captured what it was that caused Blantyre Mission to differ from the prevailing colonialist mindset:

> D. C. Scott, Hetherwick and their leading associates saw Africans as people. They saw African society as something valid; something to be built on and not something to be destroyed. They believed individual Africans to be capable of absorbing western culture, which was not something to be left for their far-distant descendants. They did not just speak and write these things but acted on them.[101]

By such action they illustrated a point made by Godwin Tasie and Richard Gray, that 'although the alliance between Christian missionaries and European colonialism was intimate, it was never complete. The message and impact of the missions could in varying degrees be distinguished from the apparatus of alien rule'.[102] The evidence assembled in this book suggests that in Hetherwick's case the distinction can be made to quite a considerable degree. It is a distinction that was rather lost on most of his contemporaries for whom 'pioneer missionary and empire builder' sat comfortably together. From a longer historical perspective a more complicated picture emerges in which he illustrates an equivocal relationship between mission and empire. John de Gruchy has observed that, '[British missionaries] were almost invariably imperialists, representatives of Victoria, even if they were sometimes problematic imperialists who sowed some of the seeds for the empire's demise'.[103] If Hetherwick was an imperialist, he was one of the problematic ones. In his day, he believed in the British Empire and was loyal to it, yet his missionary work was nurturing the people who would one day resist and overthrow the racism and imperialism that prevailed at the time.

Here his language and translation work is not to be underestimated. The imperial historian Andrew Porter has highlighted the far-reaching significance of the missionary translation project: 'the process of translation into vernacular languages ... handed effective control over the transmission and adaptation of Christianity to the indigenous peoples themselves and provided them with the means of securing their own religious identity as well as ascendancy in church and, ultimately, state'.[104] While Blantyre Mission undoubtedly played a significant part in the 'cultural imperialism' of introducing Africans to the language and norms of their colonial masters, there was all the time a movement in the opposite direction. As time went on, Hetherwick was ever more conscious that the Christianity he had been preaching was now in the hands of the African church. Quite contrary to the colonial impulse to control, his project was to empower the community with which he was working. A refrain in his post-retirement lectures was that the future direction of African Christianity was now in the hands of Africans themselves.[105] There were questions that he could not answer but he was confident that, in due time, the answers would come from the African church. When this was the direction set for the church, there were obvious implications for the state, as the Commissioners were uncomfortably aware at the Inquiry into the 'Native Rising' of 1915. Hetherwick did not share their discomfort.

When he was giving a eulogy to his friend and colleague Robert Napier, shot and killed in action towards the end of the First World War, the highest praise he could offer was that, 'He lived for the natives. Their good was the aim and end of his every action.'[106] It is unlikely that he expected anything less of himself. On the other hand, he had no time for missionaries who failed to identify with the African community. When Alexander Mauchline was invalided home in 1922, Hetherwick explained why he did not want him back: 'He has no tact – he is a bully and with no sympathy with the native point of view in things at all'.[107] His contrasting assessments of Napier and Mauchline reveal what mattered most to Hetherwick. It was the emerging African church in which he invested his hopes and imagination. 'For the first time,' he wrote in 1925, 'the number of communicant Members has topped the Ten Thousand figure – being this year 10,810 ... There are now in all 44 churches and congregations ministered to by six Native Ministers, superintended by three European Ministers.'[108]

At the ideological level, there were undoubtedly tensions and even contradictions in the mind of Alexander Hetherwick, which were not to be resolved until later history yielded a self-governing church and an independent nation. In his own time, he had to be satisfied with some degree of resolution in the relationships he enjoyed within the African community. When a group of schoolboys came from Domasi to continue their education at Blantyre in 1910, among them was the son of the very first boy who had enrolled in the school at Domasi when Hetherwick started it in 1884. He wrote with delight, 'The little lad Robert is just the size and age his father was when he came to me – to be the first scholar to enter Domasi Mission in 1884. His face and voice and attitudes are those of his father over again.'[109] Such relationships transcended the racial tensions and colonial contradictions of the time. On them the future would be built.

Notes

1. *Life and Work in British Central Africa*, April 1906.
2. Alexander Hetherwick, *The Gospel and the African: the Croall Lectures for 1930–31*, Edinburgh: T. & T. Clark, 1932, 168.
3. Ibid.
4. See e.g. Alexander Hetherwick, *The Romance of Blantyre: How Livingstone's Dream Came True*, London: James Clarke, n.d., 199–200.
5. Alexander Hetherwick, Annual Report for 1907, MNA 50/BMC/2/1/82.
6. Zomba Kirk Session Minutes, 30 July 1902, MNA 86/ZOM/3/1/2.
7. Alexander Hetherwick, *The Romance of Blantyre*, 122, my italics.
8. See further Timothy Lovering, 'Authority and Identity: Malawian Soldiers in Britain's Colonial Army, 1891–1964', PhD, University of Stirling, 2002.
9. Alexander Hetherwick, *The Romance of Blantyre*, 134.
10. Ibid.
11. J. N. Ogilvie to Alexander Hetherwick, 10 March 2016, MNA 50/BMC/2/2/9.
12. Melvin Page estimates that 191,500 men served as *tengatenga* during the war and suggests that the government figure of 4,400 deaths is an underestimate. Melvin E. Page, *The Chiwaya War*, 2nd ed., Mzuzu: Mzuni Press, 2021, 94, 151.
13. See John Chilembwe, 'The Voice of African Natives in the Present War', *Nyasaland Times*, 26 November 2014, reproduced in Kenneth R. Ross (ed.), *Christianity in Malawi: A Source Book*, 2nd ed, Mzuzu: Mzuni Press, 2020, 246–49.
14. Alexander Hetherwick, *The Romance of Blantyre*, 212.
15. Ibid., 220.
16. *Life and Work in Nyasaland*, September–December 1914.
17. https://www.channel4.com/programmes/unremembered-britains-forgotten-war-heroes accessed 26 May 2021.
18. https://www.cwgc.org/non-commemoration-report/ accessed 26 May 2021.
19. Ibid., 221.
20. The Commonwealth War Graves Commission set up a special committee which reported in 2021 that this historical neglect was due to 'entrenched prejudices, preconceptions and pervasive racism of contemporary imperial attitudes'. See David Olusoga, 'Britain's failure to honour black and Asian dead is a scandal of the present, not just the past', *The Guardian*, 25 April 2021.

21. See further Robert Boeder, *Alfred Sharpe of Nyasaland*, Blantyre: Central Africana, 1981.
22. Alexander Hetherwick to John McMurtrie, 23 January 1896, MNA 50/BMC/2/1/14.
23. Alexander Hetherwick to John McMurtrie, 9 June 1902, MNA 50/BMC/2/1/42.
24. Ibid.
25. Alexander Hetherwick to John McMurtrie, 25 June 1903, MNA 50/BMC/2/1/48.
26. Alexander Hetherwick to Rev James Robertson, Whittinghame Manse, 6 November 1904, MNA 50/BMC/2/1/63.
27. Presidential address, Proceedings of the Third General Missionary Conference of Nyasaland (1910), 4, cit. John McCracken, *Politics and Christianity*, 214.
28. Alexander Hetherwick, 'Notes on the Scheme of Readjustment of Mission Methods to Allow of the Extension Into the New Territories of Portuguese East Africa', Blantyre, 28 January 1911, MNA 50/BMC/3/18/2.
29. Alexander Hetherwick to J. D. McCallum, 3 February 1911, MNA BMC/50/2/1/113.
30. Ibid.
31. Alexander Hetherwick to James Reid, 16 September 1920, MNA BMC/50/2/1/181.
32. Alexander Hetherwick to Archibald Scott, 13 June 1892, NLS 7534/744–50.
33. Alexander Hetherwick to J. C. McCallum, 11 October 1915, BMC/50/2/1/140.
34. Jeffrey Grant Cannon, 'Church of Scotland Periodicals and the Shaping of Scottish Opinion regarding South African Apartheid and the Central African Federation, c.1912–c.1965', PhD, University of Edinburgh, 2020.
35. *The Central African Times*, 28 March 1903, quoting from the *British Weekly*, my italics.
36. Cit. H. Alan C. Cairns, *Prelude to Imperialism: British Reactions to Central African Society, 1840–1890*, London, 1965, 95, cit. John McCracken, *Politics and Christianity*, 214.
37. W. Henry Rankine, *A Hero of the Dark Continent: Memoir of Rev Wm Affleck Scott*, Edinburgh and London: William Blackwood, 1896, 233, italics original.
38. *Life and Work in British Central Africa*, January 1895.
39. George Shepperson and Thomas Price, *Independent African: John Chilembwe and the Origins, Setting and Significance of the Nyasaland Native Rising of 1915*, Edinburgh: Edinburgh University Press, 1958; Blantyre: CLAIM, 2000, 36.
40. *Life and Work in British Central Africa*, March 1895.
41. Alexander Hetherwick, cit. W. P. Livingstone, *A Prince of Missionaries: Alexander Hetherwick of Blantyre*, London: James Clarke, n.d., 106.
42. *Life and Work in British Central Africa*, December 1902, my italics.
43. *Life and Work in British Central Africa*, April 1903.
44. Alexander Hetherwick, *The Gospel and the African*, 28.
45. Alexander Hetherwick, *The Romance of Blantyre*, 75, my italics.
46. W. P. Livingstone, *Prince of Missionaries*, 169.
47. *Life and Work in British Central Africa*, March 1896.
48. *Life and Work in British Central Africa*, December 1898
49. Ibid.
50. W. P. Livingstone, *A Prince of Missionaries*, 169.

51. Jane Samson, *Race and Redemption: British Missionaries Encounter Pacific Peoples, 1797–1920*, Grand Rapids: Eerdmans, 2017, 8. Samson describes 'othering and brothering' as 'the fundamental paradox in missionary accounts of Pacific peoples'.
52. W. P. Livingstone, *A Prince of Missionaries*, v.
53. Ibid.
54. Blantyre Mission Sunday School Letter 1925, 13 April 1925, MNA 50/BMC/2/1/95.
55. W. P. Livingstone, *A Prince of Missionaries*, 156, my italics.
56. *Life and Work in British Central Africa*, February 1899.
57. Ibid.
58. Ibid.
59. Ibid.
60. *Life and Work in British Central Africa*, March 1900.
61. Ibid.
62. Ibid.
63. Alexander Hetherwick, *The Romance of Blantyre*, 233.
64. Major Pearce, Acting Commissioner to Alexander Hetherwick, 18 April 1907, MNA 50/BMC/2/1/78.
65. Alexander Hetherwick to Major Pearce, Acting Commissioner, 19 April 1907, MNA 50/BMC/2/1/78.
66. Harry H. Johnston, *The British Central Africa*, New York: Edward Arnold, 1897.
67. *Life and Work in British Central Africa*, December 1902.
68. Ibid.
69. H. L. Duff, Acting Government Secretary to Alexander Hetherwick, Confidential, 26 August 1913, MNA BMC/50/2/1/128.
70. Alexander Hetherwick to Government Secretary, Confidential, 30 August 1913, MNA BMC/50/2/1/128.
71. Ibid.
72. H. L. Duff, Acting Government Secretary to Alexander Hetherwick, Confidential, 4 September 1913, MNA BMC/50/2/1/129.
73. Alexander Hetherwick to Government Secretary, Confidential, 25 September 1913, MNA BMC/50/2/1/129.
74. 'Report on the Government Commission of Enquiry into the Recent Native Rising with Notes on the Report of the Commission by the Rev Dr Hetherwick for the Information of the Foreign Mission Committee of the Church of Scotland', February 1916, BMC/50/2/1/147.
75. John McCracken (ed.), *Voices from the Chilembwe Rising: Witness Testimonies Made to the Nyasaland Rising Commission of Inquiry, 1915*, British Academy Fontes Historiae Africanae 14, Oxford: Oxford University Press, 2015, 372–73.
76. Ibid., 375–76.
77. Ibid., 377.
78. Ibid., 378.
79. Ibid., 381
80. See e.g. Kenneth Nyamayaro Mufuka, *Mission and Policies in Malawi*, Kingston: Limestone Press, 1977, 200.
81. Alexander Hetherwick to W. M. McLachlan, 17 March 1915, BMC/50/2/1/138.
82. John McCracken, *A History of Malawi 1859–1966*, Rochester: James Currey, 2012, repr. Rochester: James Currey and Mzuzu: Mzuni Press, 2021, 139.

83. Ibid.
84. Alexander Hetherwick to W. M. McLachlan, 20 January 1922, BMC/50/2/1/195.
85. Alexander Hetherwick to Hon Lawrence Smith, 31 July 1922, BMC/50/2/1/201.
86. 'Report on the Government Commission of Enquiry into the Recent Native Rising with Notes on the Report of the Commission by the Rev Dr Hetherwick for the Information of the Foreign Mission Committee of the Church of Scotland', February 1916, BMC/50/2/1/147.
87. Alexander Hetherwick to W. M. McLachlan, 17 February 1915, BMC/50/2/1/138.
88. Alexander Hetherwick to J. F. Alexander, 2 February 1915, BMC/50/2/1/138.
89. Alexander Hetherwick to James Reid, 8 March 1915, BMC/50/2/1/138.
90. Alexander Hetherwick to W.M. McLachlan, 17 February 1915, BMC/50/2/1/138.
91. Ibid.
92. Ibid.
93. 'Report on the Government Commission of Enquiry into the Recent Native Rising with Notes on the Report of the Commission by the Rev Dr Hetherwick for the Information of the Foreign Mission Committee of the Church of Scotland', February 1916, BMC/50/2/1/147.
94. *Life and Work in Nyasaland*, January–February 1914.
95. Alexander Hetherwick, 'Notes for Annual Report, 1910', MNA BMC/50/2/1/110.
96. Alexander Hetherwick to Rev Robert Napier, 24 June 1908, MNA 50/BMC/2/1/90.
97. Alexander Hetherwick to J. D. McCallum, 24 January 1914, MNA BMC/50/2/1/131.
98. Alexander Hetherwick to J. D. McCallum, 3 March 1914, MNA BMC/50/2/1/131.
99. Alexander Hetherwick to J. D. McCallum, 8 August 1922, MNA BMC/50/2/1/202.
100. See Kenneth R. Ross and Klaus Fiedler, *A Malawi Church History 1860–2020*, Mzuzu: Mzuni Press, 2020, 273–75; Silas S. Ncozana, *Sangaya: A Leader in the Synod of Blantyre Church of Central African Presbyterian*, Blantyre: CLAIM-Kachere, 1999.
101. Andrew C. Ross, 'The African – A Child or a Man: the Quarrel between the Blantyre Mission of the Church of Scotland and the British Central Africa Administration, 1890–1905', in Eric Stokes and Richard Brown (eds), *The Zambesian Past: Studies in Central African History*, Manchester: Manchester University Press, 1966, 332–51, at 334.
102. Godwin Tasie and Richard Gray, 'Introduction', in Edward Fasholé-Luke, Richard Gray, Adrian Hastings and Godwin Tasie (eds), *Christianity in Independent Africa*, London: Rex Collings, 1978, 3.
103. John W. De Gruchy, '"Who Did They Think They Were?" Some Reflections from a Theologian on Grand Narratives and Identity in the History of Missions', in Andrew Porter (ed.), *The Imperial Horizons of British Protestant Missions, 1880–1914*, Grand Rapids and Cambridge: Eerdmans, 2003, 213–25, at 216.

104. Andrew Porter, '"Cultural Imperialism" and Protestant Missionary Enterprise, 1780–1914', *The Journal of Imperial and Commonwealth History*, 25/3 (1997), 367–91, at 379.
105. Alexander Hetherwick, *The Gospel and the African*, passim.
106. Alexander Hetherwick (ed.), *Robert Hellier Napier in Nyasaland: Being his Letters to his Home Circle*, Edinburgh and London: William Blackwood Sons, 1925, 139.
107. Alexander Hetherwick to James Reid, 7 December 1922, MNA BMC/50/2/1/206.
108. Alexander Hetherwick, 'Some Notes on Nyasaland Native Church Figures for 1925', February 1926, MNA BMC/50/2/1/240.
109. Alexander Hetherwick to J. F. Alexander, 9 November 1910, MNA BMC/50/2/1/111.

Bibliography

ARCHIVAL SOURCES

Blantyre Presbytery Minutes, Malawi National Archives.
Blantyre Mission Annual Reports, 1899–1928, Malawi National Archives.
Blantyre Mission Council Minutes, 1898–1928, Malawi National Archives.
Blantyre Mission Unclassified Correspondence, 1898–1928, Malawi National Archives.
Church of Scotland Foreign Mission Committee Convener's Letter Books, 1883–1928, National Library of Scotland, Edinburgh, Scotland.
Summary of the Proceedings of the Nyasaland Legislative Council, Held at Zomba, 1908–13, 2022–25, Malawi National Archives.
Wordsworth Poole Papers, Malawi National Archives.
World Missionary Conference, 1910, Correspondence of Commission III and Commission VIII, Ecumenical Institute, Bossey, Switzerland.
Zomba Kirk Session Minutes, Malawi National Archives.

NEWSPAPERS AND MAGAZINES

Central African Times, later *Nyasaland Times*.
Life and Work in British Central Africa 1889–1907.
Life and Work in Nyasaland 1907–1919.
The Scotsman.

PUBLICATIONS BY ALEXANDER HETHERWICK

Hetherwick, Alexander, *Blantyre Church, Nyasaland*, Edinburgh: Church of Scotland, 1926.
Hetherwick, Alexander, *The Gospel and the African: the Croall Lectures for 1930–31*, Edinburgh: T. & T. Clark, 1932.
Hetherwick, Alexander, *Introductory Handbook of the Yao Language*, Aberdeen, n.p., 1899, repr. Andesite Press (online), 2017.
Hetherwick, Alexander, 'Islam and Christianity in Nyasaland', *Muslim World* 17/2 (April 1927), 184–86.
Hetherwick, Alexander, 'Livingstone's Makololo: Pioneers of Empire before Cecil Rhodes', *Other Lands*, April 1935, 115–16.
Hetherwick, Alexander, 'My First Day in Blantyre', *Central Africa News and Views* 2/1 (July 1936), 5.

Hetherwick, Alexander, 'Nyasaland Today and Tomorrow', *Journal of the Royal African Society* 17 no. 65 (October 1917), 11–19.
Hetherwick, Alexander (ed.), *Robert Hellier Napier in Nyasaland: Being his Letters to his Home Circle*, Edinburgh and London: William Blackwood Sons, 1925.
Hetherwick, Alexander, *The Romance of Blantyre: How Livingstone's Dream Came True*, London: James Clarke, n.d.
Hetherwick, Alexander, 'Some Animistic Beliefs among the Yaos of British Central Africa', *The Journal of the Anthropological Institute of Great Britain and Ireland* 32 (January–June 1902), 89–95.
Scott, D. C. and Alexander Hetherwick, *Dictionary of the Nyanja Language*, London: Religious Tract Society, 1930.

OTHER PRIMARY SOURCES

Bismarck, Joseph, *A Brief History of Joseph Bismarck* (4 March 1932), Zomba: Occasional Papers of the Department of Antiquities, 1968.
Buchanan, John, *The Shire Highlands*, Edinburgh and London: William Blackwood, 1885; repr. Blantyre: Blantyre Print and Publishing Company, 1982.
Livingstone, W. P., *A Prince of Missionaries: Alexander Hetherwick of Blantyre*, London: James Clarke, n.d.
Scott, D. C., *A Cyclopaedic Dictionary of the Mang'anja Language*, Edinburgh: Foreign Missions Committee of the Church of Scotland, 1892.

UNPUBLISHED SECONDARY SOURCES

Boeder, Robert B., 'Malawians Abroad: The History of Labour Emigration from Malawi to Its Neighbors, 1890 to the Present', PhD, Michigan State University, 1974.
Cannon, Jeffrey Grant, 'Church of Scotland Periodicals and the Shaping of Scottish Opinion regarding South African Apartheid and the Central African Federation, c.1912–c.1965', PhD, University of Edinburgh, 2020.
Chipeta, Mapopa O. J., 'Labour in a Colonial Context: The Growth and Development of the Malawian Wage Labour Force during the Colonial Period', PhD, Dalhousie University, 1986.
Gunya, Daniel, 'Christian Missions and Land Ownership: The Case of Blantyre Mission's Land in Blantyre and Zomba Districts, 1876–1940', History Seminar Paper, Chancellor College, University of Malawi, 1994.
Lovering, Timothy, 'Authority and Identity: Malawian Soldiers in Britain's Colonial Army, 1891–1964', PhD, University of Stirling, 2002.
Macdonald, R. J., 'A History of African Education in Nyasaland, 1875–1945', PhD, University of Edinburgh, 1969.

Phiri, Gilbert Davison Foster, 'A History of Education in Blantyre Synod (1876–2018)', PhD, Mzuzu University, 2020.
Phiri, Gilbert Davison Foster, 'The Involvement of the Church in the Empowerment of the Poor through Self-Reliance Education, Health Services and Agriculture: The Case of Blantyre Synod in Domasi Presbytery', MA, University of Malawi, 2007.
Power, Joey, 'Individual Enterprise and Enterprising Individuals: African Entrepreneurship in Blantyre and Limbe, 1907–1953', PhD, Dalhousie University, 1990.

PUBLISHED SECONDARY SOURCES

Anderson, Benedict, *Imagined Communities: Reflections on the Origin and Spread of Nationalism*, London: Verso, 1983.
Banda, Kelvin N., *A Brief History of Education in Malawi*, Blantyre: Dzuka, 1982.
Bandawe, Lewis Mataka, *Memoirs of a Malawian*, Blantyre: CLAIM, 1971.
Beaton, Nick, 'Early Reminscences of Blantyre Missionary Alice de Planta and her Husband Duncan Beaton, Manager, A.L.C.', *Society of Malawi Journal* 54/2 (2001), 1–27.
Boeder, Robert, *Alfred Sharpe of Nyasaland*, Blantyre: Central Africana, 1981.
Bone, David S., 'The Development of Islam in Malawi and the Response of the Christian Churches c. 1860–1986', in David S. Bone (ed.), *Malawi's Muslims: Historical Perspectives*, Blantyre: CLAIM-Kachere, 2000, 113–51.
Breitenbach, Esther, *Empire and Scottish Society: The Impact of Foreign Missions at Home c.1790 to c.1914*, Edinburgh: Edinburgh University Press, 2009.
Cairns, H. Alan C., *Prelude to Imperialism: British Reactions to Central African Society, 1840–1890*, London: Routledge and Kegan Paul, 1965.
Carey, Hilary M., *God's Empire: Religion and Colonialism in the British World c. 1801–1908*, Cambridge: Cambridge University Press, 2011.
Colvin, Tom, *A Record of Fathers and Founders of Blantyre Synod*, Blantyre: CCAP Synod of Blantyre, 1976.
De Gruchy, John W., '"Who Did They Think They Were?" Some Reflections from a Theologian on Grand Narratives and Identity in the History of Missions', in Andrew Porter (ed.), *The Imperial Horizons of British Protestant Missions, 1880–1914*, Grand Rapids and Cambridge: Eerdmans, 2003, 213–25.
De Kock, Leon, *Civilising Barbarians: Missionary Narrative and African Textual Response in Nineteenth-Century South Africa*, Johannesburg: Witwatersrand University Press and Lovedale Press, 1996.
Doig, Andrew B., *It's People That Count*, Edinburgh: The Pentland Press, 1997.
Englund, Harri, '"Africa is an Education": Vernacular Translation and Missionary Encounter in Nineteenth Century Malawi', in Kenneth R. Ross and Wapulumuka O. Mulwafu (eds), *Politics, Christianity and*

Society in Malawi: Essays in Honour of John McCracken, Mzuzu: Mzuni Press, 2020, 138–62.

Englund, Harri, *Visions for Racial Equality: David Clement Scott and the Struggle for Justice in Nineteenth-Century Malawi*, Cambridge: Cambridge University Press, 2022.

Forster, Peter G., *T. Cullen Young: Missionary and Anthropologist*, Hull: Hull University Press, 1989 and Blantyre: CLAIM-Kachere, 2003.

Gairdner, W. H. Temple, *'Edinburgh 1910': An Account and Interpretation of the World Missionary Conference*, Edinburgh and London: Oliphant, Anderson & Ferrier and Chicago and Toronto: Fleming H. Revell, 1910.

Green, Stephen, 'Blantyre Mission', *The Nyasaland Journal* 10/2 (1957), 6–17.

Hanna, A. J., *The Beginnings of Nyasaland and Northern Rhodesia*, Oxford: Clarendon Press, 1956.

Hargreaves, John D., *Aberdeenshire to Africa: Northeast Scots and British Overseas Expansion*, Aberdeen: Aberdeen University Press, 1981.

Hastings, Adrian, *The Church in Africa 1450–1950*, Oxford: Clarendon Press, 1994.

Hiebert, Paul, 'The Flaw of the Excluded Middle', *Missiology: An International Review* 10/1 (1982), 35–47.

Houston, Tobias J., 'Utenga Wambone – the "Good News": An Exploration of Historical Ciyawo Bible Translations and Linguistic Texts', *Studia Historiae Ecclesiasticae*, 2022, 18 pages, https://doi.org/10.25159/2412-4265/11186

Johnston, Harry H., *The British Central Africa*, New York: Edward Arnold, 1897.

Kim, Kirsteen, 'Racism Awareness in Mission: Touchstone or Cultural Blind Spot?', *International Bulletin of Mission Research* 45/4 (2021), 377–86.

Krishnamurthy, B. S., 'Economic Policy: Land and Labour in Nyasaland, 1890–1914', in Bridglal Pachai (ed.), *The Early History of Malawi*, London: Longman, 1972, 384–404.

Lamport-Stokes, Barbara, *Blantyre: Glimpses of the Early Days*, Blantyre: Society of Malawi, 1989.

Langworthy, Harry W., *Africa for the African: The Life of Joseph Booth*, Blantyre: CLAIM-Kachere, 2002.

Langworthy, Harry W., 'Charles Domingo, Seventh Day Baptists and Independency', *Journal of Religion in Africa*, XV/2 (1985), 96–121, repr. Klaus Fiedler and Kenneth R. Ross (eds), *Christianity in Malawi: A Reader*, Mzuzu: Mzuni Press, 2021, 170–205.

Lohrentz, Kenneth P., 'Joseph Booth, Charles Domingo, and the Seventh Day Baptists in Northern Nyasaland, 1910–12', *Journal of African History*, XII/3 (1971), 461–480, repr. Klaus Fiedler and Kenneth R. Ross (eds), *Christianity in Malawi: A Reader*, Mzuzu: Mzuni Press, 2021, 206–38.

McCracken, John, *A History of Malawi 1859–1966*, Rochester: James

Currey, 2012, repr. Rochester: James Currey and Mzuzu: Mzuni Press, 2021.
McCracken, John, 'Class, Violence and Gender in Early Colonial Malawi: The Curious Case of Elizabeth Pithie', *Society of Malawi Journal* 64/2 (2011), 1–16.
McCracken, John, 'Mungo Murray Chisuse and the Early History of Photography in Malawi', *Society of Malawi Journal* 61/2 (2008), 1–18.
McCracken, John, *Politics and Christianity in Malawi 1875–1940: The Impact of the Livingstonia Mission in the Northern Province*, Cambridge: Cambridge University Press, 1977; 2nd ed., Blantyre: CLAIM, 2000.
McCracken, John (ed.), *Voices from the Chilembwe Rising: Witness Testimonies Made to the Nyasaland Rising Commission of Inquiry, 1915*, British Academy Fontes Historiae Africanae 14, Oxford: Oxford University Press, 2015.
Macdonald, Roderick J., 'Rev Dr Daniel Sharpe Malekebu and the Re-Opening of the Providence Industrial Mission 1926–39', in Roderick J. Macdonald (ed.), *From Nyasaland to Malawi*, Nairobi: East African Publishing, 1971, 215–33.
McIntosh, Hamish, *Robert Laws: Servant of Africa*, Edinburgh: Handsel Press and Blantyre: Central Africana, 1993.
Matecheta, Harry Kambwiri, *Blantyre Mission: Stories of its Beginning*, ed. by Thokozani Chilembwe and Todd Statham, Mzuzu: Luviri Press, 2020 (trsl. from Harry Kambwiri Matecheta, *Blantyre Mission: Nkhani za Ciyambi Cace*, Blantyre: Hetherwick Press, 1951).
Morrow, Sean, '"War Came from the Boma": Military and Police Disturbances in Blantyre, 1902', *Society of Malawi Journal* 41/2 (1988), 16–29.
Mufuka, Kenneth Nyamayaro, *Mission and Politics in Malawi*, Kingston: Limestone Press, 1977.
Müller, Retief, *The Scots Afrikaners: Identity Politics and Intertwined Religious Cultures in Southern and Central Africa*, Edinburgh: Edinburgh University Press, 2022.
Munyenyembe, Rhodian, *Pursuing an Elusive Unity: A History of the Church of Central Africa Presbyterian as a Federative Denomination (1924–2018)*, London: Langham, 2019.
Murray, A. C., *Ons Nyasa-akker: Geskiedenis van die Nyasa sending van die Nederd. Geref. Kerk in Suid-Afrika*, Stellenbosch: Pro Ecclesia, 1931.
Ncozana, Silas S., *Sangaya: A Leader in the Synod of Blantyre Church of Central African Presbyterian*, Blantyre: CLAIM-Kachere, 1999.
Nihoka, M. Ali, *Cristo em Moçambique através da missão escocesa: Surgimento e desenvolvimento da Igreja Evangelica de Cristo em Moçambique 1894–2013*, São Paulo: Scortecci, 2014.
Oldham, J. H., *Christianity and the Race Problem*, London: SCM, 1924.
Olusoga, David, 'Britain's failure to honour black and Asian dead is a scandal of the present, not just the past', *The Guardian*, 25 April 2021.
Pachai, Bridglal, 'A History of Colonial Education for Africans in Malawi',

in A. T. Mugomba and M. Nyaggah (eds), *Independence without Freedom: Colonial Education in Southern Africa*, Oxford: Clio Press, 1980.

Pachai, Bridglal, *Land and Politics in Malawi, 1875–1975*, Kingston: The Limestone Press, 1978.

Pachai, Bridglal, *Malawi: The History of the Nation*, London: Longman, 1973.

Page, Melvin E., *The Chiwaya War*, 2nd ed., Mzuzu: Mzuni Press, 2021.

Paterson, Richard, *Blantyre*, Sketches of the Fields No. 9, Edinburgh: Church of Scotland Foreign Mission Committee, n.d.

Porter, Andrew, '"Cultural Imperialism" and Protestant Missionary Enterprise, 1780–1914', *The Journal of Imperial and Commonwealth History*, 25/3 (1997), 367–91.

Rankine, W. Henry, *A Hero of the Dark Continent: Memoir of Rev Wm Affleck Scott*, Edinburgh and London: William Blackwood, 1896.

Reijnaerts, Hubert, Ann Nielsen and Matthew Schoffeleers, *Montfortians in Malawi: Their Spirituality and Pastoral Approach*, Blantyre: CLAIM-Kachere, 1997; repr. Mzuzu: Luviri Press, 2018.

Retief, M. W., *William Murray of Nyasaland*, [Alice]: The Lovedale Press, 1958.

Robertson, William, *The Martyrs of Blantyre: Henry Henderson, Dr John Bowie, Robert Cleland. A Chapter from the Story of Missions in Central Africa*, London: James Nisbet, 1892.

Robinson, Ronald E. and Jack Gallagher, *Africa and the Victorians: the Official Mind of Imperialism*, London: Macmillan, 1961.

Ross, Andrew C., 'The African – A Child or a Man: the Quarrel between the Blantyre Mission of the Church of Scotland and the British Central Africa Administration, 1890–1905', in Eric Stokes and Richard Brown (eds), *The Zambesian Past: Studies in Central African History*, Manchester: Manchester University Press, 1966, 332–51.

Ross, Andrew C., 'Alexander Hetherwick', in Gerald H. Anderson (ed.), *Biographical Dictionary of Christian Missions*, New York: Simon & Schuster, 1998, 291.

Ross, Andrew C., *Blantyre Mission and the Making of Modern Malawi*, Blantyre: CLAIM-Kachere, 1996, repr. Mzuzu: Luviri Press, 2018.

Ross, Andrew C., 'The Blantyre Mission and the Problems of Land and Labour, 1891–1915', in Roderick J. Macdonald (ed.), *From Nyasaland to Malawi*, Nairobi: East African Publishing, 1975, 86–107

Ross, Andrew C., 'Christian Missions and Mid-Nineteenth-Century Change in Attitudes to Race: the African Experience', in Andrew Porter (ed.), *The Imperial Horizons of British Protestant Missions, 1880–1914*, Grand Rapids: Eerdmans, 2003, 85–105.

Ross, Andrew C., 'The Mzungu Who Mattered', *Religion in Malawi* 8 (1998), 3–7.

Ross, Kenneth R., 'The African Church and Eastern Orthodoxy: Reflections on the Centenary of St Michael and All Angels', *Africa Theological Journal* 22/1 (1993), 10–20, also in Kenneth R. Ross, *Gospel Ferment in*

Malawi: Theological Essays, Gweru: Mambo-Kachere, 1995, repr. Mzuzu: Luviri Press, 2018, 127–38.

Ross, Kenneth R. (ed.), *Christianity in Malawi: A Sourcebook*, 2nd ed., Mzuzu: Mzuni Press, 2020.

Ross, Kenneth R., 'Crisis and Identity: Presbyterian Ecclesiology in Southern Malawi 1891–1993', *Missionalia* 25/3 (1997), 375–91, also in Kenneth R. Ross, *Here Comes Your King! Christ, Church and Nation in Malawi*, Blantyre: CLAIM-Kachere, 1998, repr. Mzuzu: Luviri Press, 2020, 85–106.

Ross, Kenneth R., *Malawi and Scotland: Together in the Talking Place since 1859*, Mzuzu: Mzuni Press, 2013.

Ross, Kenneth R., *Mission as God's Spiral of Renewal*, Mzuzu: Mzuni Press, 2019.

Ross, Kenneth R., 'Vernacular Translation in Christian Mission: the Case of David Clement Scott and the Blantyre Mission 1888–98', *Missionalia* 21/1 (April 1993), 5–18, also in Kenneth R. Ross, *Gospel Ferment in Malawi: Theological Essays*, Gweru: Mambo-Kachere, 1995, repr. Mzuzu: Luviri Press, 2018, 107–26.

Ross, Kenneth R., 'Where were the Prophets and Martyrs in Banda's Malawi: Four Presbyterian Ministers', *Missionalia* 24/2 (August 1996), 113–28, also in Kenneth R. Ross, *Here Comes Your King! Christ, Church and Nation in Malawi*, Blantyre: CLAIM-Kachere, 1998, repr. Mzuzu: Luviri Press, 2020, 154–74.

Ross, Kenneth R. and Klaus Fiedler, *A Malawi Church History 1860–2020*, Mzuzu: Mzuni Press, 2020.

Samson, Jane, *Race and Redemption: British Missionaries Encounter Pacific Peoples, 1797–1920*, Grand Rapids: Eerdmans, 2017

Shepperson, George and Thomas Price, *Independent African: John Chilembwe and the Origins, Setting and Significance of the Nyasaland Native Rising of 1915*, Edinburgh: Edinburgh University Press, 1958; repr. Blantyre: CLAIM-Kachere, [6]2000 and Mzuzu: Luviri Press, [7]2020.

Sinclair, Margaret, *Salt and Light: The Letters of Jack and Mamie Martin in Malawi 1921–28*, Blantyre: CLAIM-Kachere, 2002.

Smith, Edwin W., *The Religion of the Lower Races*, New York: Macmillan, 1923.

Stanley, Brian, 'Church, State, and the Hierarchy of "Civilization": The Making of the "Missions and Governments" Report at the World Missionary Conference, Edinburgh 1910', in Andrew Porter (ed.), *The Imperial Horizons of British Protestant Missions, 1880–1914*, Grand Rapids and Cambridge: Eerdmans, 2003, 58–84.

Stanley, Brian, *The World Missionary Conference, Edinburgh 1910*, Grand Rapids and Cambridge: Eerdmans, 2009.

Statham, Todd, 'Scott, David Clement', *Dictionary of African Christian Biography*, https://dacb.org/stories/malawi/scott-davidc/

Stokes, Eric, 'Malawi Political Systems and the Introduction of Colonial Rule, 1891–1896', in Eric Stokes and Richard Brown (eds), *The*

Zambesian Past: Studies in Central African History, Manchester: Manchester University Press, 1966, 352–75.

Tasie, Godwin and Richard Gray, 'Introduction', in Edward Fasholé-Luke, Richard Gray, Adrian Hastings and Godwin Tasie (eds), *Christianity in Independent Africa*, London: Rex Collings, 1978.

Taylor, Charles, *A Secular Age*, Cambridge, MA and London: The Belknap Press of Harvard University Press, 2007.

Walls, Andrew F., *The Missionary Movement in Christian History: Studies in the Transmission of Faith*, Maryknoll, NY: Orbis and Edinburgh: T. & T. Clark, 1996.

Warhurst, P. R., 'Portugal's Bid for Southern Malawi', in Bridglal Pachai, G. W. Smith and Roger K. Tangri (eds), *Malawi Past and Present*, Blantyre: Christian Literature Association in Malawi, 1971, 20–36.

Weller, John and Jane Linden, *Mainstream Christianity to 1980 in Malawi, Zambia and Zimbabwe*, Gweru: Mambo Press, 1984.

Young, W. John, *The Quiet Wise Spirit: Edwin W. Smith [1876–1957] and Africa*, Peterborough: Epworth Press, 2002.

Index

Aberdeen, 6, 21, 43, 65, 78, 116, 124–5, 140, 142, 159
Acts of the Apostles, 102
Adialeiptos, 122, 136
African Lakes Company, 44, 64, 66
Africanised, 113
Alexander VI, Pope, 63
Alexander, Frederick, 46, 145
Alexander, Nita, 46
alien culture, 12
Alma mater, 116
Anderson, Melville, 18, 46
Anglicanism, 29, 142
Angoniland (Ntcheu), 50, 52, 101, 106, 108
anti-Christian, 28, 163
anti-mission, 28, 163
anti-native, 28, 163
Apostles' Creed, 153
Armed Forces, 72
Ashanti, 162
atonement, 112
Auneau, Bishop, 57
Authorized Version of the Bible, 105

bairns (Scots: children), 43
Bamba, 19
Bandawe, Grace, 149
Bandawe, Lewis Mataka, 51, 149
Bantu, 101, 134
baptism, 19–20
Basutoland, 130
Battle of Karonga, 162
Bechuanaland, 130
Beck, Janet, 25, 42–3, 45–6, 122–3, 150
Berlin Mission, 151
Bible, 6, 101–17, 119–20, 124, 176
Bismarck, Joseph, 11–13
Blake, Robert, 105

Blantyre Mission Council, 30, 35, 44, 49, 55, 84, 106, 125, 144, 146
Blantyre Presbytery, 36, 143, 147–8, 152–3, 157
Blantyre Synod, 4–5, 36, 182
Board of Education, 151
Bororo, 55
Borrowman, Patrick, 156
Bowie, John, 42
Bowman, Ernest, 46
Bowman, Frank, 46
Bowring, Charles, 57
Britain, 24, 64, 66, 95, 133, 148, 162, 170, 184
British Administration, 110, 25–8, 35, 37–8, 62, 66–73, 75, 89, 95, 121, 158–9, 166, 168, 171–2, 181
British and Foreign Bible Society, 101, 116–17
British Central Africa, 73, 86–7, 163, 174
British Central Africa Company, 92
British Consul, 12, 64
British Empire, 161–3, 167–8, 171–2, 177, 179–83
British Government, 64, 66, 69–72, 83, 86–7, 92, 94
British Protectorate, 27–8, 38, 62, 64–9, 73, 83–6, 88, 91–2, 94–5, 121, 159, 172, 180–1
British South Africa Company, 66–7
Bruce Estates, 179
Buchanan, John, 12, 65, 101
Byzantine domes, 141

Calvinist, 131
Cambridge University, 6
Cape Colony, 64
Cape to Cairo railway, 92
Cassius, Dion, 170

Catechumens, 19, 53
Catholics, 29, 56–7, 141–2, 176
centralisation, 52–3, 56, 127–8
Chamber of Commerce, 37–9, 65, 72–3, 85, 91, 113, 122, 159, 163, 166
Chancery, 169
Chartered Company, 66–7, 84, 95
Chikuse, Chief, 13
Chikuse, Wilibes, 106
Chikwana, George, 19
Chilembwe, Charles, 77
Chilembwe, Donald, 77
Chilembwe, John, 74, 76–7, 162, 177, 179
Chilembwe Rising, 75–6, 171, 175, 177–9, 183
Chinde, 65
Chindio, 93
Chinyanja, 10, 32, 41, 51, 106, 108, 111, 115, 117, 145, 176
Chiradzulo, 53–4, 127
Chiromo, 52, 71, 92–3, 126
Chisi, 19
Chisuse, Mungo Murray, 50
Chitete, Alexander, 19
Chitsitsimutso (revival meeting), 19
Cholo (now Thyolo), 38
Christian Native Marriage Ordinance, 135, 180
Christianised, 101, 113, 134
Christie, Margaret, 121, 150
Church of Central Africa Presbyterian (CCAP), 4, 36, 139, 151–6
Church of Scotland, 1, 19, 27, 29, 35–6, 55, 64–5, 75, 86, 97, 125, 140, 143, 151, 154, 159, 176, 178
Cinderella, 82–4, 91, 96
civilisation, 3, 9, 27, 38, 53, 82, 85, 122, 160, 163, 167, 169–70, 180–1
civilised tongues, 111
Cleland, Robert, 42
collective punishment, 68
Colonial Office, 86, 95
Colonial rule, 1–2, 34, 66, 71–4, 77, 90, 94, 159–61, 165–6, 168–9, 171, 180–1
Colonialist, 26, 28, 50–2, 114–15, 147–8, 156, 171, 173, 178–9, 181–2

Commission of Inquiry (General Assembly – Blantyre Mission, 1897), 29–30, 35–6, 42, 49
Commission of Inquiry (Chilembwe Rising, 1915), 76, 142, 145, 171, 175, 178–9, 182–3
Commonwealth War Graves Commission, 163, 184
Communion, 29, 53, 124, 141–2, 145, 148
coronation, 161
Creed, 107, 153
Crown Colony, 26, 73–4, 160
cultural hubris, 170
Currie, Hamilton, 50, 175

Dark Continent, 36–8, 85
Darwin, Charles, 2
Department of Education, 46, 130
doctrine, 29
Domasi Mission, 4, 8–23, 25, 30–1, 45, 52, 69, 110, 126, 128, 144, 147–8, 150, 161, 164, 180, 184
Domingo, Charles, 74
Downing Street, 87
Drummond, Henry, 10
Duff, Hector, 174–5, 179
Dundee, 65
Dutch Reformed Church, 105–6, 108–9, 139, 151–3, 171

Easter Sunday, 19–20
Edinburgh, 3, 30, 35, 42, 45, 52, 54–5, 57–9, 64–5, 68, 70, 84, 86, 107, 125, 141–3, 151–2, 154, 164
education, 2, 4, 6, 8–9, 21–3, 52–4, 57, 76–7, 85, 102, 117, 127, 129–32, 150–1, 172–3, 175, 177–8, 181
Educational Code, 5, 151
Edward VIII, King, 161
Englund, Harri, 7, 26–7, 111, 113–16, 133
English law, 68
esprit de corps, 67, 131
Ethiopianism, 179
ethnic, 115, 133
Europeans, 1–3, 6, 10–11, 14–15, 33–4, 37–8, 46–55, 57, 63, 69–70, 72, 75–6, 87–9, 91–2, 94, 96, 101, 110, 114–15,

123, 127–8, 130, 132, 143–9, 153–5, 159, 162–71, 173, 177–83
evangelical, 124–5, 180
evangelisation, 47, 55, 126, 133
Examinations Board, 10
excluded middle, 14

Federated Board, 110, 151–2
Fenwick, George, 21, 32
First World War, 47, 77–8, 84, 90, 94, 104, 127, 140, 149, 154, 161–3, 183
Foreign Mission Committee, 6, 27–9, 35, 40, 45, 53–5, 60, 64, 84, 140, 143, 148, 163–4, 180
Foreign Office (British Government), 34, 64, 66, 86
Fort Johnston (now Mangochi), 83, 105, 109, 174
Fraser, Donald, 122, 125, 152–4
Free Church of Scotland, 65, 86, 125, 140, 151, 154
furlough, 22, 25, 31, 63, 104, 107, 116, 125, 139–40, 149, 159

General Assembly (Church of Scotland), 29, 35–6, 49, 87, 143, 146, 154
General Synod (CCAP), 152
German East Africa, 76, 151
Glasgow, 65
gospel, 12–13, 16–17, 36, 85, 88, 122, 124, 126, 134–5, 148
grant-in-aid, 173
Greek, 33, 102, 111, 112

Head of the Mission, 1, 3, 27, 43, 46–8, 50–1, 139, 172
heathenism, 11, 17–18, 20, 128, 182
Hebrew, 102
Henderson, Henry, 7, 9, 12, 43
Henry Henderson Institute, 54
Herd, Henry, 28–9
Hetherwick, Clement, 22, 29, 139–40
Hetherwick, Elizabeth (Pithie, Fenwick), 21–2, 29, 32, 55, 66, 139–41
Hofmeyer, A. L., 108
Holy Week, 125
House of Lords, 64

hymns, hymnody, 51, 103, 109–10, 118
Hynde, R. S., 25, 73

Imperial War Graves Commission, 162–3
incarnation, 112
India, Indian, 7, 83, 130, 132, 161
indigenous culture, 10
infantalising, 51, 167
inferiority, 51, 170, 181
Inverleith Row, 58
Inwood, Charles, 125
Islam, 9, 22

Jesuit Mission, 128
Jesus Christ, 132, 153
Johnston, Harry, 28, 64–6, 70, 73, 83, 89, 91, 97, 174

Kalimbuka, 14
Kalungwe, John Williard M., 175
Kaso, 108
Kasonga, 19
Kaunde, Joseph, 148
Kaungulu, 18
Kawinga, Chief, 69
Keswick Convention, 125
Kidney, Dorothy, 140
Kikuyu, 31, 34
King's African Rifles, 161
Kingdom of God, 96, 122, 145, 153
Kirk Session, 143–4, 147
Knoxhill, 6
Kufa, John Gray, 51, 55, 177, 179
Kundecha, Stephen, 20, 51, 147–9
Kydd, Elsie, 175

Lake Chilwa, 9–11
Lake Malawi, 65, 83, 93, 102
Land Commission, 90–1
land tenure, 39, 63, 74, 88, 90–1
Landsdowne, Marquess of, 97
Latin, 76, 80, 102, 118, 170
Laus Deo (Praise God), 106, 109, 161
Laws, Robert, 1, 3–4, 6, 43, 75, 122, 140, 144, 153–4
Legislative Council, 37, 73–6, 82–3, 88, 90, 97, 113, 122, 135, 159, 163, 178

Life and Work in British Central Africa, 22, 107, 121
lingua franca, 101, 115–16
Lisbon, 64–5
lisoka (soul), 15
Livingstone, David, 2, 4–9, 38, 47, 63, 83, 92, 160
Livingstonia Mission, 3, 6, 9, 22, 48–9, 53, 63, 78, 86, 105, 110, 122–3, 125, 139–40, 147, 151–5, 158
Lomweland, 55–6
London, 64, 66, 86
London Missionary Society, 151
Lovedale, 9, 12

McAlpine, A. G., 105
McCallum, J. D., 159, 182
McCurrach, Elizabeth, 31, 47, 125, 150
McGillivray, Elizabeth, 45, 123
McIlwain, John, 11, 25, 42, 46, 123, 140
McMurtrie, John, 19, 28–9, 45, 54, 58, 70, 73, 85–8, 92–3
Maganga, 49
Magna Carta, 91
Magomero, 58, 179
Mahomet (Muhammad), 124
Makololo, 7, 21, 65, 82, 148
Malabvi Mountain, 13
Malekebu, Daniel, 77
Malemia, Chief, 10
Malosa, 10
Malunga, Chief, 70
Mandala, 179
Mang'anja, 32, 40, 101–5, 109, 111–12, 114, 119, 126
Maori, 172
Martin, Mamie, 48
Maseya, Thomas, 148
Matecheta, Harry Kambwiri, 4, 13, 20, 48–51, 147, 149
Matope Road, 70
Mauchline, Alexander, 183
Maunde, Ralph, 177
mfumu (chief), 39
Missionary Conference, 22, 53, 55–6, 96, 110, 123, 128, 151, 153–4, 165
Mitchell, Mitford, 6
Mkwatula, John, 19
Mlanda, 106
Mlanje *see* Mulanje
Moir, John, 44
Montfortian Mission, 56
Moorish towers, 141
Moravian Mission, 151
Mothela, David, 19
Mpinganjira, James, 19
Mpyupyu, 19
Mtuwa, Harry, 52, 148
Mulanje, 28, 38, 52, 55–6, 69, 148, 180
Mulungu, 15–16, 110, 134
Mulunguzi, 12, 18
Murchision Cataracts, 83
Murray, Andrew C., 105–7
Murray, W. A., 108
Murray, W. H., 62, 105–9, 171
Mvera, 27, 108–10, 152–4, 165
Mwale, Ismael, 106

Napier, Robert, 46–7, 56, 107–8, 149, 162, 181, 183
National Bible Society of Scotland, 106
native church, 52, 54, 85, 105, 107, 110, 127, 132, 134–5, 143–49, 151–2, 155–6, 180, 182–4
Native Locations Ordinance, 89
Native Marriage Ordinance, 135, 149, 180
Native Rising *see* Chilembwe Rising
Natives on Private Estates Ordinance, 99
Ndirande Mountain, 69–70, 72
Ndombo, Che, 115
New Testament, 102, 106–9, 116, 161
Ngoni, 13–14, 50, 52, 71–2, 101, 105–6, 108
Nicene Creed, 153
Nkanda River, 13
North Livingstonia Presbytery, 158
Northern Rhodesia, 95
Nsondole, 19
Nthumbi, 50, 52, 54, 127
Nyanja, 10, 32, 40–1, 43, 51, 102, 104–13, 115–17, 119, 145, 176
Nyanja Bible, 110–11, 116, 176
Nyanja Bible Translation Committee, 104–6, 110–11

Nyasaland, 34, 37, 51, 55, 57, 62, 64, 73, 75, 77, 82–7, 91–7, 107, 109, 117, 127–8, 130–1, 154, 159–61, 163, 165–7, 170–5, 178
Nyasaland Gazette, 75
nyimbo za chamba, 110
Nyimbo za Mulungu, 110

Ogilvie, James, 6, 8, 162
Old Testament, 107–9
Oldham, J. H., 3
O'Neill, Lieutenant, 82
ordained ministers, 52, 146, 148, 153

Palmerstonian, 26
paternalism, 3, 26, 48, 73, 111, 113–15, 155, 167–71, 180, 182
Peden, Alexander, 54
Pentateuch, 108
Pentecostalisation, 155
Phalombe, 9
Phelps-Stokes Commission, 131
Philip, John, 2
Pinto, Major Serpa, 65
Poole, Wordsworth, 28
Port Herald (now Nsanje), 93
Portugal, 63–6, 95, 160
Portuguese East Africa, 47, 55–6, 60, 63, 69, 93, 102, 127–8, 137, 165
Presbyterianism, 35, 141–2, 156
Providence Industrial Mission, 76–7
public hangings, 179

Quelimane, 7, 11

racial boundaries, 144, 148
racism, 1, 3, 26, 50–2, 111, 114–15, 145, 147–8, 156, 166–8, 170–4, 178–9, 181, 183–4
racist tropes, 50, 114, 179
raiding, 11, 13, 69, 72
Ramakukan, Chief, 21
Rand, South Africa, 84, 86–8
Rankin, D. J., 29, 65
Reid, James, 42, 74, 156, 166
resurrection, 112
Rhodes, Cecil, 8, 66–7, 92
ritualism, 25, 29, 142
Robertson, George, 25, 28–9

Robertson, James, 52, 57
Ross, Andrew, 2–4, 8, 25, 29, 37–8, 43, 46–7, 67, 73, 75, 89, 109, 155, 182

sacrament, 37, 151
St Michael and All Angels, 31, 36, 141
Sakata, 19
Salisbury, Lord, 64–5
Sande, Jonathan, 106
Sangaya, Jonathan, 182
Scotland, 5–7, 10, 12, 21–2, 25, 27–9, 31–2, 36, 42, 46, 50, 56, 63–4, 104, 116, 122, 125, 128, 139–40, 142, 148, 150, 154, 162–4, 175, 178–9
Scott, Archibald, 28, 35, 42, 52, 65, 143, 167
Scott, Bella, 21, 32, 40
Scott, David Clement, 3–6, 9, 11–13, 21–2, 26–43, 46–8, 50–2, 54–5, 63–7, 70–1, 76, 84, 88–9, 101–4, 109, 111–12, 114–15, 117, 121–2, 124, 133, 141–2, 144–8, 151, 154–6, 169, 172, 182
Scott, Henry, 11, 144, 161, 164
Scott, William Affleck, 42, 168
scramble for Africa, 63, 65, 160
sexual morality, 173–4
Sharpe, Alfred, 28, 67, 71, 74, 86–7, 90, 121, 163
Shire Highlands, 9–11, 13, 37, 52, 55–6, 63–4, 70, 83, 86, 89, 101, 134–5, 160, 165, 177
Shire River, 7, 13, 64, 93
Simpson Mathematical Prize, 6
slavery, 11, 70
Smith, George, 77, 91, 149, 179
Soche Mountain, 13, 72
Somaliland, 71, 161–2
South Africa, 63–7, 74, 82–8, 93, 130, 165, 173
South African Standard Time, 82
South African Colonies, 85, 87–8, 94
Southern Rhodesia, 94
spirituality, 123–6
stadialism, 2, 167–9, 171, 180
Stewart, James, 9
Stirling, 140
Stone Age, 169
Sunday School, 140, 171

taxation, 67, 165
tengatenga (carriers), 71, 92, 162–3, 184
Tonga, 106
Transvaal, 74, 88, 94
tribal mark, 20
Tumbuka, 106, 110

Uganda, 91, 95
United Presbyterian Church, 125
Universities Mission to Central Africa (UMCA), 151
University of Aberdeen, 6, 116, 125

verities of faith, 112
Victoria Cross, 18

Wands, Revd and Mrs, 45
West Church of St Nicholas, 6, 159
West Shire District, 52
Whyte, Alexander, 124
Women's Department, 45
Women's Foreign Mission Committee, 45

World Missionary Conference (Edinburgh 1910), 55, 112, 125, 129, 132, 150–2
worship, 15–16, 29, 49, 109–10, 122, 134, 141, 143–6, 153, 155

Yao, 9–10, 13–15, 24, 43, 49, 69, 101–4, 106, 109, 113, 126, 161
Yaoland, 161

Zambezi Industrial Mission, 56
Zambezi River, 7, 55, 63, 65, 82–3, 93, 110, 128
Zambezia, 64
Zambezi-Shire Waterway, 65
Zanzibar, 95
Zion, 107
Zomba, 9–10, 12, 14, 46, 68–9, 80, 82, 92, 101, 116, 144–5, 148, 150, 161, 164–5, 178, 180
Zomba Mean Time, 82
Zulu, 172

EU representative:
Easy Access System Europe
Mustamäe tee 50, 10621 Tallinn, Estonia
Gpsr.requests@easproject.com

www.ingramcontent.com/pod-product-compliance
Lightning Source LLC
Chambersburg PA
CBHW070354240426
43671CB00013BA/2500